GAMBLING: WHAT'S AT STAKE?

ISSN 1543-4915

GAMBLING: WHAT'S AT STAKE?

Stephen Meyer

INFORMATION PLUS® REFERENCE SERIES
Formerly Published by Information Plus, Wylie, Texas

GALE
CENGAGE Learning·

Detroit • New York • San Francisco • New Haven, Conn • Waterville, Maine • London

Gambling: What's at Stake?

Stephen Meyer

Kepos Media, Inc.: Paula Kepos and Janice Jorgensen, Series Editors

Project Editors: Kathleen J. Edgar, Elizabeth Manar, Kimberley McGrath

Rights Acquisition and Management: Sheila Spencer

Composition: Evi Abou-El-Seoud, Mary Beth Trimper

Manufacturing: Rita Wimberley

Cover photograph: © Vuk Nenezic/Shutterstock.com.

While every effort has been made to ensure the reliability of the information presented in this publication, Gale, a part of Cengage Learning, does not guarantee the accuracy of the data contained herein. Gale accepts no payment for listing; and inclusion in the publication of any organization, agency, institution, publication, service, or individual does not imply endorsement of the editors or publisher. Errors brought to the attention of the publisher and verified to the satisfaction of the publisher will be corrected in future editions.

Gale
27500 Drake Rd.
Farmington Hills, MI 48331-3535

ISBN-13: 978-0-7876-5103-9 (set)
ISBN-13: 978-1-4144-8141-8

ISBN-10: 0-7876-5103-6 (set)
ISBN-10: 1-4144-8141-1

ISSN 1543-4915

This title is also available as an e-book.
ISBN-13: 978-1-5730-2285-9 (set)
ISBN-10: 1-5730-2285-3 (set)
Contact your Gale sales representative for ordering information.

Printed in the United States of America
1 2 3 4 5   17 16 15 14 13

TABLE OF CONTENTS

PREFACE

Gambling: What's at Stake? is part of the *Information Plus Reference Series*. The purpose of each volume of the series is to present the latest facts on a topic of pressing concern in modern American life. These topics include the most controversial and studied social issues of the 21st century: abortion, capital punishment, care for the elderly, crime, education, the environment, health care, immigration, minorities, national security, social welfare, women, youth, and many more. Even though this series is written especially for high school and undergraduate students, it is an excellent resource for anyone in need of factual information on current affairs.

By presenting the facts, it is the intention of Gale, Cengage Learning to provide its readers with everything they need to reach an informed opinion on current issues. To that end, there is a particular emphasis in this series on the presentation of scientific studies, surveys, and statistics. These data are generally presented in the form of tables, charts, and other graphics placed within the text of each book. Every graphic is directly referred to and carefully explained in the text. The source of each graphic is presented within the graphic itself. The data used in these graphics are drawn from the most reputable and reliable sources, such as from the various branches of the U.S. government and from private organizations and associations. Every effort has been made to secure the most recent information available. Readers should bear in mind that many major studies take years to conduct and that additional years often pass before the data from these studies are made available to the public. Therefore, in many cases the most recent information available in 2013 is dated from 2010 or 2011. Older statistics are sometimes presented as well, if they are landmark studies or of particular interest and no more-recent information exists.

Although statistics are a major focus of the *Information Plus Reference Series*, they are by no means its only content. Each book also presents the widely held positions and important ideas that shape how the book's subject is discussed in the United States. These positions are explained in detail and, where possible, in the words of their proponents. Some of the other material to be found in these books includes historical background, descriptions of major events related to the subject, relevant laws and court cases, and examples of how these issues play out in American life. Some books also feature primary documents or have pro and con debate sections that provide the words and opinions of prominent Americans on both sides of a controversial topic. All material is presented in an evenhanded and unbiased manner; readers will never be encouraged to accept one view of an issue over another.

HOW TO USE THIS BOOK

Gambling has long been a favorite pastime worldwide, and its history in the United States dates back to the founding of the nation. It has been estimated that Americans spend more than $1 trillion per year on charitable gambling, betting on horse and greyhound races, lottery purchases, casino wagering, and other legal and illegal gambling activities. Much controversy surrounds the gambling industry. While pro-gambling elements argue that the economic benefits of gambling far outweigh any potential risks, some individuals oppose gambling on moral grounds or argue that it can cause an increase in various types of social problems. This book presents in-depth information on how casino gambling, sports gambling, lotteries, and Internet gambling work, provides up-to-date financial data for each, and addresses the effects of these and other gambling activities on the communities in which they take place. Also profiled are American attitudes toward gambling.

Gambling: What's at Stake? consists of nine chapters and three appendixes. Each chapter is devoted to a particular aspect of gambling in the United States. For a summary of the information covered in each chapter, please see the synopses provided in the Table of Contents. Chapters generally begin with an overview of the basic facts and background information on the chapter's topic, then proceed to examine subtopics of particular interest. For example, Chapter 9: Internet Gambling starts with a discussion of the legal and historical context of online gaming and then follows with a brief historical overview of online casinos, beginning with the licensing of online gaming sites in Antigua and Barbuda during the mid-1990s. Next, the chapter provides an overview of various online casino games, including poker, blackjack, and slot machines. The chapter then examines statistics relating to online gamblers in the United States before turning to an in-depth analysis of the complex legal history of online gaming, from the passage of the Interstate Wire Act in 1961 to the controversy surrounding the Unlawful Internet Gambling Enforcement Act of 2006. The chapter also surveys several legislative attempts to regulate Internet gambling and discusses several notable law enforcement cases linking online gaming operations to such crimes as bank fraud and money laundering. The chapter concludes by considering the relationship between online casinos and problem gambling, as well as the unique risks posed by Internet gaming sites to underage gamblers. Readers can find their way through a chapter by looking for the section and subsection headings, which are clearly set off from the text. They can also refer to the book's extensive Index, if they already know what they are looking for.

Statistical Information

The tables and figures featured throughout *Gambling: What's at Stake?* will be of particular use to readers in learning about this topic. These tables and figures represent an extensive collection of the most recent and valuable statistics on gambling, as well as related issues—for example, the sales and profits of state lotteries, the demographics of gamblers, twenty questions designed to determine whether a person is a compulsive gambler, and an estimate of tribal gaming revenues. Gale, Cengage Learning believes that making this information available to readers is the most important way to fulfill the goal of this book: to help readers understand the issues and controversies surrounding gambling in the United States and reach their own conclusions.

Each table or figure has a unique identifier appearing above it, for ease of identification and reference. Titles for the tables and figures explain their purpose. At the end of each table or figure, the original source of the data is provided.

To help readers understand these often complicated statistics, all tables and figures are explained in the text. References in the text direct readers to the relevant statistics. Furthermore, the contents of all tables and figures

are fully indexed. Please see the opening section of the Index at the back of this volume for a description of how to find tables and figures within it.

Appendixes

Besides the main body text and images, *Gambling: What's at Stake?* has three appendixes. The first is the Important Names and Addresses directory. Here, readers will find contact information for a number of government and private organizations that can provide further information on different aspects of gambling. The second appendix is the Resources section, which can also assist readers in conducting their own research. In this section, the author and editors of *Gambling: What's at Stake?* describe some of the sources that were most useful during the compilation of this book. The final appendix is the Index. It has been greatly expanded from previous editions and should make it even easier to find specific topics in this book.

ADVISORY BOARD CONTRIBUTIONS

The staff of Information Plus would like to extend its heartfelt appreciation to the Information Plus Advisory Board. This dedicated group of media professionals provides feedback on the series on an ongoing basis. Their comments allow the editorial staff who work on the project to continually make the series better and more user-friendly. The staff's top priority is to produce the highest-quality and most useful books possible, and the Information Plus Advisory Board's contributions to this process are invaluable.

The members of the Information Plus Advisory Board are:

- Kathleen R. Bonn, Librarian, Newbury Park High School, Newbury Park, California

- Madelyn Garner, Librarian, San Jacinto College, North Campus, Houston, Texas

- Anne Oxenrider, Media Specialist, Dundee High School, Dundee, Michigan

- Charles R. Rodgers, Director of Libraries, Pasco-Hernando Community College, Dade City, Florida

- James N. Zitzelsberger, Library Media Department Chairman, Oshkosh West High School, Oshkosh, Wisconsin

COMMENTS AND SUGGESTIONS

The editors of the *Information Plus Reference Series* welcome your feedback on *Gambling: What's at Stake?* Please direct all correspondence to:

Editors
Information Plus Reference Series
27500 Drake Rd.
Farmington Hills, MI 48331-3535

CHAPTER 1
GAMBLING IN THE UNITED STATES: AN OVERVIEW

Gambling is an activity in which something of value is risked on the chance that something of greater value might be obtained, based on the uncertain outcome of a particular event. Organized gambling has become an industry because so many people are willing and even eager to risk their money in exchange for a chance at something bigger and better. The elements of risk and uncertainty actually add to gambling's appeal—and to its danger. Throughout history, various cultures have considered gambling alternately harmless and sinful, respectable and corrupt, and legal and illegal. Societal attitudes are dependent on customs, traditions, religion, morals, and the context in which gambling occurs.

Lawmakers have struggled to define gambling and determine which activities should be legal and which should not. For example, betting activities with an element of skill involved (such as picking a horse in a race or playing a card game) might be more acceptable than those based entirely on chance (such as spinning a roulette wheel or playing slot machines). Acceptability also depends on who profits from gambling. Bingo games held for charity and lotteries that fund state programs are more often legally allowed than casinos run for corporate profit.

Sam Skolnik estimates in *High Stakes: The Rising Cost of America's Gambling Addiction* (2011) that Americans lost approximately $92 billion while gambling in 2007. So why do people gamble? Common sense suggests that risking something of value on an event with an uncertain outcome is irrational. Scientists postulate a variety of reasons for gambling, including the lure of money, the excitement and fun of the activity, and the influence from peers. At its deepest level, gambling may represent a human desire to control the randomness that seems to permeate life. Whatever the drive may be, it must be strong, because an entire gambling culture has developed in the United States in which entrepreneurs (legal and otherwise) offer people opportunities to gamble, and business is booming.

THE HISTORY OF GAMBLING
Ancient Times

Archaeologists have discovered evidence that people in Egypt, China, Japan, and Greece played games of chance with dice and other devices as far back as 2000 BC. According to *Encyclopaedia Britannica*, loaded dice—which are weighted to make a particular number come up more often than others—have been found in ancient tombs in Egypt, the Far East, and even North and South America.

Dice are probably the oldest gambling implements known. They were often carved from sheep bones and known as knucklebones. They are mentioned in several historical documents, including the *Mahabharata*, the epic poem and philosophy text written in India approximately 2,500 years ago. A story in the New Testament of the Bible describes Roman soldiers throwing dice to determine who would get the robe of Jesus (4? BC–AD 29?). Roman bone dice have been found dating from the first to the third centuries AD. The Romans also gambled on chariot races, animal fights, and gladiator contests.

The Medieval Period

During medieval times (c. 500–c. 1500) gambling was legalized by some governments, particularly in areas of modern-day Germany, Italy, the Netherlands, and Spain. England and France were much less permissive, at times outlawing all forms of gambling. For example, King Louis IX (1215–1270) of France prohibited gambling during his reign for religious reasons. Still, illegal gambling continued to thrive.

During this period Christian powers in Europe launched the Crusades (military expeditions against Muslim powers that controlled lands considered holy by Christians). They also permitted gambling, but only by knights and people of higher rank. Violators were subject to severe whippings. Nevertheless, even among the titled gamblers there was a legal limit on how much money could be lost, a concept that later would come to be known as limited-stakes gambling.

English knights returned from the Crusades with long-legged Arabian stallions, which they bred with sturdy English mares to produce Thoroughbred racehorses. Betting on private horse races became a popular pastime among the nobility. Card games also became popular in Europe around the end of the 14th century. According to the International Playing-Card Society, in "History of Playing-Cards" (June 8, 2000, http://i-p-c-s.org/history.html), one of the earliest known references to playing cards in Europe dates from 1377. During the late 1400s and early 1500s lotteries were used in Europe to raise money for public projects. In "Lottery History" (2012, http://www.naspl.org/index.cfm?fuseaction=content&menuid=11&pageid=1016), the North American Association of State and Provincial Lotteries states that Queen Elizabeth I (1533–1603) established the first English state lottery in 1567.

Precolonial America and the Colonial Era

Native Americans played games of chance as part of tribal ceremonies and celebrations hundreds of years before the Europeans arrived in North America. One of the most common was a dice and bowl game in which five plum stones or bones carved with different markings were tossed into a bowl. Wagers were placed before the game began, and scoring was based on the combination of markings that appeared after a throw. The Cheyenne called the game *monshimout*. A similar game was called *hubbub* by the Arapaho and New England tribes.

European colonists brought gambling traditions with them to the New World. Historical accounts report that people in parts of New England gambled on horse racing, cockfighting, and bullbaiting. Bullbaiting was a blood sport in which a bull was tethered to a stake and attacked by dogs. The dogs were trained to torment the bull, which responded by goring the dogs. Spectators gambled on how many of the dogs the bull would kill.

In 1612 King James I (1566–1625) of England created a lottery to provide funds for Jamestown, Virginia, the first permanent British settlement in North America. Lotteries were later held throughout the colonies to finance the building of towns, roads, hospitals, and schools and to provide other public services.

Many colonists, however, disapproved of gambling. The Pilgrims and Puritans fled to North America during the 1620s and 1630s to escape persecution in Europe for their religious beliefs. They believed in a strong work ethic that considered labor morally redeeming and viewed gambling as sinful because it wasted time that could be spent on productive endeavors.

Cockfighting, bear- and bullbaiting, wrestling matches, and footraces were popular gambling sports throughout Europe during the 16th and 17th centuries. The predecessors of many modern casino games were also developed and popularized during this period. For example, the invention of the roulette wheel is often attributed to the French mathematician Blaise Pascal (1623–1662).

Gambling among British aristocrats became so customary during the early years of the 18th century that it presented a financial problem for the country. Gentlemen gambled away their belongings, their country estates, and even their titles. Cuthbert William Johnson noted in *The Law of Bills of Exchange, Promissory Notes, Checks, &c* (1839) that large transfers of land and titles were disruptive to the nation's economy and stability, so the reigning monarch, Queen Anne (1665–1714), responded in 1710 with the Statute of Anne, which made large gambling debts "utterly void, frustrate, and of none effect, to all intents and purposes whatsoever." In other words, large gambling debts could not be legally enforced. This prohibition prevailed in common law for centuries and is still cited in U.S. court cases. Queen Anne is also known for her love of horse racing, which became a popular betting sport (along with boxing) during her reign.

A surge of evangelical Christianity swept through England, Scotland, Germany, and the North American colonies during the mid- to late 1700s. Historians refer to this period as the Great Awakening, a time when conservative moral values became more prevalent and widespread. Evangelical Christians considered gambling to be a sin and dangerous to society, and religion became a powerful tool for bringing about social change.

In October 1774 the Continental Congress of the North American colonies issued the Articles of Association (2008, http://avalon.law.yale.edu/18th_century/contcong_10-20-74.asp), which stated in part that the colonists "will discountenance and discourage every species of extravagance and dissipation, especially all horse-racing, and all kinds of games, cock fighting, exhibitions of shews [sic], plays, and other expensive diversions and entertainments." The purpose of the directive was to "encourage frugality, economy, and industry."

The 19th Century

In general, gambling was tolerated as long as it did not upset the social order. According to James R. Westphal et al., in "Gambling in the South: Implications for Physicians" (*Southern Medical Journal*, vol. 93, no. 9, September 2000), Georgia, South Carolina, and Virginia passed versions of the Statute of Anne during the colonial period to prevent gambling from getting out of hand. New Orleans became a gambling mecca in the 1700s and 1800s, even though gambling was outlawed during much of that time. During the 1830s almost all southern states outlawed gambling in public places; some exceptions, however, were made for "respectable gentlemen."

In 1823, 11 years after becoming a state, the Louisiana legislature passed a licensing act that legalized several forms of gambling and licensed several gambling halls in New Orleans. Even though this act was repealed in 1835, casino-type gambling continued to prosper and spread to riverboats traveling the Mississippi River. Professional riverboat gamblers soon developed an unsavory reputation as cheats and scoundrels. Several historians trace the popularization of poker and craps in the United States to Louisiana gamblers of that period. Riverboat gambling continued to thrive until the outbreak of the Civil War (1861–1865).

Andrew Jackson (1767–1845) was president of the United States from 1829 to 1837. The Jacksonian era was associated with renewed attention to social problems and a focus on morality. A wave of evangelical Christianity swept the country. According to I. Nelson Rose of Whittier Law School, in "The Rise and Fall of the Third Wave: Gambling Will Be Outlawed in Forty Years" (William R. Eadington and Judy A. Cornelius, eds., *Gambling and Public Policy: International Perspectives*, 1991), gambling scandals and the spread of a conservative view of morality led to an end to most legal gambling in the United States by the mid-1800s.

Across the country private and public lotteries were plagued by fraud and scandal and fell into disfavor. During the 1840s most southern states banned lotteries based on moral grounds. By 1862 only two states, Missouri and Kentucky, had legal lotteries. Lotteries, however, were reinstated after the Civil War to raise badly needed funds. In 1868 Louisiana implemented a lottery known as the Serpent. Even though it was extremely popular, the lottery was plagued with fraud and was eventually outlawed by the state in 1895. Casino gambling, which had been legalized again in Louisiana in 1869, was outlawed at the same time as the lottery.

Frontier gambling in the Old West, both legal and illegal, peaked during the mid- to late 19th century. Saloons and other gambling houses were common in towns catering to cowboys, traders, and miners. Infamous gamblers of the time included Doc Holliday (1851–1887), Bat Masterson (1853–1921), Alice Ivers Tubbs (1851–1930), and James Butler "Wild Bill" Hickok (1837–1876). Hickok was shot while playing poker in 1876. At the time, he held a hand of two black aces and two black eights, which came to be known as the "dead man's hand."

Gambling in general fell into disfavor as the 19th century ended. In England, Queen Victoria (1819–1901) ruled from 1837 to 1901; her rule was characterized by concern for morality and by the spread of conservative

values. These attitudes permeated American society as well. Gambling fell out of favor as a pastime for respectable people. Many eastern racetracks and western casinos were pressured to close for moral and ethical reasons. As new states entered the Union, many included provisions against gambling in their constitutions. By federal law, all state lotteries were shut down by 1900.

GAMBLING IN THE UNITED STATES SINCE 1900

At the turn of the 20th century, there were 45 states in the Union. The territories of Arizona, New Mexico, and Oklahoma gained statehood between 1907 and 1912. According to Rose, the closure of casinos in Arizona and New Mexico was a precondition for statehood. In 1910 Nevada outlawed casino gambling. That same year horse racing was outlawed in New York, and almost all gambling was prohibited in the United States. The only legal gambling options at the time were horse races in Maryland and Kentucky and a few isolated card clubs.

Legalized Casinos in Nevada

The 1930s were a time of reawakening for legal gambling interests. Many states legalized horse racing and charitable gambling. Nevada went even further. In 1931 its legislature made casino gambling legal again. It seemed like a logical step: frontier gambling was widely tolerated in the state, even though gambling was officially illegal. More important, Nevada, like the rest of the country, was suffering from a deep recession, and it sought to cash in on two events. The state's divorce laws were changed during the early 1930s to allow the granting of a divorce after only six weeks of residency, so people from other states temporarily moved into small motels and inns to satisfy the residency requirement. At the same time, construction began on the massive Hoover Dam, only 30 miles (48 km) to the east of Las Vegas. Thousands of construction workers—much like the people waiting for their divorces to become final—were all potential gamblers.

Small legal gambling halls opened in Reno (in the northern part of the state), but they catered mostly to cowboys and local residents and had a reputation for being raunchy and wild. In April 1931 the first gambling licenses were issued in Las Vegas. The first big casino, El Rancho Vegas, was opened in 1941 on what would later be known as the Strip.

Many in the business world doubted that casino gambling in Nevada would be successful. Most of the casino hotels were small establishments operated by local families or small private companies (some were dude ranches—western-style resorts that offered horseback riding). They were located in hot and dusty desert towns far from major cities, had no air conditioning, and offered few amenities to travelers. Also, there was no state oversight of gambling activities.

However, the end of Prohibition—which had made it illegal to import or sell alcoholic beverages in the United States—brought another element to Las Vegas. During the Prohibition Era (1920–1933) organized crime syndicates operated massive bootlegging rings and became very powerful and wealthy. When Prohibition ended, they switched their focus to gambling. Organized criminals in New York and Chicago were among the first to see the potential of Nevada. Meyer Lansky (1902?–1983) and Frank Costello (1891–1973) sent fellow gangster Benjamin "Bugsy" Siegel (1906–1947) west to develop new criminal enterprises. Siegel invested millions of dollars of the mob's money in a big and lavish casino in Las Vegas that he was convinced would attract top-name entertainers and big-spending gamblers. The Flamingo Hotel and Casino opened in 1946. It was a failure at first, and Siegel was soon killed by his fellow mobsters.

POST–WORLD WAR II. Nevada's casinos grew slowly until after World War II (1939–1945). Postwar Americans were full of optimism and had spending money. Tourism began to grow in Nevada. Las Vegas casino resorts attracted Hollywood celebrities and famous entertainers. The state began collecting gaming taxes during the 1940s. The growing casinos in Las Vegas provided good-paying jobs to workers who brought their families with them, building a middle-class presence. In 1955 the state legislature created the Nevada Gaming Control Board within the Nevada Tax Commission. Four years later, the Nevada Gaming Commission was established.

CORPORATE GROWTH: THE 1960S. The Las Vegas casinos continued to grow during the 1960s. By that time, organized crime syndicates used respectable front men in top management positions while they manipulated the businesses from behind the scenes. Publicly held corporations had been largely kept out of the casino business by a provision in Nevada law that required every individual stockholder to be licensed to operate a casino.

One corporation that was able to get into the casino business was Summa Corporation, a spin-off of Hughes Tool Company, which had only one stockholder: Howard Hughes (1905–1976). Hughes was a wealthy and eccentric businessman who owned the very profitable Hughes Aircraft Company. He spent a lot of his time in Las Vegas during the 1940s and 1950s and later moved there. In 1966 he bought the Desert Inn, a casino hotel on the Strip in Las Vegas. Later, he bought the nearby Sands, Frontier, Castaways, and Silver Slipper casinos.

Legend has it that mobsters threatened Hughes to drive him out of the casino business in Las Vegas, but he refused to leave. He invested hundreds of millions of dollars in Las Vegas properties and predicted that the city would be an entertainment center by the end of the century. In 1967 the Nevada legislature changed the law to make it easier for corporations to own casinos.

To combat organized crime, federal statutes against racketeering (the act of extorting money or favors from businesses through the use of intimidating tactics or by other illegal means) were enacted in 1971, and Nevada officials overhauled the casino regulatory system, making it more difficult for organized crime figures to be involved. Corporations and legitimate financiers began investing heavily in casino hotels in Las Vegas and in other parts of the state.

The Development of Gambling beyond Nevada

During the early 1970s the U.S. Commission on the Review of the National Policy toward Gambling studied Americans' attitudes about gambling and their gambling behavior. The commission found that 80% of Americans approved of gambling and that 67% engaged in gambling activities. In its final report, *Gambling in America* (1976), the commission concluded that state governments that were considering the legalization of gambling should set gambling policy without interference from the federal government, unless problems developed from the infiltration of organized crime or from conflicts between states.

In 1978 the first legal casino hotel outside of Nevada opened in Atlantic City, New Jersey. By the mid-1990s nine additional states had legalized casino gambling: Iowa (1989), South Dakota (1989), Colorado (1990), Illinois (1990), Mississippi (1990), Louisiana (1991), Indiana (1993), Missouri (1993), and Michigan (1996). The American Gaming Association reports in *2012 State of the States: The AGA Survey of Casino Entertainment* (May 2012, http://www.americangaming.org/files/aga/uploads/docs/sos/aga_sos_2012_web.pdf) that by 2011, 15 states allowed commercial casinos to operate.

STATE-SPONSORED LOTTERIES. In 1964 New Hampshire was the first state to again legalize a state lottery. Called the New Hampshire Sweepstakes, it was tied to horse-race results to avoid laws that prohibited lotteries. New York established a lottery in 1967. Twelve other states followed suit during the 1970s. These legal lottery states were concentrated in the Northeast: New Jersey (1970), Pennsylvania (1971), Connecticut (1972), Massachusetts (1972), Michigan (1972), Maryland (1973), Illinois (1974), Maine (1974), Ohio (1974), Rhode Island (1974), Delaware (1975), and Vermont (1977).

An additional 23 states and the District of Columbia legalized lotteries during the 1980s and 1990s. The first multistate lottery game began operating in 1988 and included Iowa, Kansas, Oregon, Rhode Island, West Virginia, and the District of Columbia. It went through several incarnations before becoming the Powerball game in 1992. By 2012, six more states had legalized lotteries, bringing the total to 43 states and the District of Columbia. Lotteries are examined in detail in Chapter 7.

NATIVE AMERICAN GAMBLING ENTERPRISES. Native American tribes established bingo halls to raise funds for tribal operations, and these became highly popular during the 1970s. Some of the most successful were high-stakes operations in Maine and Florida, where most other forms of gambling were prohibited. However, as the stakes were raised, the tribes began facing legal opposition from state governments. The tribes argued that their status as sovereign (independent) nations made them exempt from state laws against gambling. Tribes in various states sued, and the issue was debated in court for years. Finally, the U.S. Supreme Court's landmark ruling in *California v. Cabazon Band of Mission Indians* (480 U.S. 202 [1987]) opened the door to tribal gaming when it found that gambling activities conducted on tribal lands did not fall within the legal jurisdiction of the state. In 1988 Congress passed the Indian Gaming Regulatory Act, which allowed federally recognized Native American tribes to open gambling establishments on their reservations if the states in which they were located already permitted legalized gambling.

In 2000 California voters passed Proposition 1A, which amended the state constitution to permit Native American tribes to operate lottery games, slot machines, and banking and percentage card games on tribal lands. Previously, the tribes were largely restricted to operating bingo halls. In *2012 State of the States*, the American Gaming Association reports that 29 states allowed tribal Class II or III gaming in 2011. Class II and III gaming includes bingo, lotto, card and table games, slot machines, and pari-mutuel gambling (gambling in which those who bet on the top competitors share the total amount bet and the house gets a percentage). Native American tribal casinos are examined in detail in Chapter 5.

INTERNET GAMBLING. Internet gambling sites began operating during the mid-1990s, and most of them were based in the Caribbean. By the end of the decade between 600 and 700 gambling websites were available. According to David O. Stewart of Ropes & Gray, LLP, in *Online Gambling Five Years after UIGEA* (May 2011, http://www.americangaming.org/files/aga/uploads/docs/whitepapers/final_online_gambling_white_paper_5-18-11.pdf), 2,679 gambling websites owned by 665 companies were operating in 2010; by that time Americans were spending $4 billion per year to gamble online.

Even though some countries, such as the United Kingdom, embraced Internet gambling and began regulating the industry, the United States took action to interrupt online gambling activity by U.S. gamblers. Passage of the Unlawful Internet Gambling Enforcement Act of 2006 made it illegal for banks and credit card companies to process payments from U.S. customers to online gambling websites. Many websites immediately stopped accepting customers in the United States. In the press release "After Months of Steady Growth, U.S. Online Gambling Shows Decline in October" (November 14, 2006, http://www.netratings.com/pr/pr_061114.pdf), Nielsen/NetRatings reports a 67% drop in traffic at PartyPoker.com, the most popular online gambling website, from September to October 2006, the month in which the U.S. law was passed. Overall, Nielsen/NetRatings indicates that the top-10 online gaming websites experienced a 56% decline in traffic from September to October 2006.

Despite the fact that some online gaming sites turned away U.S. customers and many credit card companies stopped accepting charges from online gaming sites, final enforcement of the Unlawful Internet Gambling Enforcement Act was delayed several times until June 1, 2010. Gary Wise reports in "A Positive Delay" (ESPN.com, December 2, 2009) that this enforcement was delayed because of the vagueness of the act, which called for banks to block "unlawful Internet gambling transactions" without much guidance as to what transactions were unlawful.

Enjoli Francis reports in "Online Gambling, Casinos to 'Sweep' U.S. in 2012" (ABC News, December 28, 2011) that in December 2011 the U.S. Department of Justice reversed a longtime ban of many types of online gambling, making it legal within state borders. In "Delaware to Allow Online Gambling" (*USA Today*, June 28, 2012), Doug Denison notes that in June 2012 Delaware became the first state to approve legislation offering full-service casino websites. Delaware aimed to launch online gambling in 2013. Nevada began accepting applications for online gambling licenses, and California and New Jersey were considering allowing Internet gambling as well. Internet gambling is examined in depth in Chapter 9.

GAMBLING ISSUES AND SOCIAL IMPACT

In 1957 two men addicted to gambling decided to meet regularly to discuss the problems gambling had caused them and the changes they needed to make in their life to overcome it. After meeting for several months, each realized that the moral support offered by the other was allowing them to control their desire to gamble. They started an organization that was based on the spiritual principles used by Alcoholics Anonymous and similar groups to control addictions. The first group meeting of Gamblers Anonymous was held in September 1957 in Los Angeles, California.

As gambling became more widespread throughout the country, efforts were undertaken to help those whose lives had been negatively affected by gambling. In recognition of the wide social impact of the gambling industry, the American Psychiatric Association officially recognized pathological gambling as a mental health disorder in 1980. Pathological gambling was listed under disorders of impulse control and described as a "chronic and progressive failure to resist impulses to gamble." During the 1980s many states began setting up programs to offer assistance to compulsive gamblers. Harrah's Entertainment became the first commercial casino company to officially address problem gambling when it instituted the educational campaigns Operation Bet Smart and Project 21 to promote responsible gaming and raise awareness about problems associated with underage gambling, respectively.

In 1996 Congress authorized the National Gambling Impact Study Commission to investigate the social and economic consequences of gambling in the United States. The federally funded group included nine commissioners representing pro- and antigambling positions. Existing literature was reviewed and new studies were ordered. The commission held hearings around the country at which a variety of people involved in and affected by the gambling industry testified. In June 1999 the commission concluded in *Final Report* (http://govinfo.library .unt.edu/ngisc/reports/fullrpt.html) that with the exception of Internet gambling, gambling policy decisions were best left up to state, tribal, and local governments. The commission also recommended that legalized gambling not be expanded further until all related costs and benefits were identified and reviewed.

Also during 1999 the National Academies Press published *Pathological Gambling: A Critical Review*, which identified and analyzed all available scientific research studies dealing with pathological and problem gambling. The researchers estimated that about 1.5% of American adults had been pathological gamblers at some point during their life, with about 1.8 million compulsive gamblers actively gambling during a given year. Even though the researchers were able to draw some general conclusions about the prevalence of pathological gambling in the United States, they cited a lack of scientific evidence as a limiting factor in their ability to draw more specific conclusions. For example, they found that men were more likely than women to be pathological gamblers, but they lacked the data to estimate the prevalence of problem gambling among demographic subgroups such as the elderly or those with low incomes.

PUBLIC OPINION

In May 2012 the Gallup Organization conducted a nationwide poll to determine the moral acceptability of a variety of social issues. Overall, gambling was considered to be morally acceptable by 64% of those asked. (See Table 1.1.) Roughly the same percentage of people believed divorce (67%), buying and wearing animal fur (60%), sex between an unmarried man and woman (59%), medical research using stem cells obtained from human embryos (58%), and the death penalty (58%) were morally acceptable.

TABLE 1.1

Public opinion on the moral acceptability of 18 issues, May 2012

Ranked by "Difference"

	Morally acceptable %	Morally wrong %	Difference pct. pts.
Birth control	89	8	81
Divorce	67	25	42
Gambling	64	31	33
Buying and wearing clothing made of animal fur	60	35	25
Medical research using stem cells obtained from human embryos	58	33	25
The death penalty	58	34	24
Sex between an unmarried man and woman	59	38	21
Medical testing on animals	55	38	17
Gay or lesbian relations	54	42	12
Having a baby outside of marriage	54	42	12
Doctor assisted suicide	45	48	−3
Abortion	38	51	−13
Cloning animals	34	60	−26
Pornography	31	64	−33
Suicide	14	80	−66
Polygamy, when a married person has more than one spouse at the same time	11	86	−75
Cloning humans	10	86	−76
Married men and women having an affair	7	89	−82

SOURCE: Frank Newport, "U.S. Perceived Moral Acceptability of Behaviors and Social Policies," in *Americans, Including Catholics, Say Birth Control Is Morally OK*, The Gallup Organization, May 22, 2012, http://www.gallup.com/poll/154799/Americans-Including-Catholics-Say-Birth-Control-Morally .aspx (accessed August 15, 2012). Copyright © 2012 Gallup, Inc. All rights reserved. The content is used with permission; however, Gallup retains all rights of republication.

Frank Newport of the Gallup Organization reports in *Americans, Including Catholics, Say Birth Control Is Morally OK* (May 22, 2012, http://www.gallup.com/poll/ 154799/americans-including-catholics-say-birth-control-morally.aspx) that in 2012 Democrats, Independents, and Republicans were found to differ on the moral acceptability of gambling. Approximately two-thirds of Democrats (67%) and Independents (68%) believed gambling was morally acceptable, compared with 57% of Republicans. (See Table 1.2.) Concerning morality in general, Alyssa Brown of the Gallup Organization notes in *Americans' Negativity about U.S. Moral Values Inches Back Up* (May 18, 2012, http://www.gallup.com/poll/154715/ Americans-Negativity-Moral-Values-Inches-Back.aspx) that Democrats (53%) were less likely than Republicans (82%) or Independents (72%) to say that the overall moral values in the United States were poor.

Between February and March 2006 the Pew Research Center polled 2,250 adults and asked them about their attitudes toward legalized gambling. The results were published by Paul Taylor, Cary Funk, and Peyton Craighill in *Gambling: As the Take Rises, So Does Public Concern* (May 23, 2006, http://pewresearch.org/assets/ social/pdf/Gambling.pdf). In 2006, 71% of adults approved of cash lotteries and 66% approved of bingo for cash prizes. (See Figure 1.1.) Casino gambling (51%)

TABLE 1.2

Perceived moral acceptability of 18 moral issues by political party affiliation, 2012

% morally acceptable, sorted by "Gap"

	Republicans %	Independents %	Democrats %	Gap, Republicans minus Democrats pct. pts.
The death penalty	73	62	42	31
Medical testing on animals	69	50	48	21
Buying and wearing clothing made of animal fur	71	55	55	16
Cloning animals	32	37	32	0
Birth control	87	89	90	−3
Cloning humans	10	9	13	−3
Married men and women having an affair	3	10	8	−5
Polygamy, when a married person has more than one spouse at the same time	5	14	11	−6
Divorce	60	71	69	−9
Gambling	57	68	67	−10
Suicide	9	12	21	−12
Doctor-assisted suicide	33	51	49	−16
Pornography	21	32	39	−18
Sex between an unmarried man and woman	42	68	66	−24
Medical research using stem cells obtained from human embryos	44	57	72	−28
Having a baby outside of marriage	35	60	64	−29
Gay or lesbian relations	36	58	66	−30
Abortion	22	40	52	−30

SOURCE: Frank Newport, "Perceived Moral Acceptability of 2012's Most Controversial Issues—by Party ID," in *Americans, Including Catholics, Say Birth Control Is Morally OK*, The Gallup Organization, May 22, 2012, http://www.gallup.com/poll/154799/Americans-Including-Catholics-Say-Birth-Control-Morally.aspx (accessed August 15, 2012). Copyright © 2012 Gallup, Inc. All rights reserved. The content is used with permission; however, Gallup retains all rights of republication.

and offtrack betting on horse races (50%) received less support. Legalized betting on professional sports (42%) received the lowest approval rating.

Overall, a smaller percentage of Americans approved of gambling in the 2006 Pew poll than did in a similar survey that was conducted by the Gallup Organization in April 1989 and cited by Taylor, Funk, and Craighill. Approval of legalized lotteries and bingo dropped the most between 1989 and 2006. (See Figure 1.1.) Taylor, Funk, and Craighill suggest that the change in Americans' attitudes about gambling has less to do with moral values and more to do with economic values. Less than one-third (28%) of respondents in the 2006 Pew poll thought gambling is immoral, but 70% of respondents believed legalized gambling causes people to spend more money than they can afford. (See Figure 1.2.) This represented an increase of eight percentage points from the 62% of respondents who felt the same way in 1989.

The Pew Research Center took a closer look in 2006 at the demographics of those who believed gambling is morally wrong, morally acceptable, or not a moral issue. Women (38%) were more likely than men (33%) to believe gambling is morally wrong, and more than half (52%) of adults aged 65 years and older condemned gambling on moral grounds, compared with 30% of adults aged 18 to 49 years. (See Table 1.3.)

Education, income, and church attendance were also associated with how people thought about gambling. On the whole, people who are better educated, wealthier, and seldom attend church tended to view gambling as not a moral issue. (See Table 1.3.) By contrast, people with a high school education or less (46%); with family incomes of less than $30,000 (43%); who attend church at least once per week (50%); or who are white, evangelical Protestants (57%) tended to view gambling as morally wrong.

FIGURE 1.1

Public approval of legalized gambling, 1989 and 2006

[By percentage]

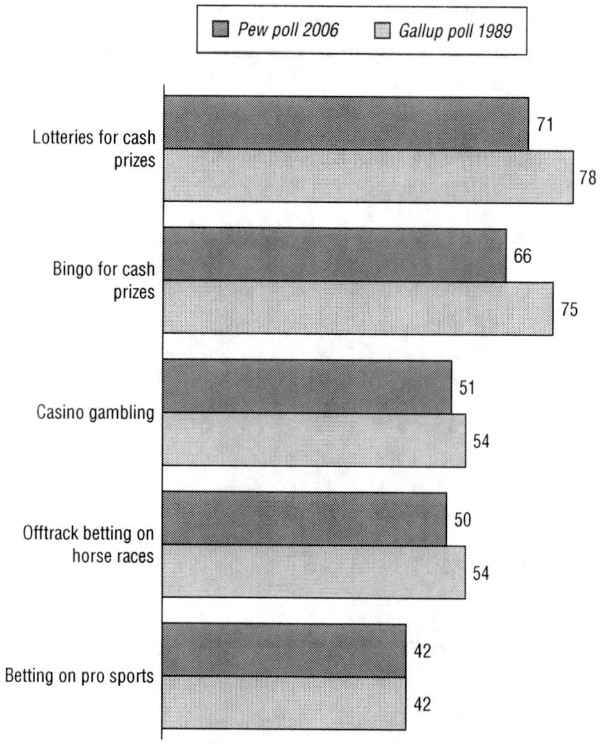

Pew poll 2006
Gallup poll 1989
Lotteries for cash prizes
71
78
Bingo for cash prizes
66
75
Casino gambling
51
54
Offtrack betting on horse races
50
54
Betting on pro sports
42
42

SOURCE: Paul Taylor, Cary Funk, and Peyton Craighill, "Approval of Legalized Gambling down Slightly," in *Gambling: As the Take Rises, So Does Public Concern*, Pew Research Center, May 23, 2006, http://pewresearch.org/assets/social/pdf/Gambling.pdf (accessed August 15, 2012). Data from The Gallup Organization. Copyright © 1989 Gallup, Inc. All rights reserved. The content is used with permission; however, Gallup retains all rights of republication.

FIGURE 1.2

Poll respondents who say legalized gambling encourages people to gamble more than they can afford, 1989 and 2006

[By percentage]

100
0
62
70
Gallup poll 1989
Pew poll 2006

SOURCE: Paul Taylor, Cary Funk, and Peyton Craighill, "More See a Downside to Gambling," in *Gambling: As the Take Rises, So Does Public Concern*, Pew Research Center, May 23, 2006, http://pewresearch.org/assets/social/pdf/Gambling.pdf (accessed August 15, 2012). Data from The Gallup Organization. Copyright © 1989 Gallup, Inc. All rights reserved. The content is used with permission; however, Gallup retains all rights of republication.

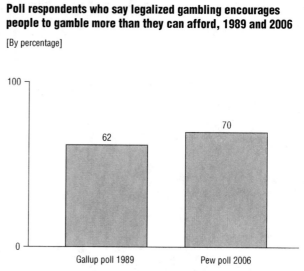

TABLE 1.3

Views of gambling by demographic characteristics, 2006

PERCENT WHO BELIEVE THIS BEHAVIOR IS. . .

	Morally wrong	Morally acceptable	Not a moral issue	(Vol.) Depends	Don't know	N
	%	%	%	%	%	
All adults	35	17	42	3	3=100	745
Gender						
Men	33	20	42	3	2=100	359
Women	38	13	43	3	3=100	336
Age						
18–49	30	19	45	3	3=100	357
50–64	33	13	43	3	3=100	230
65+	52	15	27	3	3=100	147
Education						
College grad	24	17	53	3	3=100	304
Some college	26	17	50	5	2=100	188
High school or less	46	17	33	1	3=100	249
Family income						
$75,000 or more	23	19	53	2	3=100	234
$30,000 to $75,000	37	16	43	3	1=100	254
Less than $30,000	43	16	34	4	3=100	180
Marital status						
Married	39	16	39	4	2=100	447
Not married	30	19	47	2	2=100	292
Church attendance						
Weekly or more	50	13	31	3	3=100	290
Monthly or less	29	21	46	3	1=100	246
Seldom or never	21	17	56	2	4=100	193
Religion						
White Evangelical Protestant	57	7	29	4	3=100	173
White mainline Protestant	30	20	46	2	2=100	172
Catholic	24	24	48	3	1=100	173
Ideology						
Conservative	47	14	35	2	2=100	301
Moderate	30	18	45	4	3=100	291
Liberal	19	17	58	4	2=100	126
Party identification						
Republican	43	16	37	3	1=100	242
Democrat	34	22	38	2	4=100	239
Independent	27	11	55	4	3=100	228
Region						
Northeast	23	19	52	4	2=100	128
Midwest	35	14	46	2	3=100	177
South	49	17	30	2	2=100	254
West	26	17	49	4	4=100	186

N = Population.

SOURCE: Paul Taylor, Cary Funk, and Peyton Craighill, "Gambling," in *A Barometer of Modern Morals: Sex, Drugs, and the 1040*, Pew Research Center, March 28, 2006, http://www.pewsocialtrends.org/2006/03/28/a-barometer-of-modern-morals/77-2/ (accessed August 15, 2012)

CHAPTER 2
SUPPLY AND DEMAND: WHO OFFERS GAMBLING? WHO GAMBLES?

Like any business in a capitalist society, the gambling industry is driven by the principles of supply and demand. Gambling proponents argue that demand drives supply. In other words, the industry grows and spreads into new markets because the public is eager to gamble. Furthermore, opinion polls show that most Americans support legal gambling opportunities, particularly lotteries and casinos.

Gambling is one of the most popular leisure activities in the country. According to the American Gaming Association (AGA), in *2012 State of the States: The AGA Survey of Casino Entertainment* (May 2012, http://www.americangaming.org/files/aga/uploads/docs/sos/aga_sos_2012_web.pdf), commercial casinos generated revenues of $35.6 billion in 2011. In addition, tribal casinos took in $27.2 billion that same year, according to the National Indian Gaming Commission, in "Gaming Revenues by Region 2010 and 2011" (2012, http://www.nigc.gov/Portals/0/NIGC%20Uploads/Tribal%20Data/GamingRevenuesByRegion2010and2011.pdf). These numbers dwarf, for example, box office sales of the U.S. motion picture industry, which the Motion Picture Association of America indicates in *Theatrical Market Statistics, 2011* (2012, http://www.mpaa.org/Resources/5bec4ac9-a95e-443b-987b-bff6fb5455a9.pdf) earned $10.2 billion in the domestic market and $32.6 billion worldwide in 2011.

However, gambling opponents argue that supply drives demand. They surmise that people would not be tempted to gamble or to gamble as often if opportunities were not so prevalent and widespread. They view gambling as an irresistible temptation with potentially dangerous consequences. It bothers them that gambling opportunities are presented, promoted, and supported not only by the business world but also by government leaders and politicians—people who are supposed to represent the best interests of the public they serve.

Whatever the driving reason, gambling has become a big business and a popular pastime for many Americans.

SUPPLY: GAMBLING OPPORTUNITIES AND OPPORTUNISTS

A variety of gambling opportunities are available in the United States, both legal and illegal. Gambling is a moneymaking activity for corporations, small businesses, charities, governments, and, in some cases, criminals. The legal gambling industry employs hundreds of thousands of people across the country. In addition, it generates business in a variety of related industries, including manufacturing companies that provide slot machines and other supplies; travel and tourism companies that provide transportation, food, and lodging for gamblers; advertising agencies that promote gambling enterprises; and breeders who raise and train greyhounds and racehorses.

According to the *Statistical Abstract of the United States: 2012* (2012, http://www.census.gov/compendia/statab/2012/tables/12s1259.pdf), the legal gambling industry's gross revenue increased from $62.2 billion in 2000 to $92.3 billion in 2007, before dipping to $89.3 billion in 2009; these figures include revenues for commercial casinos, racetracks, lotteries, and other forms of betting. Gross gambling revenue is the money that is taken in by the industry minus the winnings paid out. In other words, it is equivalent to sales. From this number, then, operating expenses such as wages, benefits, and taxes must be subtracted to gauge the profits that are realized by the industry. In *2012 State of the States*, the AGA estimates that, of the $35.6 billion in gross revenue earned by the commercial casino industry in 2011, $12.9 billion was paid out in wages (including benefits and tips), and $7.9 billion was paid in taxes.

Casino Owners and Operators

Corporations have profited the most from legalized gambling since they took over the small casinos of Las

Vegas, Nevada, during the late 1960s. The government had pushed out organized crime, which enabled the corporations to bring their management practices to an increasingly profitable business. They invested money in new and bigger properties in Las Vegas and throughout the state of Nevada and then, in 1978, opened the first casino hotel in Atlantic City, New Jersey. As of 2013, most corporations in the industry owned or operated several commercial casinos. Casino City Press estimates in *North American Gaming Almanac* (2012, http://www.casinocitypress.com/pdfs/naga/naga2012_na.pdf) that in 2010 commercial casinos and card rooms controlled 46% of the legal gambling revenue in the United States and Canada, compared with 24% controlled by lotteries and 27% by tribal casinos. Some companies, such as Caesars Entertainment Corporation, also manage casinos for Native American tribes. The tribes are increasingly partnering with large, well-known corporations to take advantage of their name recognition and corporate experience.

Many of the nation's gambling properties are controlled by five well-known corporations: Caesars Entertainment Corporation, MGM Resorts International, Boyd Gaming Corporation, Penn National Gaming, and Station Casinos.

CAESARS ENTERTAINMENT CORPORATION. According to the Caesars Entertainment Corporation's 2011 10-K filing with the U.S. Securities and Exchange Commission (SEC; March 15, 2012, http://investor.caesars.com/secfiling.cfm?filingID=1193125-12-115625), in 2011 the company owned or managed 52 casinos in seven countries. The majority of the company's casinos were in the United States, with 10 casinos in Las Vegas alone. In the United States, the company's holdings were operated primarily under the Harrah's, Caesars, Bally's, and Horseshoe brand names. The company also owned the World Series of Poker tournament, and in 2010 it acquired Planet Hollywood. In 2011 it employed approximately 70,000 people and had net revenues of $8.8 billion.

In Las Vegas the company owned Bally's Las Vegas, Bill's Gamblin' Hall and Saloon, Caesars Palace, Flamingo Las Vegas, Harrah's Las Vegas, Hot Spot Oasis, Imperial Palace Hotel and Casino, Paris Las Vegas, Planet Hollywood Resort and Casino, and Rio All-Suite Hotel and Casino. Elsewhere in Nevada the company owned Harrah's Lake Tahoe, Harrah's Laughlin, Harrah's Reno, and Harvey's Lake Tahoe. Caesars also owned several properties in Atlantic City, New Jersey, including Bally's Atlantic City, Caesars Atlantic City, Harrah's Resort Atlantic City, and Showboat Atlantic City. The company also owned casinos in Arizona, California, Illinois, Indiana, Iowa, Louisiana, Mississippi, Missouri, North Carolina, and Pennsylvania, as well as

horse racing facilities in Kentucky, Massachusetts, and Ohio. In addition, the company owned casinos in Canada, Egypt, South Africa, the United Kingdom, and Uruguay.

MGM RESORTS INTERNATIONAL. MGM Resorts International reports in *The Astonishing World of MGM Resorts International: 2011 Annual Report* (2012, http://mgmresorts.investorroom.com/file.php/288/2011%2BAnnual%2BReport.MGMResortsInternational.pdf) that in 2011 the company generated $7.8 billion in revenue, up from $6.1 billion in 2010, an increase of nearly 30%. According to the company's website (2012, http://mgmresorts.com/company/company-overview.aspx), in 2012 MGM Resorts International operated 15 casino resorts in Michigan, Mississippi, and Nevada and co-owned three others in Illinois and Nevada. Notable MGM establishments included ARIA, the Bellagio, Circus Circus Las Vegas, Excalibur, Luxor, Mandalay Bay, MGM Grand Las Vegas, The Mirage, Monte Carlo, New York–New York, and Vdara, all in Las Vegas. The company also owned a 51% stake in MGM China Holdings Limited, which operated the MGM Macau resort and casino.

BOYD GAMING CORPORATION. Boyd Gaming Corporation (http://boydgaming.investorroom.com/) is a Las Vegas–based company that owned 22 casinos in eight states as of 2012. The company's properties included nine casinos in Las Vegas, among them the Fremont Hotel and Casino, the Gold Coast Hotel and Casino, and the Orleans Hotel and Casino, as well as casinos in Illinois, Indiana, Iowa, Kansas, Louisiana, Mississippi, and New Jersey. In 2012 the company acquired Peninsula Gaming, operator of five casinos in three states, while also entering into a strategic partnership with Bwin.Party Digital Entertainment, a leading online gaming corporation. According to Boyd's 2011 10-K filing with the SEC (2012, http://www.sec.gov/Archives/edgar/data/906553/000090655312000005/byd10k2011.htm), Boyd Gaming generated net revenues of $2.3 billion in 2011, up from $2.1 billion in 2010. Of these earnings, nearly $830 million came from the company's gaming operations in Las Vegas, approximately $730 million were generated by its casino in Atlantic City, and just over $770 million from its operations in other states.

PENN NATIONAL GAMING. According to the company's website (2012, http://www.pngaming.com/About/Company%20Fact%20Sheet), in 2012 Penn National Gaming owned and operated 22 casinos, 11 horse- and dog-racing facilities, and six offtrack betting properties in Colorado, Florida, Illinois, Indiana, Iowa, Kansas, Louisiana, Maine, Maryland, Mississippi, Missouri, Nevada, New Jersey, New Mexico, Ohio, Pennsylvania, Texas, West Virginia, and Ontario, Canada. The company acquired several of its establishments from Argosy Gaming Corporation in October 2005 for $2.3 billion. In its

12   Supply and Demand: Who Offers Gambling? Who Gambles?

Gambling

2011 annual report (2012, http://phx.corporate-ir.net/External.File?item=UGFyZW50SUQ9MTMxNTQzfENoaWxkSUQ9 LTF8VHlwZT0z&t=1), Penn National Gaming reported net earnings of $2.7 billion in 2011, compared with $2.4 billion in 2010. As of December 31, 2011, Penn National Gaming employed 16,740 people.

STATION CASINOS. Station Casinos reports in its 2011 10-K filing (2012, http://www.secinfo.com/d1DSAk.pd.htm) that in 2011 it owned nine major hotel/casino properties under the Station and Fiesta brand names, as well stakes in eight smaller casino properties in the Las Vegas area. Properties owned included Boulder Station, Fiesta Henderson Hotel and Casino, Fiesta Rancho, Gold Rush Casino, Palace Station, Red Rock Casino Resort & Spa, Santa Fe Station, Sunset Station, Texas Station, Wildfire Boulder, and Wild Wild West Gambling Hall & Hotel. The company also managed the Thunder Valley Casino for the United Auburn Indian Community in Lincoln, California, and the Gun Lake Casino in Allegan County, Michigan.

In November 2007 the company was taken private through a management buyout. In July 2009 Station Casinos filed for Chapter 11 bankruptcy, blaming its losses on the recession; the company's reorganization plan was approved in August of that year. As Chris Sieroty reports in "Station Casinos Emerges from Bankruptcy" (June 17, 2011, http://www.lvrj.com/business/station-casinos-emerges-from-bankruptcy-124086429.html), the company finally emerged from bankruptcy protection in June 2011, becoming Station Casinos LLC. For that year, the company had net revenues of $1.2 billion, up from $945 million in 2010. As of February 29, 2012, Station Casinos LLC employed 11,800 people.

OTHER GAMBLING CORPORATIONS. Different companies play important roles in other realms of the gambling industry. Churchill Downs is the major organization in the Thoroughbred horse racing business. Churchill Downs notes in *2011 Annual Report* (March 12, 2012, http://ir.churchilldownsincorporated.com/secfiling.cfm?filingID=1193125-12-109920), its annual report to the SEC, that in 2011 it operated racetracks in Florida, Illinois, Kentucky (including its namesake venue, home of the famed Kentucky Derby), and Louisiana. In addition, Churchill Downs owned Harlow's Casino Resort & Hotel in Greenville, Mississippi, slot and video poker machine facilities in Florida and Louisiana, and the online wagering entity TwinSpires, among other holdings. In 2011 the company had revenues of $696.9 million, up from $585.3 million in 2010.

Many corporations directly support the gambling industry by providing equipment, goods, supplies, and services. They may be members of the Gaming Standards Association (2012, http://www.gamingstandards.com/?page=about_us/vision_and_mission), an international organization that

is "the leading standards forum that creates value by facilitating innovation and efficiencies for the gaming community." Some examples of these corporations are:

- GTECH Corporation (a subsidiary of the Lottomatica Group), which introduced the first lottery terminal in 1982 and now provides technology services to lotteries in 23 states

- Bally Technology, which introduced its first slot machine in 1936 and is now a successful machine manufacturer and distributor

- Konami Gaming, a Japanese producer of high-tech video slot machines and multisite casino management systems that entered the U.S. gaming market in 2000

- WMS Gaming, which is engaged entirely in the manufacture, sale, leasing, and licensing of gambling machines

GAMBLING AS AN INVESTMENT. The investment firm USA MUTUALS sells shares in its Vice Fund, a mutual fund that consists entirely of companies in the alcohol, tobacco, gambling, and defense industries. In the fact sheet "Vice Fund—VICEX" (September 30, 2012, http://www.usamutuals.com/vicefund/docs/VICEXcomplete.pdf), the firm states that, after suffering a sharp decline in value in the aftermath of the financial crisis of 2007–08, by September 2012 Vice Fund's returns were up more than 30% over the previous year, and 9.15% since the fund was established in 2002.

Small Businesses

Many small casinos and racetracks, minicasinos, and card rooms around the country are owned or operated by small companies, families, and entrepreneurs. Other ways in which small businesses are engaged in or serve the gambling industry include:

- Selling lottery tickets and operating electronic gaming devices at independently owned convenience stores, markets, service stations, bars, restaurants, bowling alleys, and newsstands

- Manufacturing and distributing equipment such as slot machines, roulette wheels, lottery tickets, dice, and cards

- Providing services such as advertising, marketing, public relations, accounting, information technology, and food

- Breeding, training, and caring for horses and greyhounds

Most small businesses that offer gambling do so through lottery ticket sales or electronic gaming devices, such as slot machines. These are considered forms of convenience gambling because patrons do not have to travel to special destinations, such as casinos and racetracks. Convenience gambling has been more controversial than destination gambling. Critics argue that allowing gambling in stores and restaurants and other places that people visit as part of their everyday routine makes it too easy for them to gamble. The same criticism is leveled against Internet gambling, which patrons can do at home.

Internet Gambling Businesses

At the beginning of the 21st century, online betting in the United States was subject to regulation under the Federal Wire Act of 1961, which declared it illegal to place wagers on sporting events via any form of wire communication. In 2006 Congress passed the Unlawful Internet Gambling Enforcement Act (UIGEA), which explicitly prohibited gambling companies from receiving wagering money over the Internet. In spite of the ban on Internet gambling, Americans still managed to gamble online during these years. As the AGA notes in "Now Is the Time to Create a Safe, Regulated Online Gambling Experience" (June 1, 2011, http://www.americangaming .org/newsroom/op-eds/now-time-create-safe-regulated-online-gambling-experience-0), roughly 15% of the $30 billion generated worldwide by online gambling in 2010 came from the United States. The federal interpretation of online gambling laws changed in 2011, when the U.S. Justice Department announced that only online sports betting was prohibited under the UIGEA, opening the door for individual states to pass their own statutes regarding other forms of Internet gaming. As Alexandra Bruell reports in "Jackpot! Online Casinos to Drop Billions on Ads" (October 29, 2012, http://adage.com/article/ digital/jackpot-online-casinos-drop-billions-ads/238012/), in 2012 Nevada became the first state to legalize online gambling, while other states, among them California and New Jersey, were exploring the possibility of legalizing some forms of online gaming in the near future.

Criminals

Gambling has had a checkered legal history in the United States. At various times it has been legal, illegal but tolerated, or illegal and actively prosecuted. During times when gambling opportunities have been outlawed, entrepreneurs have stepped in to offer them anyway. These entrepreneurs range from mobsters running million-dollar betting rings to grandmothers running neighborhood bingo games. Either way, the illegal nature of the activity makes these entrepreneurs criminals.

Organized crime groups have often been associated with gambling, which is a cash business with high demand and good profits. Crime syndicates on the East Coast were among the first to see the potential of Las Vegas, invest in it, and profit from it. At times, they infiltrated other segments of the legal gambling industry, such as horse racing. However, strict regulations and crackdowns by law enforcement were put into place to push them out. The federal Racketeer Influenced and Corrupt Organizations (RICO) Act of 1970 was designed to combat infiltration by organized crime into legitimate businesses, including gambling enterprises. Most analysts believe RICO has been largely successful at keeping mobsters from establishing or taking over legal gambling businesses.

However, even though they have been denied casino ownership and management roles, some organized crime figures have infiltrated casinos in other ways, such as through labor unions and maintenance or food services. Law enforcement officials also believe organized crime families have been involved in bribing state officials who were considering the extension or expansion of gambling options, particularly relating to electronic gambling machines.

The Nevada Gaming Commission and State Gaming Control Board maintain a list of people who are prohibited from gambling in Nevada. The List of Excluded Persons, more commonly known as "Nevada's Black Book," includes known cheaters, crime family bosses, mob associates, and others who are linked in some way to organized crime. These people are considered so dangerous to the integrity of legal gambling that they are not allowed to set foot in Nevada casinos. In "GCB Excluded Person List" (2013, http://gaming.nv.gov/index.aspx? page=72), the Nevada Gaming Commission and State Gaming Control Board provide photographs of these excluded people.

The most lucrative sector of the gambling industry for organized crime has been and continues to be illegal bookmaking and numbers games. Bookmaking is a gambling activity in which a bookmaker takes bets on the odds that a particular event will occur or that an event will have a particular outcome. The vast majority of bookmaking revolves around sporting events, such as college and professional football and basketball games. Such wagering is extremely popular in the United States. Because sports bookmaking is legal only in Nevada, there is a large illegal market for it across the country. As the AGA explains in "Sports Wagering" (2012, http://www .americangaming.org/industry-resources/research/fact-sheets/sports-wagering), the state of Nevada reported that nearly $2.9 billion was wagered in legal sports betting in 2011; by comparison, illegal sports wagers totaled an estimated $380 billion nationally that year.

Illegal numbers games are similar to lottery games in that players wager money on particular numbers to be selected in a drawing or by other means. Illegal numbers operators thrive in many parts of the country, especially large cities—even those where legal lotteries are offered.

Not all bookmaking is done through mobsters. Many enterprising entrepreneurs run small-time illegal gambling books, mostly related to sporting events. Office

14   Supply and Demand: Who Offers Gambling? Who Gambles?

Gambling

pools, in which coworkers pool small wagers on sports or office events (e.g., when a baby is going to be born) are common. Even though society does not generally consider private wagers and small-stakes office pools to be illegal gambling, the laws in most states do.

Despite widespread illegal gambling, few people are actually arrested for engaging in it. Authorities made only 9,941 arrests for gambling in 2010 out of 13.1 million total arrests that year. (See Table 2.1.) The number was even lower in 2011 as reported by the Federal Bureau of Investigation in *Crime in the United States 2011* (October 29, 2012, http://www.fbi.gov/about-us/cjis/ucr/crime-in-the-u.s/2011/crime-in-the-u.s.-2011), when 8,596 arrests were made for gambling offenses out of a total 12.4 million arrests that year in the United States.

Charities

Charitable gambling is the most widely practiced form of gambling in the United States. In 2013 it was legal in 48 states and the District of Columbia (only Hawaii and Utah prohibited it). In charitable gambling,

TABLE 2.1

Estimated arrests by type of crime, 2010

Total[a]	13,120,947
Murder and nonnegligent manslaughter	11,201
Forcible rape	20,088
Robbery	112,300
Aggravated assault	408,488
Burglary	289,769
Larceny-theft	1,271,410
Motor vehicle theft	71,487
Arson	11,296
Violent crime[b]	552,077
Property crime[b]	1,643,962
Other assaults	1,292,449
Forgery and counterfeiting	78,101
Fraud	187,887
Embezzlement	16,616
Stolen property; buying, receiving, possessing	94,802
Vandalism	252,753
Weapons; carrying, possessing, etc.	159,020
Prostitution and commercialized vice	62,668
Sex offenses (except forcible rape and prostitution)	72,628
Drug abuse violations	1,638,846
Gambling	9,941
Offenses against the family and children	111,062
Driving under the influence	1,412,223
Liquor laws	512,790
Drunkenness	560,718
Disorderly conduct	615,172
Vagrancy	32,033
All other offenses	3,720,402
Suspicion	1,166
Curfew and loitering law violations	94,797

[a]Does not include suspicion.
[b]Violent crimes are offenses of murder and nonnegligent manslaughter, forcible rape, robbery, and aggravated assault. Property crimes are offenses of burglary, larceny-theft, motor vehicle theft, and arson.

SOURCE: "Table 29. Estimated Number of Arrests, United States, 2010," in *Crime in the United States, 2010*, U.S. Department of Justice, Federal Bureau of Investigation, September 2011, http://www.fbi.gov/about-us/cjis/ucr/crime-in-the-u.s/2010/crime-in-the-u.s.-2010/tables/10tbl29.xls (accessed August 15, 2012)

a specified portion of the money that is raised (minus prizes, expenses, and any state fees and taxes) goes to qualified charitable organizations. Such organizations include religious groups, fraternal organizations, veterans groups, volunteer fire departments, parent-teacher organizations, civic and cultural groups, booster clubs, and other nonprofit organizations.

Generally, a charitable organization has to have been in existence for several years and has to obtain a state license for the gambling activity. Most states will only issue licenses to organizations that have been recognized by the Internal Revenue Service as exempt from federal income tax under Tax Code section 501(c). Thousands of charitable organizations are registered to conduct gambling throughout the country.

Most charitable gambling is regulated by state governments, although not uniformly by the same department—it may be the department of revenue, the state police, the alcohol control board, or the lottery, gaming, or racing commission. Administrative fees and taxes are levied in most states. In some states charitable gambling activity is unregulated.

Typical games allowed include bingo (the most common), pull tabs (lottery tickets with tabs that gamblers pull open to reveal cash prizes), raffles, and card games such as poker or blackjack. Slot machines and table games such as roulette and craps are generally not permitted. Limits are usually placed on the size of cash prizes that can be awarded. States allow different games for charity fundraising. For example, as of 2012 California allowed charitable raffles, bingo, and poker and other controlled games.

Because of the inconsistencies in state oversight, it is difficult to determine the complete extent of charitable gambling in the United States. In *Charity Gaming in North America: 2011 Annual Report* (2012, http://www.naftm.org/vertical/sites/%7B10B16680-A509-4D78-B468-8A1901FC0CF7%7D/uploads/NAFTM_2011.pdf), the National Association of Fundraising Ticket Manufacturers (NAFTM), a trade association representing companies that manufacture bingo paper, pull tabs, and other supplies used in the charitable gambling industry, notes that, among states that participated in the organization's annual survey, in 2011 the 10 highest-earning states generated $5.3 billion in gross receipts through charitable gaming. As Table 2.2 reveals, in 2010 the top five states by gross receipts were Minnesota ($973.6 million), Texas ($699.4 million), Michigan ($560.5 million), Washington ($556.3 million), and Indiana ($484 million). New Jersey reported the highest percentage of net earnings through charitable gaming in 2010, generating $51.7 million in net proceeds out of $139.6 million in gross receipts, or 37%; by comparison, South Carolina

Gambling

Supply and Demand: Who Offers Gambling? Who Gambles? **15**

TABLE 2.2

Gross receipts and proceeds from charitable gaming in top 10 participation states, 2010

Top states by gross receipts		Top states by net receipts	
State	Total gross receipts	State	Net receipts
Minnesota	$973,632,000	Minnesota	$78,237,000
Texas	$699,391,264	Michigan	$73,942,586
Michigan	$560,542,356	Indiana	$65,240,196
Washington	$556,284,212	New Jersey	$51,715,000
Indiana	$484,026,932	Kentucky	$44,952,100
Kentucky	$406,310,500	Wisconsin	$39,439,300
New York	$316,536,752	Nebraska	$30,305,551
Virginia	$276,866,332	Virginia	$28,346,390
North Dakota	$249,468,404	Texas	$25,673,203
Nebraska	$232,462,466		

SOURCE: "Top Ten States by Gross Receipts" and "Top Ten States by Net Receipts," in *Charity Gaming in North America: 2010 Annual Report*, National Association of Fundraising Ticket Manufacturers, 2012, http://www.naftm.org/vertical/sites/%7B10B16680-A509-4D78-B468-8A1901FC0CF7%7D/uploads/NAFTM_2010_annual_report_final.pdf (accessed August 15, 2012)

reported net proceeds of only $617,399, or 1% of gross receipts totaling $120.5 million. (See Table 2.3.)

The NAFTM notes that nearly all states charge licensing fees to conduct charitable gambling events. In 2011 Washington charged nearly $12.3 million in licensing fees, more than any other state. A few states base licensing fees on the amount of gross receipts, so the fees can be thousands of dollars. Most states also impose a gaming tax on the proceeds from charitable gambling and/or collect administrative fees. A majority of states allocate all or a portion of these revenues to their general funds or to the agencies that oversee charitable gambling. A few states split the money with local law enforcement agencies.

The Government

Federal, state, local, and tribal agencies collect money from gambling operations through the assessment of taxes and fees and, in some cases, by directly supplying gambling opportunities. Because the money raised is spent on public programs, many Americans are ultimately affected by the government's involvement in gambling. In states facing budget deficits, the expansion of gambling often seems an attractive solution. Stephen C. Fehr reports in "Tracking the Recession: Gambling Revisited" (January 20, 2009, http://www.infozine.com/news/stories/op/storiesView/sid/33330/) that in 2009 states that outlawed gambling were considering allowing it and other states were considering expanding it as a way to deal with the budget crises that resulted from the recession. For example, in 2009 Maine expanded casino hours into Sunday morning. As Kyle Smith reports in "Legalize Sports Betting, and Let Gov. Chris Christie Spike the Football" (August 23, 2012, http://www.forbes.com/sites/kylesmith/2012/08/23/legalize-sports-betting-

and-let-gov-chris-christie-spike-the-football/), the state of New Jersey's decision to legalize sports betting in 2012 prompted lawsuits from the four major professional sports leagues and the National Collegiate Athletic Association (NCAA), which charged that the new law was in violation of the Professional and Amateur Sports Protection Act of 1992. However, as Dan Wetzel reports in "New Jersey's Plan to Legalize Sports Betting Incurs Laughable Response from NCAA" (October 16, 2012, http://sports.yahoo.com/news/nfl-new-jersey-s-plan-to-legalize-sports-betting-ncaa-pulls-events.html), in spite of these legal challenges the state still intended to legalize sports betting in 2013.

THE FEDERAL GOVERNMENT. The primary means by which the federal government makes money from the gambling industry is by taxing winning gamblers and gambling operators. Gamblers must declare gambling earnings when they file their personal income taxes. They get to subtract their gambling losses, but they must keep thorough records and have receipts, if possible, to prove their losses. For racetrack gamblers, this means saving losing betting slips and keeping a gambling diary of dates, events, and amounts. Casino gamblers who join so-called slot clubs can get a detailed printout of their gambling history from the casino.

Gambling operators, like all companies, are subject to corporate taxes. They are required to report winnings that meet certain criteria to the Internal Revenue Service. (See Table 2.4.) The gambling operator must withhold income tax from winnings of more than $5,000, usually at a withholding rate of 25%. Gamblers who win noncash prizes, such as cars or other merchandise, have to pay taxes on the fair market value of the item.

The federal government is also in the gambling business. John H. Tucker reports in "Our Military Has a Gambling Problem" (May 2, 2012, http://www.seattleweekly.com/2012-05-02/news/our-military-doesn-t-have-a-gambling-problem/) that, through its Recreation Machine Program, the U.S. armed forces operated 2,189 video gambling machines on marine, army, and naval bases overseas; the U.S. Air Force administered an additional 1,100 machines. Between 2010 and 2011, the military generated net revenues of $142.3 million through its gaming machines. Tucker writes that easy access to video gambling on military bases played a role in the rise in gambling addiction among U.S. service members during this time. To address this issue, in 2008 Representative Lincoln Davis (1943–; D-TN) introduced in the U.S. House of Representatives the Warrant Officer Aaron Walsh Stop DOD Sponsored Gambling Act, which would prohibit slot machines on U.S. military bases. The bill died in subcommittee.

STATE GOVERNMENTS. State governments make money from legal gambling enterprises that are operated

16 Supply and Demand: Who Offers Gambling? Who Gambles?

Gambling

TABLE 2.3

Receipts by game, charitable gaming, 2010

State	Bingo gross	Pull tab gross	Raffles gross	Other games	Total gross receipts	Total net proceeds	% net proceeds/ gross receipts
Colorado	$45,238,937	$58,573,919	$9,511,240	$—	$113,324,096	$18,000,000	16%
Connecticut	$19,273,816	$6,923,240	$11,291,966	$459,317	$37,948,339	$13,562,793	36%
Illinois	$—	$—	$—	$—	$—	$—	N/A
Indiana	$82,388,278	$366,900,025	$21,562,501	$13,176,128	$484,026,932	$65,240,196	13%
Kentucky	$82,566,200	$303,608,300	$13,133,200	$7,012,800	$406,310,500	$44,952,100	11%
Lousiana	$100,760,500	$93,561,800	$2,887,100	$19,276,600	$216,486,000	$21,310,500	10%
Maine	$17,203,701	$—	$—	$55,607,957	$72,811,658	$—	0%
Massachusetts	$42,727,347	$16,960,200	$20,049,717	$1,360,689	$81,097,953	$14,467,498	18%
Michigan	$119,991,416	$201,839,683	$53,615,439	$181,892,459	$560,542,356	$73,942,586	13%
Minnesota	$59,109,000	$886,673,000	$7,512,000	$20,338,000	$973,632,000	$78,237,000	8%
Missouri	$59,060,997	$44,023,801	N/A	N/A	$103,084,799	$10,584,482	11%
Nebraska	$9,427,780	$30,752,495	$6,820,938	$185,461,253	$232,462,466	$30,305,551	13%
New Hampshire	$17,419,081	$63,484,904	$53,817,700	$32,887,446	$113,791,431	$—	0%
New Jersey	$41,997,400	$43,771,400	$6,603,334	$872,370	$139,586,500	$51,715,000	37%
New York	$73,926,547	$235,134,501	$4,348,675	$76,686,706	$316,536,752	$—	0%
North Dakota	$31,976,605	$136,456,418	$6,349,918	$732,034	$249,468,404	$24,733,952	10%
Oregon	$32,717,992	$—	$—	$—	$39,799,943	$7,481,386	19%
Pennsylvania	$—	$—	$—	$—	$—	$—	N/A
South Carolina	$120,500,719	$—	$—	$—	$120,500,719	$617,399	1%
Texas	$372,206,404	$327,184,860	$—	$—	$699,391,264	$25,673,203	4%
Virginia	$114,437,868	$156,477,860	$5,536,410	$414,194	$276,866,332	$28,346,390	10%
Washington	$40,683,419	$43,289,509 (non-profit) $217,739,289 (commercial)	$7,281,248	$365,780 (non-profit) $246,924,967 (commercial)	$91,619,956 (non-profit) $464,664,256 (commercial)	NA	NA
Wisconsin	$18,030,200	$—	$62,091,800	$19,000	$80,141,000	$39,439,300	49%
Province							
Alberta	$139,845,000	$75,808,000	$170,137,000	$1,013,636,000	$1,399,426,000	$151,247,000	11%
Manitoba	$44,174,145	$4,179,006	$27,979,514	$1,438,842	$77,771,508	$17,703,759	23%
Newfoundland	$189,316	$145,697	$187,265	$18,682	$540,661	$30,738	6%
Ontario	$609,000,000	$317,000,000	$284,000,000	$—	$1,200,000,000	$406,000,000	34%

Notes: This table will provide the reader with a breakdown on how much is wagered by state or province in bingo, pull tabs, raffles and other games sponsored by charities ("gross receipts"). It will also identify the amount of money ("net proceeds") charities will have derived from the play of those games during the 2009 fiscal year for that jurisdiction, and which they may use for their programs. Finally, a calculation is made to show the percentage of net proceeds to gross receipts so the reader may make comparisons among the reporting jurisdictions. Canadian receipts are reported in Canadian dollars.

SOURCE: "Receipts by Game," in *Charity Gaming in North America: 2010 Annual Report*, National Association of Fundraising Ticket Manufacturers, 2012. http://www.naftm.org/vertical/sites/%7B10B16680-A509-4D78B468-8A1901FC0CF7%7D/uploads/NAFTM_2010_annual_report_final.pdf (accessed August 15, 2012)

Gambling

Supply and Demand: Who Offers Gambling? Who Gambles?   17

TABLE 2.4

Gambling winnings that must be reported to the Internal Revenue Service (IRS), 2012

Type of game	Amount of prize paid is equal to or greater than
Lotteries sweepstakes, horse races, dog races, instant bingo game prizes, and other wagering transactions	$600 and prize is at least 300 times wager
Bingo	$1,200
Slot machines	$1,200
Keno	$1,500
Poker tournaments	$5,000

SOURCE: Adapted from *2012 Instructions for Forms W-2G and 5754*, U.S. Department of the Treasury, Internal Revenue Service, September 2011, http://www.irs.gov/pub/irs-pdf/iw2g.pdf (accessed August 15, 2012)

within their borders, including lotteries, commercial casinos, horse and dog races, jai alai games, card rooms, charitable gambling, and video machine gambling. Until 2010 only lotteries were operated by state governments; however, Stephanie Simon reports in "(State) House Rules in Kansas Casino" (*Wall Street Journal*, February 4, 2010) that in February 2010 Kansas opened Boot Hill Casino and Resort in Dodge City, the only state-run casino in the nation. The state government will collect 27% of the revenue from the casino and local governments will collect 5%. The state has plans to build an additional three casinos in the future.

According to the North American Association of State and Provincial Lotteries, in "Sales and Profits" (2012, http://www.naspl.org/index.cfm?fuseaction=content&menuid=17&pageid=1025), 43 states and the District of Columbia operated lotteries in 2012; Alaska, Alabama, Hawaii, Mississippi, Nevada, Utah, and Wyoming did not. State lotteries had approximately $68.8 billion in sales in fiscal year 2012 and a profit of $19.4 billion. Generally, after paying expenses and the winners and retailers who sell the tickets, states have about a 30% profit to spend on government programs, such as education.

TRIBAL GOVERNMENTS. Native American tribes that have been officially recognized by the U.S. government are considered sovereign nations; in other words, to a certain extent they govern themselves. In 1988 Congress passed the Indian Gaming Regulatory Act, which allows federally recognized tribes to open gambling establishments if the state in which they are located already permits certain types of legalized gambling.

The National Indian Gaming Commission indicates in the press release *2011 Indian Gaming Revenues Increased 3%* (July 17, 2012, http://www.nigc.gov/LinkClick.aspx?fileticket=cXMGE3FkCog%3d&tabid=36&mid=345) that 237 tribes were engaged in gaming operations in 2011, generating $27.2 billion in gross revenues; this figure was nearly double the $14.7 billion in

gross revenues earned by tribal casinos in 2002. Net revenues fund tribal government operations or programs, provisions for the general welfare of the tribe and its members, tribal economic development, charitable contributions, and operations of local government agencies. Tribal governments have used gambling revenues to build health clinics, schools, houses, and community centers and to provide educational scholarships and social services for their members.

LOCAL GOVERNMENTS. In some states local governments collect taxes and fees from gambling activities that are operated within their jurisdictions. This is particularly true for casinos and racetracks.

Between 1970 and 2010 New York City was particularly active in the gambling industry. The New York City Off-Track Betting Corporation was founded in 1970 to provide a legal alternative to the widespread offtrack wagering that was offered by organized crime syndicates. Even though the corporation was a quasi-governmental entity, it operated as a private enterprise that turned profits over to state and local governments. According to a report by Russ Buettner in "OTB Is in Financial Trouble, but It's Ready to Roll" (*New York Times*, September 2, 2009), the corporation routinely handled over $1 billion annually in offtrack wagers. However, the costs of keeping the parlors open were higher than the city's share of the corporation's revenue. The city narrowly averted a shutdown of the corporation's parlors in June 2008, when the state agreed to take over the corporation. In "Bleeding Cash and Deep in Debt, OTB Files for Bankruptcy Protection" (*New York Times*, December 3, 2009), A. G. Sulzberger notes that the corporation finally filed for bankruptcy protection in December 2009, which allowed it to reorganize, close some parlors, and shift its emphasis to telephone and online betting operations. By the end of 2010, however, the New York City Off-Track Betting Corporation officially closed. As Matt Hegarty writes in "Governor Vetoes New York City Offtrack Betting Proposal" (December 17, 2012, http://www.drf.com/news/governor-vetoes-new-york-city-off-track-betting-proposal), in late 2012 several companies were vying for the right to resurrect offtrack betting in the city, including the state-owned New York Racing Association. Some state and city politicians, notably Governor Andrew Cuomo (1957–; Democrat) and New York City mayor Michael Bloomberg (1942–; Independent), remained wary of supporting new proposals for offtrack betting until legislation regulating the business could be put in place.

DEMAND: THE GAMBLERS

Gambling is a leisure activity. People gamble because they enjoy it. Proponents say there is no difference between spending money at a theme park and

18   Supply and Demand: Who Offers Gambling? Who Gambles?

Gambling

spending it at a casino: the money is exchanged for a good time in either case. However, gambling has a powerful allure besides fun: the dream of wealth, which is a strong motivator. Some options, such as lotteries, offer the chance to risk a small investment for an enormous payoff. This potential is too appealing for many people to pass up.

Adults

In a March 2012 interview with *Los Angeles Times* columnist David Lazarus ("March Madness and American Gambling Habits," March 15, 2012, http://www.market place.org/topics/life/march-madness-and-american-gam bling-habits), Jeremy Hobson of American Public Media states that 86% of Americans participate in some form of gambling at least once per year; 16% of Americans gamble on a weekly basis. Overall, Americans who gamble lose roughly $100 billion annually.

Paul Taylor, Cary Funk, and Peyton Craighill of the Pew Research Center note in *Gambling: As the Take Rises, So Does Public Concern* (May 23, 2006, http://pewre search.org/assets/social/pdf/Gambling.pdf) that approximately two-thirds (67%) of Americans gambled between March 2005 and March 2006. (See Table 2.5.) Men (72%) were more likely than women (62%) to have gambled during this period. Those with a college education were slightly less likely to have gambled than were those with only some college or with a high school diploma or less. The participation rate for people with higher incomes (greater than $100,000 per year) was higher than for other income groups. Only 59% of those making less than $30,000 per year reported gambling between March 2005 and March 2006, compared with 79% of those making more than $100,000 per year.

Taylor, Funk, and Craighill indicate that gambling participation rates also vary with religion. Protestants (61%) reported less gambling activity between March 2005 and March 2006 than Catholics (77%) or those who were identified as secular (72%). (See Table 2.5.) Among Protestants, members of mainline denominations, such as Methodists, were more likely to gamble than those who identified with evangelical denominations. Northeasterners were more active gamblers than those living in other regions of the country. A larger percentage of whites (68%) than African-Americans (62%) or Hispanics (62%) reported gambling between March 2005 and March 2006. Differences in participation by age were minor, although poll participants over the age of 65 years were less likely to gamble than were younger people.

SENIOR CITIZENS. According to Taylor, Funk, and Craighill, 58% of people aged 65 years and older reported gambling between March 2005 and March 2006. (See Table 2.5.) Other studies show similar, or even higher, rates of participation. For example,

TABLE 2.5

Gamblers by demographic characteristics, March 2005–March 2006

	Any type of gambling	Bought lottery ticket	Visited casino	Bet[a] on sports	Played cards for money
	%	%	%	%	%
All adults	67	52	29	23	17
Gender					
Men	72	56	31	32	25
Women	62	48	27	15	10
Race/ethnicity					
White	68	53	30	23	18
Black	62	45	24	24	14
Hispanic[b]	62	47	22	16	12
Age					
18–29	71	48	30	30	32
30–49	69	56	30	25	17
50–64	68	55	31	22	11
65+	58	43	22	13	10
Education					
College grad	65	48	31	25	15
Some college	71	55	32	23	21
H.S. grad or less	66	52	27	22	17
Family income					
$100,000+	79	57	40	39	24
$50K–$99K	74	60	37	27	22
$30K–$49K	67	54	27	22	21
Less than $30K	59	44	21	16	11
Region					
Northeast	77	63	31	26	20
Midwest	64	52	26	23	18
South	62	48	24	21	15
West	68	47	38	23	17
Religion					
Protestant	61	48	24	19	13
Catholic	77	62	39	30	23
Secular	72	52	29	24	23
White Protestants					
Evangelical	50	40	19	14	11
Mainline	73	58	29	24	17

[a]Betting on sports includes professional sports, college sports or an office pool.
[b]Hispanics are of any race.

SOURCE: Paul Taylor, Cary Funk, and Peyton Craighill, "Profile of Gamblers," in *Gambling: As the Take Rises, So Does Public Concern*, Pew Research Center, May 23, 2006, http://pewresearch.org/assets/social/pdf/Gambling.pdf (accessed August 15, 2012)

Suzi Levens et al. reveal in "Gambling among Older, Primary-Care Patients" (*American Journal of Geriatric Psychiatry*, vol. 13, no. 1, January 2005) that in 2005 nearly 70% of Americans older than 65 years reported gambling in the previous 12 months. This study, which was based on a survey of 843 elderly patients, also finds that nearly 11% of those questioned were at risk for problem gambling.

For older adults not at risk for gambling problems, the activity may have a positive impact. In "Health Correlates of Recreational Gambling in Older Adults" (*American Journal of Psychiatry*, vol. 161, no. 9, September 2004), Rani A. Desai et al. indicate that a correlation exists between gambling and good health among

Gambling

Supply and Demand: Who Offers Gambling? Who Gambles? **19**

people older than the age of 65. The researchers do not find a similar correlation in those aged 18 to 64 years. The study, which is based on interviews with 2,417 older adults, focuses only on recreational gamers and does not include subjects who exhibited gambling addiction.

Young People

The minimum legal age for placing a legal bet ranges from 18 to 21 years, depending on the state and the activity. For example, most states limit the sale of lottery tickets to those who are 18 years and older, although most allow minors to receive lottery tickets as gifts. All commercial casinos have a minimum gambling age of 21 years as set by state law. Tribal casinos are allowed to set their own minimum gambling age as long as it is at least 18 years. The minimum age to participate in charitable gambling activities, such as bingo games, is 18 years in most states. A few states allow people as young as 16 years to participate.

Each year the Annenberg Public Policy Center at the University of Pennsylvania releases the National Annenberg Survey of Youth. In "Internet Gambling Grows among Male Youth Ages 18 to 22" (October 14, 2010, http://www.annenbergpublicpolicycenter.org/Downloads/Releases/ACI/Card%20Playing%202010%20Release%20final.pdf), the center notes that roughly one-third (33.3%) of young men aged 18 to 22 years played cards for money at least once per month in 2010, up slightly from the 31.7% who gambled on cards monthly in 2008. On the other hand, the percentage of young men between the ages of 18 and 22 who gambled on the Internet once a month nearly quadrupled during this same span, from 4.4% in 2008 to 16% in 2010. According to Annenberg Adolescent Communication Institute director Dan Romer, roughly 1.7 million college-age males gambled online once per month in 2010; over 400,000 gambled on the Internet once a week. While the center recorded that no young women between 18 and 22 gambled on the Internet in 2008, by 2010, 4.4% of females in that age group reported gambling online at least once per month. The most striking increase in gambling occurred among high school girls between the ages of 14 and 17. As the center reports, 9.5% of females aged 14 to 17 gambled on sports once a month or more in 2008; by 2010 this proportion had grown to 22%. Overall, more than one-quarter (28.2%) of girls aged 14 to 17 participated in some form of gambling at least once per month in 2010.

Problem Gamblers

Problem gambling is a broad term that covers all gambling behaviors that are harmful to people in some way—financially, emotionally, socially, and/or legally. The harmful effects of problem gambling include:

- Financial difficulties, such as unpaid bills, loss of employment, large debts, and even bankruptcy

- Emotional problems, such as depression, anxiety, addictions, and thoughts of suicide

- Social problems, as evidenced by strained or broken relationships with spouses, family, friends, and coworkers

- Legal problems related to neglect of children or commission of criminal acts to obtain money

Taylor, Funk, and Craighill indicate that in 2006, 6% of those asked said gambling had been a source of problems for their family. (See Table 2.6.) This percentage was up slightly from those reported by the Gallup Organization in 1989, 1992, and 1996, but down slightly from the percentage reported in 1999. The researchers note that there is a marked difference in answers by age. Only 5% of those aged 50 years and older said gambling had been a problem for their family, compared with 12% of adults younger than 50.

In general, scientists characterize gambling behavior by the level of harm that it causes. People who experience no harmful effects are called nonproblem gamblers, or social, casual, or recreational gamblers. Those who gamble regularly and may be prone to a gambling problem are called at-risk gamblers, and those who experience minor to moderate harm from their gambling behavior are called problem gamblers. Pathological gamblers are severely harmed by their gambling activities.

TABLE 2.6

Poll respondents who have experienced family problems related to gambling, selected years 1989–2006

DO YOU SOMETIMES GAMBLE MORE THAN YOU THINK YOU SHOULD?

	Yes	No	Don't know
All gamblers	%	%	%
March 2006	9	90	1=100
December 2003	10	90	0=100
May 1999	11	88	1=100
June 1996	7	93	=100
November 1992	9	91	0=100
April 1989	10	90	0=100

HAS GAMBLING EVER BEEN A SOURCE OF PROBLEMS WITHIN YOUR FAMILY?

All adults			
March 2006	6	93	1=100
December 2003	6	94	=100
May 1999	9	91	=100
June 1996	5	95	=100
November 1992	5	94	1=100
April 1989	4	96	=100

Note: Based on people who gambled in past year. March 2006 figures are from Pew Research Center; data from all other years are from the Gallup Organization.

SOURCE: Paul Taylor, Cary Funk, and Peyton Craighill, "Gamble Too Much? Has Gambling Ever Been a Source of Problems within Your Family?" in *Gambling: As the Take Rises, So Does Public Concern*, Pew Research Center, May 23, 2006, http://pewresearch.org/assets/social/pdf/Gambling.pdf (accessed August 15, 2012). Data from The Gallup Organization. Copyright © 1989–2003 Gallup, Inc. All rights reserved. The content is used with permission; however, Gallup retains all rights of republication.

20   Supply and Demand: Who Offers Gambling? Who Gambles?

Gambling

Scientists use a screening process to determine which category fits a particular gambler. One of the most common is the South Oaks Gambling Screen (SOGS), a 16-item questionnaire that was developed during the 1980s by Henry R. Lesieur and Sheila B. Blume. A detailed description of the questionnaire and its development was first presented by Lesieur and Blume in "The South Oaks Gambling Screen (SOGS): A New Instrument for the Identification of Pathological Gamblers" (*American Journal of Psychiatry*, vol. 144, no. 9, September 1987). The researchers used information from 1,616 subjects to develop the SOGS, including patients with substance abuse and pathological gambling problems, Gamblers Anonymous members, university students, and hospital employees. Because potential problem gamblers fill out the questionnaires themselves, scores depend entirely on the truthfulness of the people answering the questions. Jeffrey N. Weatherly et al. indicate in "Assessing the Reliability of the Gambling Functional Assessment: Revised" (*Journal of Gambling Studies*, June 2012) that as of 2012 the SOGS continued to be the most widely used instrument to identify pathological gamblers. They advocate that once probable pathological gambling has been identified, a 20-item test should be used to identify what about gambling has made it addictive: to get attention from others, to experience the sensory stimulation, to escape from stress or personal problems, or to feel the excitement it brings. Once this assessment is completed, an appropriate treatment can be devised.

Another means of defining problem gamblers was created by the self-help organization Gamblers Anonymous, which prefers the term *compulsive gambling*. In "Questions & Answers about Gamblers Anonymous" (January 2013, http://www.gamblersanonymous.org/qna .html), the organization explains that compulsive gamblers exhibit certain characteristic behaviors, such as:

- An "inability and unwillingness to accept reality"

- A belief that they have a "system" that will eventually pay off

- A lot of time spent daydreaming about what they will do when they finally make a big win

- Feelings of emotional insecurity when they are not gambling

- Immaturity and a desire to escape from responsibility

- Wanting all the good things in life without expending much effort for them

- Wanting to be a "big shot" in the eyes of other people

Gamblers Anonymous provides a list of 20 questions that gamblers can use to determine if they have a gambling problem. (See Table 2.7.) The organization indicates that compulsive gamblers are likely to answer yes to at least seven of the questions.

TABLE 2.7

Twenty questions designed to determine whether a person is a compulsive gambler

1. Did you ever lose time from work or school due to gambling?
2. Has gambling ever made your home life unhappy?
3. Did gambling affect your reputation?
4. Have you ever felt remorse after gambling?
5. Did you ever gamble to get money with which to pay debts or otherwise solve financial difficulties?
6. Did gambling cause a decrease in your ambition or efficiency?
7. After losing did you feel you must return as soon as possible and win back your losses?
8. After a win did you have a strong urge to return and win more?
9. Did you often gamble until your last dollar was gone?
10. Did you ever borrow to finance your gambling?
11. Have you ever sold anything to finance gambling?
12. Were you reluctant to use "gambling money" for normal expenditures?
13. Did gambling make you careless of the welfare of yourself or your family?
14. Did you ever gamble longer than you had planned?
15. Have you ever gambled to escape worry, trouble, boredom or loneliness?
16. Have you ever committed, or considered committing, an illegal act to finance gambling?
17. Did gambling cause you to have difficulty in sleeping?
18. Do arguments, disappointments or frustrations create within you an urge to gamble?
19. Did you ever have an urge to celebrate any good fortune by a few hours of gambling?
20. Have you ever considered self-destruction or suicide as a result of your gambling?

SOURCE: "20 Questions: Are You a Compulsive Gambler?" Gamblers Anonymous, 2012, http://www.gamblersanonymous.org/ga/content/20-questions (accessed August 15, 2012)

PATHOLOGICAL GAMBLERS. In general, pathological gambling is a disorder characterized by irrational thinking in which people continuously (or periodically) lose control over their gambling behavior. Pathological gamblers become preoccupied with gambling by constantly thinking about their next bet or how to raise more money with which they can gamble. This behavior continues even if the gambler suffers adverse consequences, such as financial difficulties or strained relationships with family and friends.

The American Psychiatric Association (APA) officially recognized pathological gambling as a mental health disorder in 1980 and listed it in its publication *Diagnostic and Statistical Manual of Mental Disorders* (*DSM*). Pathological gambling was associated with gambling at an early age, with problems typically beginning in the 20s and persisting for a decade. A variety of other *DSM* disorders were associated with pathological gambling, including anxiety, mood, impulse control, and kleptomania.

Pathological Gambling: A Critical Review was published in 1999 by the National Academies Press. The book identifies and analyzes all available scientific research studies that deal with pathological and problem gambling. The studies are reviewed by dozens of researchers on behalf of the National Research Council, an organization that is administered by the National Academy of Sciences, the National Academy of Engineering, and the

Gambling

Supply and Demand: Who Offers Gambling? Who Gambles? **21**

Institute of Medicine. The researchers estimate that 1.5% of U.S. adults have been pathological gamblers at some point in their life. In any given year, 0.9% of U.S. adults (approximately 1.8 million people) and 1.1 million adolescents aged 12 to 18 years are pathological gamblers. The following general conclusions are drawn:

- Men are more likely than women to be pathological gamblers.

- Pathological gambling often occurs concurrently with other behavioral problems, such as drug and alcohol abuse and mood and personality disorders.

- The earlier in life a person starts to gamble, the more likely he or she is to become a pathological gambler.

- Pathological gamblers are more likely than those without a gambling problem to have pathological gamblers as parents.

- Pathological gamblers who seek treatment generally get better.

However, the researchers are unable to determine from available studies whether any particular treatment technique is more effective than most others or even if some pathological gamblers are able to recover on their own. They are also unable to determine whether particular groups, such as the elderly and the poor, have disproportionately high rates of pathological gambling. The researchers conclude that further studies are needed to provide a detailed understanding of pathological gambling.

As Constance Holden writes in "Behavioral Addictions Debut in Proposed *DSM-V*" (*Science*, February 2010), in 2013 the APA was preparing to reclassify pathological gambling under a new category, "behavioral addiction." This change was scheduled to appear in the fifth edition of the *DSM*, due to be published in May 2013. According to Holden, under these new guidelines pathological gambling "would join substance-use disorders as a full-fledged addiction." In "Disordered Gambling: Etiology, Trajectory, and Clinical Considerations" (*Annual Review of Clinical Psychology*, April 2011), Howard J. Shaffer and Ryan Martin assert that this shift in category was based on new discoveries concerning "commonalities in clinical expression, etiology, comorbidity, physiology, and treatment with substance use disorders." Shaffer and Martin also note that that the APA was planning to create a broader category known as "disordered gambling" for the *DSM-V*, which would encompass both pathological and problem (or subclinical) gambling.

TREATMENT ORGANIZATIONS. A variety of treatment methods are available to problem gamblers through organizations and private counselors. For example, Gamblers Anonymous is open to all people who want to stop gambling. At its meetings, which are held throughout the United States, gamblers remain anonymous by using only

their first name. The group method offers compulsive gamblers moral support and an accepting environment where they can talk about their experiences and the problems that gambling creates in their life. Gambling is not treated as a vice but as a progressive illness.

Peter Ferentzy, Wayne Skinner, and Paul Antze explain in "Changing Spousal Roles in and Their Effects on Recovery in Gamblers Anonymous: GamAnon, Social Support, Wives and Husbands" (*Journal of Gambling Studies*, vol. 26, September 2010) that Gamblers Anonymous is a society based on "mutual aid," through which gambling addicts recover by following the organization's 12-step recovery program. (See Table 2.8.) These steps are similar to those employed by support groups such as Alcoholics Anonymous. Even though the steps have a spiritual aspect, Gamblers Anonymous is not affiliated with any religious group or institution, and the organization is funded by donations. The premise of Gamblers Anonymous is that a recovering compulsive gambler cannot gamble at all without succumbing to the gambling compulsion, so it advocates a "cold turkey" approach to quitting (the gambler just stops gambling) rather than a gradual reduction in gambling activity.

The National Council on Problem Gambling is a nonprofit organization that was founded to increase public awareness about pathological gambling and to encourage the development of educational, research, and treatment programs. It sponsors the *Journal of Gambling Studies*, an academic journal that is dedicated to scientific research, and operates a confidential hotline (1-800-522-4700) for problem gamblers who need help. In "NCPG Affiliate Member List" (November 20, 2012, http://www.ncpgambling.org/files/public/Affiliate_List.pdf), the council notes that as of 2012 it had 35 state affiliate chapters.

TABLE 2.8

Gamblers Anonymous 12-Step Recovery Program

1. We admitted we were powerless over gambling—that our lives had become unmanageable.
2. Came to believe that a power greater than ourselves could restore us to a normal way of thinking and living.
3. Made a decision to turn our will and our lives over to the care of this power of our own understanding.
4. Made a searching and fearless moral and financial inventory of ourselves.
5. Admitted to ourselves and to another human being the exact nature of our wrongs.
6. Were entirely ready to have these defects of character removed.
7. Humbly asked God (of our understanding) to remove our shortcomings.
8. Made a list of all persons we had harmed and became willing to make amends to them all.
9. Make direct amends to such people wherever possible, except when to do so would injure them or others.
10. Continued to take personal inventory and when we were wrong, promptly admitted it.
11. Sought through prayer and meditation to improve our conscious contact with God as we understood Him, praying only for knowledge of His will for us and the power to carry that out.
12. Having made an effort to practice these principles in all our affairs, we tried to carry this message to other compulsive gamblers.

SOURCE: "Recovery Program," Gamblers Anonymous, 2012, http://www.gamblersanonymous.org/ga/content/recovery-program (accessed August 15, 2012)

The council also directs the National Certified Gambling Counselor program and offers a database of counselors throughout the United States who have completed its certification program. Other organizations that certify gambling counselors include the American Compulsive Gambling Certification Board and the American Academy of Health Care Providers in the Addictive Disorders.

TREATMENT METHODS. Many problem gamblers seek professional counseling. The most common treatment method, in both group and individual counseling sessions, is cognitive behavior therapy. The cognitive portion of the therapy focuses attention on the person's thoughts, beliefs, and assumptions about gambling. According to Timothy W. Fong of the Semel Institute for Neuroscience and Human Behavior at the University of California, Los Angeles, in "Pathological Gambling: Update on Assessment and Treatment" (*Psychiatric Times*, vol. 26, no. 9, August 27, 2009), the primary goal is recognizing and changing faulty thinking patterns, such as a belief that gambling can lead to great riches. Behavior therapy focuses on changing harmful behaviors. Most counselors favor complete abstinence from gambling during treatment. For those with mild to moderate gambling problems, treatment usually involves weekly meetings with a support group and/or individual counseling sessions.

Nicki Dowling, David Smith, and Trang Thomas find in "A Comparison of Individual and Group Cognitive-Behavioural Treatment for Female Pathological Gambling" (*Behaviour Research and Therapy*, vol. 45, no. 9, September 2007) that individual treatment seems to be more effective than group treatment at least among some gamblers, although Tony Toneatto and Rosa Dragonetti indicate in "Effectiveness of Community-Based Treatment for Problem Gambling: A Quasi-experimental Evaluation of Cognitive-Behavioral vs. Twelve-Step Therapy" (*American Journal on Addictions*, vol. 17, no. 4, July–August 2008) that 12-step programs are also effective. Those with severe gambling problems usually check into addiction treatment centers to curb their addiction. Such treatment centers isolate patients from the outside world, so they can focus on overcoming their addiction. Some treatment centers even forbid patients from keeping cash on them or from using laptops, phones, or any device that could allow them to gamble. As Bojana Knezevic and David M. Ledgerwood report in "Gambling Severity, Impulsivity, and Psychopathology: Comparison of Treatment- and Community-Recruited Pathological Gamblers" (*American Journal of Addictions*, vol. 21, no. 6, November/December

2012), pathological gamblers generally exhibit a strong tendency toward impulsive behavior, suggesting such restrictions are crucial in the treatment process. In "Resilience and Self-Control Impairment," published in the second edition of the *Handbook of Resilience in Children* (2013; Sam Goldstein and Robert B. Brooks, editors), Wai Chen and Eric Taylor study potential links between lack of self-control and attention deficit hyperactivity disorder (ADHD) in gambling and other forms of impulsive activity.

Increasingly, mental health professionals and gambling treatment centers are using antidepressants along with cognitive therapy to treat compulsive gambling. Researchers speculate that some compulsive gamblers experience highly elevated levels of euphoria-causing chemicals, such as dopamine, in the brain when they gamble. A number of antidepressant drugs have been proven to prevent such chemicals from interacting with the brain. For example, in "Multicenter Investigation of the Opioid Antagonist Nalmefene in the Treatment of Pathological Gambling" (*American Journal of Psychiatry*, vol. 163, no. 2, February 2006), Jon E. Grant et al. report that the antidepressant nalmefene significantly lowers the need to gamble among people diagnosed with compulsive gambling.

In "Opiate Antagonists in Treatment of Pathological Gambling" (*Brown University Psychopharmacology Update*, vol. 20, no. 3, March 2009), Jon E. Grant et al. find that subjects with a family history of alcoholism had the strongest response to the opiate antagonists that are used to treat pathological gambling. Donald W. Black, Martha C. Shaw, and Jeff Allen of the University of Iowa find in "Extended Release Carbamazepine in the Treatment of Pathological Gambling: An Open-Label Study" (*Progress in Neuro-Psychopharmacology and Biological Psychiatry*, vol. 32, no. 5, July 1, 2008) that carbamazepine, an antiseizure drug that is sometimes used to treat bipolar disorder, appears to be effective in treating pathological gambling. Jochen Mutschler et al. report in "Disulfiram, an Option for the Treatment of Pathological Gambling?" (*Alcohol and Alcoholism*, vol. 45, no. 2, December 16, 2010) that disulfiram, which is typically used to treat alcoholism, might also be an effective treatment for pathological gambling. In "Amantadine in the Treatment of Pathological Gambling: A Case Report" (*Frontiers in Psychiatry*, vol. 3, November 2012), Mauro Pettorruso et al. find that the antiviral drug amantadine has the potential to reduce symptoms in pathological gamblers by between 43% and 64%.

Gambling

Supply and Demand: Who Offers Gambling? Who Gambles?   **23**

CHAPTER 3
AN INTRODUCTION TO CASINOS

When most people picture a casino, they probably imagine one of the megaresorts in Las Vegas—a massive hotel and entertainment complex, blazing with neon lights, games, and fun—however, casinos come in all sizes. Some casinos are huge, whereas others are small businesses defined more by the types of gambling they offer than by glitz and glamour.

The federal government classifies all businesses and industries operated within the United States by using the North American Industry Classification System (NAICS), which issues a six-digit code for each type of business and industry. In *2012 NAICS Definition* (2012, http://www.census.gov/eos/www/naics/index.html), the U.S. Census Bureau defines the NAICS code for casinos, 713210, as follows: "This industry comprises establishments primarily engaged in operating gambling facilities that offer table wagering games along with other gambling activities, such as slot machines and sports betting. These establishments often provide food and beverage services. Included in this industry are floating casinos (i.e., gambling cruises, riverboat casinos)." Casino hotels—that is, hotels with a casino on the premises—fall under the code 721120. They typically offer a variety of amenities, including dining, entertainment, swimming pools, and conference and convention rooms.

For practical purposes, casino gambling encompasses games of chance and skill that are played at tables and machines. Casino games can take place in massive resorts as well as in small card rooms. There are also floating casinos operating on boats and barges on waterways across the country. Casino game machines have been introduced at racetracks to create racinos. In some states casino-type game machines are also allowed in truck stops, bars, grocery stores, and other small businesses.

Successful casinos take in billions of dollars each year for the companies, corporations, investors, and Native American tribes that own and operate them. State and local governments also reap casino revenues in the form of taxes, fees, and other payments.

THE HISTORICAL AND CURRENT STATUS OF CASINOS

Gambling was illegal for most of the nation's history. This did not keep casino games from being played, sometimes openly and with the complicity of local law enforcement, but it did keep casinos from developing into a legitimate industry. Even after casino gambling was legalized in Nevada in 1931, its growth outside that state was stifled for decades. It took 47 years before a second state, New Jersey, decided to allow casino gambling within its borders.

As Atlantic City, New Jersey, opened casinos in 1978, a shift occurred in the legality of gambling elsewhere in the country, much of it due to the efforts of some Native American tribes. A string of legal victories allowed the tribes to convert the small-time bingo halls they had been operating into full-scale casinos. Other states also wanted to profit from casino gambling. Between 1989 and 1996 nine other states authorized commercial casino gambling: Colorado, Illinois, Indiana, Iowa, Louisiana, Michigan, Mississippi, Missouri, and South Dakota.

The American Gaming Association (AGA) estimates in *2012 State of the States: The AGA Survey of Casino Entertainment* (May 2012, http://www.americangaming.org/files/aga/uploads/docs/sos/aga_sos_2012_web.pdf) that commercial casinos had revenues of $35.6 billion in 2011, up 3% from 2010. In the press release "2011 Indian Gaming Revenues Increased 3%" (July 17, 2012, http://www.nigc.gov/LinkClick.aspx?fileticket=cXMGE3FkCog%3d&tabid=36&mid=345), the National Indian Gaming Commission states that tribal casino revenues totaled $27.2 billion in 2011, up slightly from $26.5 billion in 2010. According to the AGA, 445 commercial casinos, 459 tribal casinos, and 47 racetrack casinos (or racinos) operated nation-wide in 2011. Additionally, 517 card rooms operated in five states.

By 2011 commercial casinos operated in 15 states: Colorado, Illinois, Indiana, Iowa, Kansas, Louisiana, Maryland, Michigan, Mississippi, Missouri, Nevada, New Jersey, Pennsylvania, South Dakota, and West Virginia. Tribal casinos operated in 29 states. Besides the full-scale casinos, racetrack casinos operated in 13 states: Delaware, Florida, Indiana, Iowa, Louisiana, Maine, Maryland, New Mexico, New York, Oklahoma, Pennsylvania, Rhode Island, and West Virginia. An additional six states offered electronic gaming devices in noncasino locations: Louisiana, Montana, Nevada, Oregon, South Dakota, and West Virginia.

CASINO ACCEPTABILITY

Each year the AGA releases results of a survey on the attitudes of Americans toward casino gambling. In *2012 State of the States*, the AGA indicates that nearly half of the people surveyed in 2012 considered casino gambling acceptable: 46% of respondents found casino gambling to be acceptable for anyone and 35% considered it acceptable for others but not for themselves. Only 16% of respondents thought casino gambling was not acceptable for anyone. Since 2003 the percentage of those who believed casino gambling was acceptable for anyone had dropped from 57%, whereas the percentage of those who said it was acceptable for others but not themselves had risen from 28%. In other words, even though the percentage of those who thought gambling was acceptable for themselves or for others in total had not changed, a slight shift had occurred in views of the personal acceptability of gambling.

CASINO GAMES

Casinos offer a variety of games, including card games, dice games, domino games, slot machines, and gambling devices (such as the roulette wheel). Some games are banked games, meaning that the house has a stake in the outcome of the game and bets against the players. Banked games include blackjack, craps, keno, roulette, and traditional slot machines. A nonbanked game is one in which the payout and the house's cut depend on the number of players or the amount that is bet, not the outcome of the game. In percentage games the house collects a share of the amount wagered.

For example, in nonbanked poker players bank their own games. Each player puts money into the "pot" and competes against the other players to win the pot. A portion of the pot is taken by the house. In house-banked poker the players compete against the house rather than each other. Another type of house-banked poker game is one in which there is a posted payout schedule for winning hands rather than for a pot.

Gaming machines are by far the most popular type of casino activity. Electronic slot machines offer many different games (poker is one of the most popular) and are called by a variety of names: electronic gaming devices, video gaming terminals, video gaming devices, video poker machines, or just slots. Harrah's Entertainment explains in *Profile of the American Casino Gambler: Harrah's Survey 2006* (June 2006, http://www.harrahs.com/images/PDFs/Profile_Survey_2006.pdf) that slot machines can be played for a variety of denominations—from a penny up to more than $5. The $0.25 and $0.50 slot machines are the most popular. In *2012 State of the States*, the AGA reports that in 2011, 53% of casino-goers indicated that electronic gaming machines were their favorite activity, followed by blackjack (23%), poker (7%), and craps and roulette (both 3%). David Stewart of Ropes & Gray, LLP, notes in *Demystifying Slot Machines and Their Impact in the United States* (July 27, 2010, http://www.americangaming.org/files/aga/uploads/docs/whitepapers/demystifying_slot_machines_and_their_impact.pdf) that the widespread popularity of slot machines led casinos to increase the floor space devoted to slots from about 40% in the 1970s to about 70% in 2010.

Gaming machines are simple to operate and can offer large payouts for small wagers. Introduced in 1896, the first commercial gambling machines were called slot machines because the gambler inserted a coin into a slot to begin play. Each slot machine consisted of a metal box housing three reels, each of which was decorated all around with symbols (usually types of fruit or spades, hearts, diamonds, and clubs). When the player pulled the handle on the machine, the reels spun randomly until stoppers within the machine slowed them. If a matching sequence of symbols appeared when the reels stopped, the player won. Each reel had many symbols, so literally thousands of outcomes were possible. Because of their construction, ease of play, and low odds, slot machines came to be known as "one-armed bandits."

Some casinos still offer old-fashioned slot machines, but most gaming machines in the 21st century are electronic and computer controlled. They are manufactured to strict technical specifications and use a computer programming technique called random number generation. A computer chip in each machine determines the percentage of payout. Similar to high-tech video games, the gaming machines offer sophisticated graphics and sound. Some are even designed to mimic the look and feel of reel-type machines. Patrons may have a choice of a modern push button or an old-fashioned handle to activate play.

Some casinos have slot machines with progressive jackpots—in other words, the jackpot grows with continued play. Most progressive jackpot machines are connected to others in a computerized network. Play on any one machine within the group causes the jackpot to increase. On March 21, 2003, a man playing a progressive slot machine at the Excalibur Hotel and Casino in Las Vegas won $39.7 million, the largest slot machine payout in U.S. history (as of October 2012).

Odds against Gamblers

Because casinos are businesses and must make money to survive, the mathematical odds are always against players in casino games. For example, in "Easy Money!" (June 10, 1997, http://www.pbs.org/wgbh/pages/frontline/shows/gamble/), *Frontline* explains that a person betting $100 an hour on roulette will lose an average of $5.26 per hour in the long run. The "long run" is a concept often overlooked by gamblers. This is especially true of gamblers who play games of chance such as roulette.

Most roulette wheels have two colors: red and black. On each spin of the wheel, the odds of red or black coming up are 50-50. Many gamblers believe this means the number of black results will equal the number of red results over the course of time they are playing the game. Thus, when several consecutive spins have come up red, gamblers feel that black is overdue, so they bet on that color.

This belief is false and is known as the gambler's fallacy. Each spin of the roulette wheel is independent of the spins that came before and has the same 50-50 chance of being red or black. The fact that four or five results in a row have been red does not change the odds for the next spin. Therefore, even though it is true that over the long run the number of red and black results will be roughly equal, during that long run there may be many periods in which large numbers of spins come up red or black.

The same holds true for slot machines. Many gamblers believe that if they have bet on a slot machine many times in a row and lost, this increases the odds of the next bet being a winner. This is not the case. The Colorado Division of Gaming explains slot machines in "Understanding Slot Machines" (2012, http://www.colorado.gov/cs/Satellite/Rev-Gaming/RGM/1213781235400). The division notes that a slot machine with a 97% payout would theoretically be expected to pay back 97% of all money taken in over the lifetime of the machine, which is typically seven years. Therefore, a gambler who plays on that slot machine continuously for seven years could expect to attain a 97% payout. During those seven years, however, there will likely be periods in which he wins frequently, and periods in which he loses frequently, with no way to predict when they will occur.

The casino has an edge not only on slots and roulette but also on all banked casino games. The rate at which a gambler loses money varies by game, but in all games the players' wager expectation is negative. This house advantage is the long-run percentage of all money wagered that will be retained by the casino and is alternately called the house edge, the odds, or the percentage. In "Place Your Bets: Cashing in on Probability" (2012, http://www.learner.org/interactives/dailymath/placebets.html), the Annenberg Foundation, a private foundation that provides funding and support to nonprofit organizations, explains that "the odds make it certain that, over time, the casino will consistently turn a profit."

THE CASINO GAMBLER

According to the AGA, in *2012 State of the States*, 27% of Americans surveyed had visited a casino during the past year. In the previous year's survey, *2011 State of the States: The AGA Survey of Casino Entertainment* (May 2011, http://www.americangaming.org/files/aga/uploads/docs/sos/aga-sos-2011.pdf), the AGA also finds casino customers are slightly older and have a higher income than the U.S. population as a whole. In 2011, 58% of casino visitors were 50 years old or older, compared with 53% of the general survey population. Casino visitors (16%) were less likely than survey respondents as a whole (21%) to have an annual household income of less than $35,000 and more likely to have annual incomes of $60,000 to $100,000 (22% and 17%, respectively). Approximately 30% of casino gamblers in 2010 had a college degree and 15% had a graduate degree. About 25% had some college credits. A quarter (25%) had completed high school. These percentages compare roughly with the education levels of the U.S. population as a whole.

Harrah's Entertainment explains that *Profile of the American Casino Gambler* is based on two studies: the National Profile Study by Roper Reports GfK NOP and the U.S. Gaming Panel by TNS. The National Profile Study included face-to-face interviews with 2,000 American adults, and the U.S. Gaming Panel had a questionnaire that was mailed to 100,000 adults (57,205 responded). Harrah's Entertainment finds that in 2005 the typical casino gambler was a 46-year-old female from a household with an above-average income. Older adults over the age of 45 years, who often have more vacation time and available spending money than younger adults, made up the largest group (23%) of casino gamblers in 2005. Harrah's Entertainment also finds that participation in casino gambling dropped with decreasing income: 31% of Americans with annual household incomes more than $95,000 per year were casino gamblers, whereas only 20% of Americans with annual household incomes less than $35,000 per year participated.

Harrah's Entertainment finds that in 2005 female casino gamblers showed a marked preference for electronic gaming, with 79% of those surveyed indicating that it was their favorite type of game, compared with 63% of men. Forty-one percent of women preferred machines in the $0.25- to $0.50-per-play range. Men (21%) were more likely to participate in table games than were women (9%). Game preference also varied by age; younger gamblers were more likely to prefer table games than were older gamblers.

The Popularity of Poker

With the advent of computer-simulated card games and Internet card rooms, poker surged in popularity during the first few years of the first decade of the 21st century. Gamblers were no longer required to play experienced poker players to gain experience themselves. By 2003 a particular type of poker known as Texas Hold 'Em emerged as the game of choice. In Texas Hold 'Em players attempt to make a winning hand from a combination of cards dealt to them face down and community cards revealed to all players. Individuals who had never visited a commercial poker table began spending their weekends at local casinos or in online poker rooms, trying to wrest money from each other. Furthermore, cable networks such as ESPN and the Travel Channel began broadcasting games from the World Series of Poker and the World Poker Tour, which had once been obscure competitions reserved primarily for hard-core poker players.

In *2010 State of the States: The AGA Survey of Casino Entertainment* (April 2010, http://www.americangaming .org/files/aga/uploads/docs/sos/aga-sos-2010.pdf), the AGA includes a special report on poker. Poker revenue in Nevada declined slightly from $62.7 million in 1999 to $57.5 million in 2002. Between 2002 and 2007, however, poker revenue nearly tripled, totaling $168 million in 2007. In New Jersey revenue rose from $32.5 million in 2002 to $84.4 million in 2008. The biggest increases for both states occurred between 2003 and 2005. Poker revenues declined between 2007 and 2009 in both Nevada and New Jersey due to the recession, which lasted from late 2007 to mid-2009. In addition, the AGA reports that interest in poker seemed to wane between 2005 and 2008; in 2005, 18% of Americans had played poker in person or on the Internet, but by 2008 that percentage was just 11%. However, the percentage of Americans who played poker increased significantly between 2008 and 2009, to 15%. The AGA notes in *2012 State of the States* that the proportion held steady at 15% in 2011.

HOW DO CASINOS PERSUADE PEOPLE TO GAMBLE?

Casino gambling is different from other forms of gambling, such as lotteries and Internet gambling, because of its social aspect. Players are either directly interacting with others, as in craps or poker, or surrounded by other people as they play the slot machines. Players often shout

out encouragement. Alcoholic drinks are easily accessible and delivered directly to gamblers by waitstaff that circulate throughout the casino. Nonalcoholic drinks and snacks are sometimes provided free of charge. The casino atmosphere is designed around noise, light, and excitement.

Also, casinos arrange slot machines in large groups to attract gamblers. In "The Social Contagion of Gambling: How Venue Size Contributes to Player Losses" (*Journal of Gambling Studies*, September 25, 2010), Matthew J. Rockloff, Nancy Greer, and Carly Fay study the effects of the size of the gambling venue on the behaviors of 135 gamblers. They find that the larger the crowd of gamblers, the faster gamblers played. Even though gamblers in larger crowds tended to bet slightly less than gamblers playing alone or in small crowds, increased gambler persistence led to greater gambling losses over the long term.

Most commercial casino visitors participate in activities other than gambling. The AGA notes in *2012 State of the States* that 76% of casino visitors ate in a "fine dining restaurant," 62% attended a show or a concert, 51% went to a bar or nightclub, 46% went shopping, and 28% used recreational facilities such as a spa or a golf course. In fact, 27% of those surveyed said that when they visited a casino they gambled rarely if at all. Among casino visitors who never or rarely gamble at casinos, 70% said that dining and 40% said that going to shows are their favorite activities when they visit.

Casinos use sophisticated marketing and design to attract gamblers to their facilities and to keep them gambling as long and as happily as possible. They invest millions of dollars to determine which colors, sounds, and scents are most appealing to patrons. The legend that oxygen is pumped into casinos to keep customers alert is not true—it would be an extreme fire hazard. Nevertheless, casinos do use bright and sometimes gaudy floor and wall coverings that have a stimulating and cheering effect. Red is a popular decorating color because it is thought to make people lose track of time. Also, clocks do not appear on casino walls.

In "Casinos Use TV Stars to Draw New Customers" (Associated Press, April 3, 2010), Wayne Parry explains that during the recession casino marketing campaigns used television and movie celebrities to get people in the doors. The casinos paid an appearance fee to the celebrities, who served in a variety of roles, for example, reality television chefs cooked for customers, television shows were filmed at casinos, and reality dance competition contestants danced in shows. The casinos hoped that after the celebrities made their appearance, the customers would decide to stay to gamble. Liz Benston reports in "To Slot Players, Palms' Sideshow a Freak Show" (*Las Vegas Sun*, September 18, 2010) that other casinos began offering more free shows in an attempt to attract customers.

With continuing pressures of online betting, casinos will have to find more ways to attract customers. Chuck Darrow indicates in "New Live-Entertainment Venues Energize Casinos and Their Patrons" (*Philadelphia Inquirer*, May 31, 2012) that casinos continue to open entertainment venues and large retail spaces to attract gamblers and other tourists.

According to the article "The Tech of a Casino" (*TechTV*, June 2002), casinos use a variety of tricks to attract gamblers. Slot machines and gaming tables are arranged in a mazelike fashion so that wandering patrons are continuously enticed by more gambling options. Slot machines are designed to be appealing to the senses of sight, touch, and sound—the noises of the machines are electronically tuned to the musical key of C to be pleasing to the ear. Bells, lights, whistles, and the clang of dropping coins are constant. Humans are attracted to bright lights, so more than 15,000 miles (24,100 km) of neon tubing are used to light the casinos along the Las Vegas Strip.

Casinos also focus on customer service. For example, they provide perks that are designed to encourage gamblers to spend more and to reward those who do. Most casinos offer "comps," which is short for "complimentaries" (free items). During the 1970s Las Vegas casinos were famous for their deeply discounted travel packages, cheap buffets, and free show tickets. The strategy at that time was to maximize the volume of people going to Las Vegas. Gambling revenue was driven by filling hotel rooms and the casino floor with as many people as possible.

However, in "Atlantic City Casinos Try to Market Sizzle, Sweat on Winter Nights" (pressofAtlanticCity.com, February 12, 2010), Donald Wittkowski explains that once the recession took hold of the U.S. economy there was less money to spend on marketing. Wittkowski notes that as a result, "casinos are instead trying to expand their customer base by adding more sex, sizzle and singing to the marketing mix." In "Atlantic City Casinos Turn to Discounts, Quirky Promotions to Attract Customers in Winter" (pressofAtlanticCity.com, January 22, 2011), Wittkowski notes that meal discounts and promotional giveaways also attract visitors.

In addition, casinos concentrate their comp investments on the "high rollers" (gamblers who spend much more than average). Such people often gamble in special rooms, separate from the main casino floor, where the stakes (i.e., the amount bet) can be in the tens of thousands of dollars. Casinos make much of their profit from these high-stakes gamblers. Therefore, the high rollers receive comps that are worth a great deal of money, such as free luxury suites, and are lavished with lots of personal attention.

Less expensive comps are available to smaller spenders. Most casinos offer clubs that are similar to airline frequent-flyer programs. Gamblers who join receive a card that can be swiped electronically before they play a game. Casino computers track their usage and spending habits and tally up points that can be exchanged for coupons for free slot play or for free or discounted meals, drinks, and shows. The comp programs also serve as a valuable marketing tool for the casinos because they develop a patron database that can be used for advertising and to track trends in game preference and spending.

CHAPTER 4
COMMERCIAL CASINOS

THE MARKET

Commercial casinos are profit-making businesses owned by individuals, private companies, or large public corporations. The term *commercial casino* is used in the United States to indicate a gaming facility that is not owned and operated on Native American lands by a tribal government. (See Chapter 5.) State governments closely regulate casinos. Some states allow land-based casinos, whereas others restrict casino games to floating gambling halls on barges or riverboats. A handful of states allow casino games such as slot machines at other locations, including horse and dog racetracks or other commercial establishments. Some states allow only limited-stakes gambling, in which a limit is placed on the amount that can be wagered.

In *2012 State of the States: The AGA Survey of Casino Entertainment* (2012, http://www.americangaming .org/files/aga/uploads/docs/sos/aga_sos_2012_web.pdf), the American Gaming Association (AGA) states that in 2011 there were 445 commercial casinos operating in 15 states: Colorado, Illinois, Indiana, Iowa, Kansas, Louisiana, Maryland, Michigan, Mississippi, Missouri, Nevada, New Jersey, Pennsylvania, South Dakota, and West Virginia. These included both land-based and floating casinos. Major markets for floating casinos included Illinois, Indiana, Iowa, Mississippi, and Louisiana. In addition, 13 states oversaw the operation of 47 racetrack casinos, or racinos, in 2011.

The casino industry measures its revenue by consumer spending, that is, the money gamblers spend while gambling. According to the AGA, consumer spending on gambling in 2011 totaled $35.6 billion. In gambling terminology, the *handle* is the gross amount of money wagered by gamblers. The money that the gamblers win is called the *payout*, and the money that the casinos keep is called the *casino win*.

NEVADA

Gambling has a long history in Nevada. It was common in the frontier towns of the Old West but was outlawed at the end of the 19th century, a time when conservative values predominated. Regardless, illegal gambling was widely tolerated throughout the state. In 1931 gambling was legalized again in Nevada. The country was in a deep economic depression at the time, and gambling was seen as a source of needed revenue.

Casino development was slow at first. Many business people were not convinced that the desert towns of Nevada could attract sufficient tourists to make the operations profitable. In 1941 El Rancho Vegas opened in Las Vegas. Five years later the mobster Benjamin "Bugsy" Siegel (1906–1947) opened the Flamingo Hotel and Casino, also in Las Vegas. (Siegel was eventually murdered, reportedly by his business partners because of cost overruns.) Organized crime's relationship with Las Vegas continued for 30 years and tainted casino gambling in many people's minds.

Even though the state of Nevada began collecting gaming taxes during the 1940s, regulation of the casinos was lax until the 1970s. Organized crime figures were pushed out of the casino business after Congress passed the Racketeer Influenced and Corrupt Organizations Act in 1970. Corporations moved in to take their place. In 1975 gaming revenues in the state reached $1 billion, according to the Las Vegas Convention and Visitors Authority (LVCVA), in "Stats & Facts: History of Las Vegas" (2013, http://www.lvcva.com/press/statistics-facts/ vegas-history.jsp). The AGA notes in *2012 State of the States* that by 2011 the gambling industry employed 174,381 people in Nevada and contributed $865.3 million in tax revenue to the state's general fund.

Many different forms of legal gambling are available in Nevada, including live bingo, keno, and horse racing; card rooms; casino games; and offtrack and phone betting on sports events and horse races. Establishments such as bars, restaurants, and stores are restricted to fewer than 15 slot machines. Casinos are allowed to have more than 15 machines; many have hundreds of slot machines.

According to the AGA, in 2011 there were 256 commercial casinos operating in Nevada—by far the most of any state. According to the Nevada State Gaming Control Board, the state's commercial casinos generated $10.7 billion in revenue from gambling operations during 2011, which was up from the $9.7 billion recorded in 2010, yet still short of a high of $12.3 billion posted in 2007. (See Figure 4.1.) The decline was due to the economic recession that began in late 2007 and ended in mid-2009. According to the AGA, consumers spent more money on commercial casino gaming in Nevada than in any other state in 2011.

Nevada casino revenue, or casino win, for 2011 is broken down by gambling category in Table 4.1. Slot machines accounted for $6.7 billion of the casinos' gaming revenue of $10.7 billion. Other games, such as keno, Pai gow poker, and roulette, brought in $3.8 billion in revenue that year.

As mentioned above, the recession seriously depressed Nevada's gambling industry during 2008 and 2009. Howard Stutz reports in "Nevada Economy: Gaming Revenue at 2004 Level" (*Las Vegas Review Journal*, August 12, 2009) that casino revenues fell precipitously in 2008 and 2009 as a result of the recession. He notes that on the Las Vegas Strip revenues had dropped 14.7% during the first six months of 2009, compared with the previous year. As Figure 4.1 shows, however, within two years the industry had rebounded, with overall revenues rising by $1 billion between 2010 and 2011.

Multidenomination slot machines made the most money of any game in Nevada's casinos in 2011 ($3.1 billion), followed by one-cent slot machines ($2.2 billion). (See Table 4.1.) The table game with the highest revenue was baccarat ($1.3 billion), followed by blackjack (also called twenty-one; $1 billion).

Even though casinos are located throughout the state, the major gambling markets in Nevada are in the southern part of the state in Clark County (which encompasses Las Vegas and Laughlin) and along the California border in Washoe County (which encompasses Reno) and the Lake Tahoe resort area.

Las Vegas

Perhaps no other city is more associated with casinos than Las Vegas. According to the LVCVA in "2011 Year-to-Date Executive Summary" (2012, http://www.lvcva.com/includes/content/images/media/docs/Year-end-2011.pdf), the city had 38.9 million visitors in 2011, up 4.3% from 2010. The city's hotel and motel rooms had an occupancy rate of 83.8%, up 3.4% from 2010. In *Las Vegas Visitor Profile Study 2011* (December 2011, http://www.lvcva.com/includes/content/images/media/docs/2011-Las_Vegas_Visitor_Profile.pdf), the LVCVA indicates that in 2011 most visitors to Las Vegas were married (77%) and had a household income of at least $40,000 (87%). The average age of visitors was 49 years, and 25% of visitors were retired. Well over half (55%) of the city's visitors came from the western United States; nearly one-third (31%) came from California. The LVCVA indicates in "2011 Year-to-Date Executive Summary" that in 2011, 19,029 conventions were held in Las Vegas; the number of conventions held was up 5.7% from 2010, and the percentage of convention attendees was up even more, at 8.8%.

Even in the midst of this modest growth, however, the Las Vegas gaming industry was still struggling to rebound from the global financial crisis.. According to the LVCVA (2013, http://www.lvcva.com/stats-and-

FIGURE 4.1

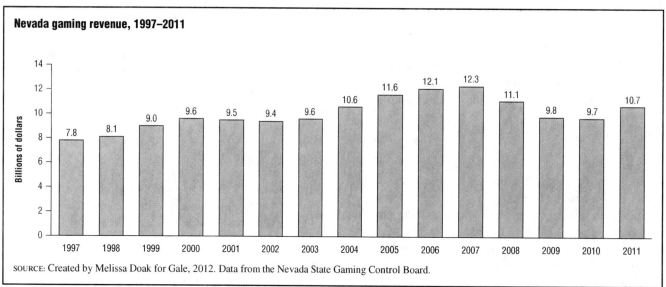

Nevada gaming revenue, 1997–2011

SOURCE: Created by Melissa Doak for Gale, 2012. Data from the Nevada State Gaming Control Board.

TABLE 4.1

Nevada gaming revenue, selected statistics, 2011

[In thousands]

| | Twelve-month summary—01/01/11 to 12/31/11
Number of reporting locations—340 | | |
	Win amount	% change	Win percent
Twenty-One	1,044,144	7.04	11.41
Craps	394,992	2.47	12.44
Roulette	323,359	4.71	16.37
3-card poker	156,394	11.83	30.05
Baccarat	1,262,087	6.25	12.48
Mini-Baccarat	89,717	19.15	10.16
Keno	32,260	0.18	27.47
Bingo	6,572	26.46	3.24
Caribbean Stud	4,404	−29.01	27.91
Let It Ride	47,153	−4.33	23.62
Pai Gow	12,528	−42.01	11.74
Pai Gow poker	107,707	4.64	20.74
Race Book (1)	59,557	−4.43	15.23
Sports Pool (2)	140,731	−6.86	4.89
Other games	149,830	16.30	20.56
Total games	**3,837,405**	**5.48**	**12.37**
Card games	131,877	−2.46	
Slot machines			
1 cent	2,198,765	11.37	9.98
5 cent	162,889	−10.21	5.6
25 cent	499,654	−8.42	5.56
1 dollar	520,508	−3.12	5.38
Megabucks	7,332	22.37	11.24
5 dollar	106,446	1.67	5.11
25 dollar	21,257	−8.41	3.46
100 dollar	18,679	−32.65	3.78
Multi-denomination	3,083,107	−0.89	5.25
Other slot machines	53,075	−28.65	
Total slot machines	**6,737,712**	**1.48**	**6.26**
Total gaming win	**10,700,994**	**2.83**	
(1) Race pari-mutuel	59,445	−6.11	16.36
(2) Sports pool detail			
Football	44,279	−21.53	3.3
Basketball	48,818	24.02	6.62
Baseball	19,642	−13.19	3.52
Sports parlay cards	17,600	−7.35	28.1
Sports pari-mutuel	1	0.00	
Other	10,391	−24.04	5.79

Notes: Columns may not foot due to rounding. Unit detail is shown separately only when there are 3 or more locations reporting specific unit information. Otherwise, information is included in "Other" categories. Figures are current as of 2/2/12.

SOURCE: Adapted from "Statewide, All Nonrestricted Locations, Twelve-Month Summary—01/01/11 to 12/31/11," in *State of Nevada Gaming Revenue Report: Year Ended December 31, 2011*, Nevada State Gaming Control Board, 2012, http://gaming.nv.gov/modules/showdocument. aspx?documentid=3975 (accessed August 16, 2012)

facts/visitor-statistics/), in 2007 Las Vegas attracted a record 39.2 million visitors; by 2009 this number had fallen to 36.4 million, a 7% decline. Gaming revenue also fell sharply during this span, from $8.4 billion in 2007 to a little over $7 billion in 2009. This economic downturn exerted a serious toll on the labor market. As G. Scott Thomas reports in "Unemployment Rises in Every Major Market since Recession" (September 7, 2012, http://www .bizjournals.com/bizjournals/on-numbers/scott-thomas/ 2012/09/unemployment-rises-in-every-major.html), the city's unemployment rate rose from 5% in July 2007 to 12.9% in July 2012, the largest increase in any major U.S. city. The city's distinctive landscape of high rise

resorts and casinos also suffered in the aftermath of the recession. David G. Schwartz reports in "The Year of Hope and Holding Steady" (December 6, 2012, http:// vegasseven.com/latest/2012/12/06/year-hope-holding-steady) that by 2012 construction of a number of high-profile real estate ventures, notably the Fontainebleau Resort on the Las Vegas strip, remained unfinished in the face of lingering economic uncertainty.

In *Las Vegas Visitor Profile Study 2011*, the LVCVA notes that in 2011, 16% of visitors to Las Vegas were first-time visitors. Seven percent of visitors stated that their primary purpose in visiting the city was to gamble, down significantly from 2008 and 2009, when 13% stated that gambling was their primary purpose. However, 77% of all visitors to Las Vegas gambled during their visit, spending an average of 2.9 hours per day gambling, with an average gambling budget of $447.63.

According to the AGA in *2012 State of the States*, the casinos on the 4-mile (6.4-km) stretch of Las Vegas Boulevard known as the Strip made up the top commercial casino market in the country in 2011. More than 30 hotel casinos line the Strip, a number of which are among the largest hotels in the United States. These lavishly decorated megaresorts offer amenities such as spas, pools, top-quality restaurants, and top-notch entertainment. The companies operating these establishments generate a substantial amount of their revenue from nongambling sources, including lodging, dining, and entertainment. As Table 4.2 shows, Las Vegas Strip casinos generated $6.1 billion in revenues in 2011. By comparison, casinos in the city's downtown area accounted for $496.7 million in revenues that same year. (See Table 4.3.)

Besides those on the Strip, casinos are located throughout Las Vegas and in other parts of Clark County, including Mesquite, Primm, and Laughlin. The Nevada State Gaming Control Board reports in *State of Nevada Gaming Revenue Report: Year Ended December 31, 2011* (2012, http://gaming.nv.gov/modules/showdocument.aspx? documentid=3975) that in total, the 181 casinos in Clark County, both on the Strip and off, had gambling revenues of $9.2 billion in 2011. This amounted to 86% of the state's total casino gambling revenues for that year.

NEW JERSEY

In June 1976 New Jersey voters legalized casino gambling in Atlantic City, making it the second state to do so. The AGA notes in *2012 State of the States* that it was the second-largest gambling market in the country in 2011.

Atlantic City

Atlantic City was a popular resort destination during the late 1800s and early 1900s. It was easily accessible by rail, and people visited the beautiful beaches and elegant hotels along the boardwalk, which stretches

TABLE 4.2

TABLE 4.3

Las Vegas Strip gaming revenue, selected statistics, 2011

[In thousands]

	Twelve-month summary—01/01/11 to 12/31/11 Number of reporting locations—20		
	Win amount	% change	Win percent
Twenty-One	791,862	9.73	10.85
Craps	281,618	5.33	11.89
Roulette	273,362	5.59	15.72
3-card poker	111,837	16.31	31.05
Baccarat	1,254,553	6.14	12.48
Mini-Baccarat	70,505	13.02	9.82
Keno	7,062	2.20	29.82
Bingo	1,420	−14.06	6.00
Caribbean Stud	4,404	−29.01	27.91
Let It Ride	29,797	−4.57	22.88
Pai Gow	9,331	−47.60	10.34
Pai Gow poker	63,887	10.15	20.46
Race Book (1)	26,126	−2.20	15.67
Sports Pool (2)	55,657	−19.73	3.84
Other games	118,070	20.16	19.64
Total games	**3,099,492**	**6.71**	**12.23**
Card games	80,940	−1.28	
Slot machines:			
1 cent	885,761	19.20	11.63
5 cent	52,789	−26.94	8.29
25 cent	232,120	−11.66	8.29
1 dollar	291,187	−2.34	6.64
Megabucks	40,830	30.96	10.88
5 dollar	71,854	6.56	5.28
25 dollar	13,941	−8.62	3.11
100 dollar	15,420	−29.72	3.64
Multi-denomination	1,257,461	1.98	6.11
Other slot machines	27,164	−39.16	
Total slot machines	**2,888,527**	**3.54**	**7.34**
Total gaming win	**6,068,959**	**5.07**	
(1) Race pari-mutuel	25,913	−2.52	15.72
(2) Sports pool detail			
Football	11,460	−55.39	1.69
Basketball	22,977	21.66	5.85
Baseball	8,744	−17.52	3.37
Sports parlay cards	5,251	−7.07	30.91
Sports pari-mutuel	1	0.00	
Other	7,224	−15.09	7.06

Notes: Columns may not foot due to rounding. Unit detail is shown separately only when there are 3 or more locations reporting specific unit information. Otherwise, information is included in "Other"categories. Figures are current as of 2/2/12.

SOURCE: Adapted from "Clark County Las Vegas Strip Area, All Nonrestricted Locations, Twelve-Month Summary—01/01/11 to 12/31/11," in *State of Nevada Gaming Revenue Report: Year Ended December 31, 2011*, Nevada State Gaming Control Board, 2012, http://gaming.nv.gov/modules/showdocument.aspx?documentid=3975 (accessed August 16, 2012)

Downtown Las Vegas gaming revenue, selected statistics, 2011

[In thousands]

	Twelve-month summary—01/01/11 to 12/31/11 Number of reporting locations—20		
	Win amount	% change	Win percent
Twenty-One	42,450	4.33	12.91
Craps	28,165	0.57	−0.57
Roulette	10,636	4.51	20.08
3-card poker	9,148	4.64	25.11
Mini-Baccarat	870	4.82	4.46
Keno	4,203	0.65	25.05
Let It Ride	5,522	3.94	23.2
Pai Gow poker	3,865	−5.49	19.95
Race Book (1)	1,630	−14.14	17.11
Sports Pool (2)	4,363	−0.20	3.21
Other games	5,975	−25.10	17.19
Total games	**116,827**	**0.20**	**12.78**
Card games	4,938	−5.13	
Slot machines			
1 cent	126,927	15.68	10.86
5 cent	13,788	−12.85	8.78
25 cent	57,728	−6.46	5.17
1 dollar	41,920	−3.90	4.63
Megabucks	5,978	17.97	10.55
5 dollar	6,715	−6.02	5.35
Multi-denomination	115,030	−5.15	5.37
Other slot machines	6,827	−5.53	
Total slot machines	**374,914**	**0.89**	**6.41**
Total gaming win	**496,678**	**0.67**	
(1) Race pari-mutuel	1,539	−16.43	16.83
(2) Sports pool detail			
Football	1,600	−28.02	2.74
Basketball	1,251	37.84	3.61
Baseball	517	−19.91	1.54
Sports parlay cards	618	72.66	26.38
Sports pari-mutuel	0	0.00	
Other	377	58.67	5.52

Notes: Columns may not foot due to rounding. Unit detail is shown separately only when there are 3 or more locations reporting specific unit information. Otherwise, information is included in "Other" categories. Figures are current as of 2/2/12.

SOURCE: Adapted from "Clark County Downtown Las Vegas Area, All Nonrestricted Locations, Twelve-Month Summary—01/01/11 to 12/31/11," in *State of Nevada Gaming Revenue Report: Year Ended December 31, 2011*, Nevada State Gaming Control Board, 2012, http://gaming.nv.gov/modules/showdocument.aspx?documentid=3975 (accessed August 16, 2012)

nearly 5 miles (8 km). During the 1960s the city lost most of its tourist trade to beaches farther south, mainly in Florida and the Caribbean, and the city fell into an economic slump. Casinos were seen as a way to revitalize the city and attract tourists again. The first casino, Resorts International, opened in 1978, followed by Caesars Atlantic and Bally's Park Place in 1979. By 1991 casino gambling was permitted 24 hours per day.

The city's 12 casinos had a casino win of $3.3 billion in 2011, down from $3.6 billion in 2010. (See Table 4.4.) As the AGA reports in *2012 State of the States*, much of this decline was fueled by increased competition from casinos in nearby Delaware and Pennsylvania.

All Atlantic City casinos are land based. According to the New Jersey Casino Control Commission in *New Jersey Casino Control Commission Annual Report 2011* (2012, http://www.nj.gov/casinos/reports/docs/2011_ccc_annual_report.pdf), as of December 31, 2011, they offered 27,048 slot machines, 1,580 table games, and 6 keno windows. (See Table 4.5.) Atlantic City casinos employed 32,823 people in 2011 and paid wages of roughly $817.2 million. (See Table 4.6 and Table 4.7).

Atlantic City differs from Las Vegas in many ways. There are far fewer hotel rooms, although the opening of three new hotels in 2008, and a fourth in 2012, increased the number of rooms from 14,500 to approximately 18,000. Regardless, the hotels do not provide as many amenities. Atlantic City is considered a "day-tripper market," meaning that it attracts people within driving

TABLE 4.4

New Jersey casino revenue, selected statistics, 2010–11

[Dollars in thousands]

Casino hotel	Casino win	Daily average casino win	Adjustments	Promotional gaming credits	Taxable gross revenue	Gross revenue tax	Market share of casino win
Atlantic Club[c]							
2011	$142,979	$392	$—	$19,713	$123,266	$9,861	4.3%
2010	163,650	448	—	16,762	146,888	11,751	4.6%
Bally's Atlantic City							
2011	378,311	1,036	—	45,551	332,760	26,621	11.4%
2010	426,005	1,167	—	38,340	387,665	31,013	12.0%
Borgata							
2011	651,814	1,786	—	60,953	590,861	47,269	19.7%
2010	647,670	1,774	—	50,667	597,002	47,760	18.2%
Caesars							
2011	403,346	1,105	(21)	43,238	360,129	28,810	12.2%
2010	408,730	1,120	(79)	36,357	372,452	29,796	11.5%
Harrah's Marina							
2011	439,812	1,205	—	43,347	396,465	31,717	13.3%
2010	453,471	1,242	(4)	36,090	417,385	33,391	12.7%
Resorts[a]							
2011	154,218	423	4	18,515	135,699	10,856	4.6%
2010	154,493	423	—	12,010	142,483	11,399	4.3%
Showboat							
2011	258,282	708	(8)	29,576	228,714	18,297	7.8%
2010	285,027	781	(11)	24,824	260,214	20,817	8.0%
Tropicana							
2011	277,153	759	—	29,407	247,746	19,820	8.4%
2010	300,443	823	—	24,543	275,900	22,072	8.4%
Golden Nugget[b]							
2011	125,194	343	147	2,612	122,729	9,818	3.8%
2010	147,386	404	—	13,737	133,649	10,692	4.1%
Trump Plaza							
2011	136,739	375	(31)	20,034	116,736	9,339	4.1%
2010	175,057	480	(50)	16,963	158,144	12,652	4.9%
Trump Taj Mahal							
2011	348,835	956	(17)	53,377	295,475	23,638	10.5%
2010	402,398	1102	(20)	33,173	369,245	29,540	11.3%
Totals							
2011	**$3,316,683**	**$9,087**	**$74**	**$366,323**	**$2,950,580**	**$236,046**	**100.0%**
2010	**$3,564,330**	**$9,765**	**$(164)**	**$303,466**	**$3,261,027**	**$260,883**	**100.0%**

[a]Resorts was under Resorts International Hotel, Inc. management until December 6, 2010 and operating as DGMB Casino, LLC since December 7, 2010.
[b]Reflects results of Trump Marina through May 23, 2011 and Golden Nugget thereafter.
[c]In March 2012 ACH changed its name to Atlantic Club.

SOURCE: "The New Jersey Casino Industry Gross Revenue Statistics for the Years Ended December 31, 2011 and 2010," in *The 2011 Annual Report of the New Jersey Casino Control Commission*, State of New Jersey Casino Control Commission, 2012, http://www.nj.gov/casinos/reports/docs/2011_ccc_annual_report.pdf (accessed August 22, 2012). Source of data: New Jersey Division of Gaming Enforcement's Quarterly Press Release and Statistical Summaries.

or train distance who visit for the day (many of them are from New York City and Philadelphia). Casino development was sluggish in Atlantic City during the 1990s; no new casinos were built. In July 2003, however, the Boyd Gaming Corporation and MGM Mirage (now known as MGM Resorts International) collaborated to open Borgata. Revel, which opened in April 2012, was the first hotel casino in Atlantic City to offer a completely smoke-free atmosphere for its customers.

Each casino in Atlantic City is assessed an 8% tax on its gross revenue (i.e., casino revenue after all winners are paid but before other expenses are paid). The tax payments go into the Casino Revenue Fund, which distributes funds among various state programs. The New Jersey Casino Control Commission indicates that in fiscal year (FY) 2011 a total of $264.7 million in taxes was

collected from the casinos. The revenue fund then disperses payments to the Department of Health and Senior Services, the Department of Human Services, the Department of Transportation, the Department of Labor and Workforce Development, and the Department of Law and Public Safety. Most of these taxes fund programs that benefit senior citizens and disabled people living in the state. In addition, casinos pay a 1.1% tax on the value of comps (complimentary accommodations, goods, or services that are provided to gamblers), a $3.00 tax for each parking space that is in use each day, and $3.00 per day for each occupied hotel room.

The casinos of Atlantic City have not changed the town into a trendy tourist destination as was originally hoped. In fact, Atlantic City has the reputation of being a slum with casinos. Industry experts point to two primary

TABLE 4.5

New Jersey casino industry facilities, games and slots, 2011

Games	Atlantic Club[a]	Bally's AC	Borgata	Caesars	Harrah's AC	Resorts	Showboat	Tropicana	Golden Nugget[b]	Trump Plaza	Trump Taj Mahal	Industry Totals
Blackjack	35	81	78	59	70	41	41	55	24	37	67	588
Craps	5	9	14	14	9	5	5	9	3	3	12	88
Roulette	7	21	20	17	12	8	9	15	6	9	14	138
Three Card Poker	4	15	15	11	14	4	9	8	4	2	6	92
Baccarat	0	1	1	4	0	0	0	0	0	0	0	6
Minibaccarat	18	16	16	9	6	14	9	9	6	11	14	128
Keno windows	0	0	0	0	4	0	0	0	0	0	2	6
Caribbean Stud poker	0	2	4	2	1	0	1	1	1	0	2	14
Let It Ride poker	2	4	5	2	4	2	2	2	2	1	3	29
Pai Gow	4	3	2	5	1	3	2	2	1	2	2	27
Pai Gow Poker	2	6	6	6	3	4	3	2	1	2	2	37
Other games[c]	4	11	9	8	3	5	4	6	1	2	7	60
Banking poker games[d]	3	11	14	10	7	3	3	4	5	2	4	66
Poker	8	26	76	32	40	0	24	27	20	0	54	307
Total games	**92**	**206**	**260**	**179**	**174**	**89**	**112**	**140**	**74**	**71**	**189**	**1,586**
Slot machines												
$0.01 and $0.02	969	1,225	1,506	1,086	737	581	636	1,067	598	769	1,315	10,489
$0.05	100	324	507	165	269	150	123	160	178	92	129	2,197
$0.25	267	572	315	265	457	360	250	211	277	389	398	3,761
$0.50	39	60	81	69	8	38	3	33	26	59	22	438
$1	210	342	225	301	198	144	173	162	125	148	317	2,345
$5	88	94	84	71	61	60	29	45	20	21	73	646
$25	6	18	22	14	16	9	3	20	9	9	12	138
$100	4	13	12	13	7	10	3	15	4	2	23	106
Multi-denominational	133	593	672	311	1,093	753	1,379	909	210	155	401	6,609
Other	22	27	51	48	26	20	5	38	7	44	31	319
Total slot machines	**1,838**	**3,268**	**3,475**	**2,343**	**2,872**	**2,125**	**2,604**	**2,660**	**1,454**	**1,688**	**2,721**	**27,048**
Casino statistics												
Casino square footage	75,416	179,678	136,667	111,812	179,753	99,030	122,454	136,980	67,150	86,923	149,239	1,345,102
Simulcasting square footage	0	9,393	23,620	28,963	569	0	17,086	0	0	0	12,483	92,114
Total gaming space	**75,416**	**189,071**	**160,287**	**140,775**	**180,322**	**99,030**	**139,540**	**136,980**	**67,150**	**86,923**	**161,722**	**1,437,216**
Number of parking spaces	**1,406**	**3,782**	**6,443**	**5,324**	**4,703**	**1,337**	**3,499**	**4,975**	**2,986**	**2,618**	**5,806**	**42,879**

[a]In March 2012 ACH changed its name to Atlantic Club.
[b]In May 2011 Trump Marina became Golden Nugget.
[c]Includes: Big Six, Sic Bo, Supreme Pai Gow, Double Attack Blackjack, Casino War, and Spanish 21.
[d]Includes: Four Card Poker, Flop Poker, Asia Poker, Mini-Tex 3 Card Hold'Em, Mississippi Stud Winner's Pot Pokker, Ultimate Texas Hold'Em, Texas Hold'Em, Bonus Poer, House Way Pai Gow Poker, 1 Bet Threat Texas Hold'Em, and Two Card Joker Poker.

SOURCE: "The New Jersey Casino Industry Facility Statistics at the Year Ended December 31, 2011," in *The 2011 Annual Report of the New Jersey Casino Control Commission*, State of New Jersey Casino Control Commission, 2012, http://www.nj.gov/casinos/reports/docs/2011_ccc_annual_report.pdf (accessed August 22, 2012). Source of data: Monthly forms—DGE 101.

factors for this perception: the town relies on day-trippers rather than on long-term vacationers and casino tax revenues have largely funded physical and mental health programs throughout the state rather than being invested in local infrastructure and economic development.

The article "Gov. Christie Pledges to Turn Atlantic City Casino District into 'Las Vegas East'" (*Newark [NJ] Star-Ledger*, July 21, 2010) reports on the results of a governor's commission, which found in 2010 that the Atlantic City local government was inept and possibly corrupt and had mismanaged hundreds of millions of dollars in tax revenues from the casinos. In July 2010 Chris Christie (1962–; Republican), the governor of New Jersey, promised that the state would take over management of the casino district in Atlantic City to create an "East Las Vegas" and shut down horse racing operations at Meadowlands Racetrack, which had been unprofitable for many years.

MISSISSIPPI

In 1989 Mississippi became the first state to permit gambling on cruise ships that were in state waters on their way to or from international waters. However, gambling in Mississippi has had a long history. Gambling along the Mississippi River and its connecting waterways was widespread during the early 1800s. The rivers were the equivalent of the modern-day interstate highway system in that they carried cash-laden farmers, merchants, and tourists to bustling towns along the riverbank. Gambling halls became notorious establishments that attracted professional gamblers, especially cardsharps, who employed various methods of cheating to earn a living at cards.

By the 1830s the cardsharps had worn out their welcome. According to Richard Dunstan in *Gambling in California* (1997), five cardsharps were lynched in Mississippi in 1835, so the professional gamblers decided to move to the riverboats that cruised up and down the

TABLE 4.6

New Jersey casino industry employment statistics, 2008–11

	2011	2010	2009	2008
Atlantic Club[a]	1,701	2,005	2,050	2,261
Bally's A.C.	3,856	4,061	4,360	4,759
Borgata	6,211	6,311	6,507	6,840
Caesars	3,090	3,246	3,353	3,645
Harrah's A.C.	4,115	3,858	3,886	4,001
Resorts/DGMB[b]	1,933	1,724	2,141	2,422
Showboat	2,488	2,541	2,513	2,710
Tropicana	2,952	3,011	3,229	3,517
Golden Nugget[c]	1,660	1,631	1,794	1,928
Trump Plaza	1,442	1,917	2,180	2,406
Trump Taj Mahal	3,375	3,840	4,069	4,096
Industry totals	**32,823***	**34,145**	**36,082**	**38,585**

*25,079 (76.4%) are full time employees, 3,958 (12.1%) are part time employees and 3,786 (11.5%) are considered other employees.
[a]In March 2012, ACH changed its name to Atlantic Club.
[b]Resorts was under Resorts International Hotel, Inc. management until December 6, 2010 and operating as DGMB Casino, LLC since December 7, 2010.
[c]In May 2011, Golden Nugget began operations after acquiring the Trump Marina property.
[d]Salaries and wages for 2010 changed to reflect new chart of accounts reporting structure per consolidation with Tropicana Entertainment.

SOURCE: "The New Jersey Casino Industry Employment Statistics for the Four Years Ended December 31, 2011," in *The 2011 Annual Report of the New Jersey Casino Control Commission*, State of New Jersey Casino Control Commission, 2012, http://www.nj.gov/casinos/reports/docs/2011_ccc_annual_report.pdf (accessed August 22, 2012). Source of data: Information supplied by each casino licensee.

TABLE 4.7

New Jersey casino industry salaries and wages, 2008–11

[Dollars in thousands]

	2011	2010	2009	2008
Atlantic Club[a]	$52,972	$58,624	$61,799	$70,098
Bally's A.C.	95,179	109,813	116,720	134,747
Borgata	149,059	152,634	154,987	164,673
Caesars	81,554	90,525	92,564	105,485
Harrah's A.C.	89,741	91,984	91,604	99,318
Resorts/DGMB[b]	47,170	50,737	56,681	62,596
Showboat	59,976	66,483	65,638	75,524
Tropicana	73,553	78,946[d]	77,804	82,777
Golden Nugget[c]	33,766	52,491	54,066	59,732
Trump Plaza	45,620	63,738	67,018	73,779
Trump Taj Mahal	88,656	108,938	110,085	109,450
Industry totals	**$817,246**	**$924,913**	**$948,966**	**$1,038,179**

[a]In March 2012, ACH changed its name to Atlantic Club.
[b]Resorts was under Resorts International Hotel, Inc. management until December 6, 2010 and operating as DGMB Casino, LLC since December 7, 2010.
[c]In May 2011, Golden Nugget began operations after acquiring the Trump Marina property.
[d]Salaries and wages for 2010 changed to reflect new chart of accounts reporting structure per consolidation with Tropicana Entertainment.

SOURCE: "The New Jersey Casino Industry Salaries and Wages for the Four Years Ended December 31, 2011," in *The 2011 Annual Report of the New Jersey Casino Control Commission*, State of New Jersey Casino Control Commission, 2012, http://www.nj.gov/casinos/reports/docs/2011_ccc_annual_report.pdf (accessed August 22, 2012). Source of data: New Jersey Division of Gaming Enforcement's Quarterly Press Release and Statistical Summaries.

rivers. Gambling was a popular pastime for riverboat passengers during the 1840s and 1850s. The onset of the Civil War (1861–1865) and then the antigambling movement around the turn of the 20th century dampened, but did not destroy, open gambling in the state.

During and after World War II (1939–1945) the Mississippi coast experienced a resurgence in illegal casino gambling, particularly in Harrison County, which is where the Keesler Air Force Base is located. For example, the officers' club at the base reportedly operated slot machines. During the 1960s the Alcohol Beverage Control Board began refusing licenses to public facilities that allowed gambling. A few private clubs and lodges continued to offer card games and slot machines, but they were shut down by the mid-1980s.

In 1987 the ship *Europa Star* and several other ships from Biloxi ports began taking gamblers on "cruises to nowhere"—cruises to international waters in the Gulf of Mexico, where passengers could gamble legally. Even though the cruises were supported by the city of Biloxi, the state initially opposed them until it became apparent that they were reviving tourism in port towns. The state was in desperate economic times; the 1980 census revealed that it was the poorest state in the country.

In 1990 the Mississippi legislature legalized casino gambling, although each county was allowed to decide whether it would permit gambling within its borders. Fourteen counties along the Gulf Coast and the Mississippi River held referenda to allow dockside casinos, and all voted them down. The next year a city-by-city vote was held, and voters in Biloxi, which was nearly bankrupt at the time, approved the referendum. In 1992 nine dockside casinos opened in Biloxi.

Casinos are grouped in three parts of the state: the northern region centered in Tunica; the central region based in Vicksburg and Natchez; and the coastal region centered in Biloxi, Gulfport, and Bay St. Louis. In *2012 State of the States*, the AGA indicates that in 2011 Biloxi was the eighth-largest casino market in the United States and Tunica the ninth largest.

Mississippi has not set a limit on the number of casinos that can be built in the state. Instead, it allows competition to determine the market size. Before Hurricane Katrina hit the state in August 2005 and devastated the area around Biloxi, casinos were required to be permanently docked in the water along the Mississippi River and the Mississippi Gulf Coast. The gambling halls of the casinos actually sat on the water, while their associated lodging, dining, and entertainment facilities were on land. After the hurricane partially or completely destroyed all 12 casinos along the Gulf Coast, the legislature passed a law allowing casino operators who had establishments on the coast in Biloxi, Gulfport, and Bay St. Louis to relocate their casinos 800 feet (244 m) inland so they would be safe from any future storm surges. Along the Mississippi River, the gambling halls sit in slips that have been cut into the riverbank. The Mississippi Band of Choctaw Indians operates the only inland casinos, which are located in Neshoba County.

As of June 2012, there were 29 commercial casinos licensed to operate in Mississippi. (See Table 4.8.) In total, they employed 21,402 people and offered over 1.4 million square feet (132,500 sq m) of gaming space, 32,597 slot machines, 857 table games, and 148 poker games. Table games offered included baccarat, blackjack, craps, keno, and roulette. The state allows round-the-clock gambling with no bet limits.

The gross casino revenue for the state was $2.2 billion in 2011, down 24% from 2007. (See Figure 4.2.) The newest property to open was the Magnolia Bluffs Casino in Natchez, which opened in December 2012.

According to the Mississippi Gaming Commission, in "Tax Revenues from Gaming" (July 1, 2012, http://www.dor.ms.gov/docs/game_gamtaxprevious.pdf), the casino industry produces a substantial percentage of the state's annual budget. In FY 2012 (July 2011 to June 2012) casinos paid $281.5 million in taxes. Approximately $151.9 million (54%) was paid into the state's general fund, $93.7 million (33%) went to local governments, and the remainder went to retire debt. In total, nearly $4.6 billion had been collected in casino taxes in Mississippi between July 1992 and June 2012.

LOUISIANA

Like Mississippi, Louisiana has a long gambling history. In 1823, 11 years after Louisiana became a state, its legislature legalized several forms of gambling and licensed six "temples of chance" in the city of New Orleans. Each was to pay $5,000 per year to fund the Charity Hospital and the College of Orleans. The casinos attracted many patrons, including professional gamblers, swindlers, and thieves. In 1835 the legislature repealed the licensing act and passed laws that made gambling hall owners subject to prison terms or large fines.

However, casino-type gambling continued and even prospered throughout the southern part of the state. By 1840 New Orleans had an estimated 500 gambling halls that employed more than 4,000 people but did not pay revenue to the city. Hundreds of professional gamblers who plied the Mississippi River between New Orleans and St. Louis frequented riverboat casinos. When the Civil War broke out, the riverboats were pressed into military service. In 1869 the legislature legalized casino gambling once more, requiring each casino to again pay the state a tax of $5,000.

In *Bad Bet on the Bayou: The Rise of Gambling in Louisiana and the Fall of Governor Edwin Edwards* (2001), Tyler Bridges credits Louisiana gamblers for popularizing craps and poker in the United States during the

19th century. Both were games of chance that had originated in Europe. The Louisiana state lottery began in 1868 but was outlawed in 1895, along with other forms of gambling, after massive fraud was uncovered. Casino gambling went underground and continued to flourish well into the 1960s, thanks to mobsters and political corruption. Two of the state's governors, Earl Kemp Long (1895–1960; Democrat) and Edwin Edwards (1927–; Democrat), were well-known gamblers. Edwards reportedly hosted high-stakes gambling games at the governor's mansion; he also went to prison in 2001 for extorting money from people who sought riverboat casino licenses.

In 1991 the state legalized gambling again, authorizing a lottery, casinos, and the operation of video poker machines in restaurants, bars, and truck stops. The legislature authorized operation of up to 15 riverboat casinos in the state; all but those along the Red River were required to make regularly scheduled cruises. The riverboat casinos were required to be at least 150 feet (46 m) long and decorated to look like 19th-century paddleboats. The first riverboat casino, the *Showboat Star*, began operating in 1993.

New Orleans received special permission from the legislature in 1993 to allow a limited number of land-based casinos. In January 1995 Harrah's Entertainment began construction on a casino in the heart of the city. By November 1995 the casino had declared bankruptcy. Following years of negotiations with the state and the city, it reopened in 1999 but threatened bankruptcy again in 2001, blaming the state's $100 million minimum tax. The legislature reduced the tax to $50 million for 2001 and to $60 million for subsequent years to help keep the casino in business.

In April 2001 the legislature ended the so-called phantom cruises of the riverboat casinos, ruling that it would actually be illegal for them to leave the docks. All riverboats were allowed to begin dockside gambling. However, their tax rate was increased from 18.5% to 21.5%.

Between July 1 and December 31, 2011, Louisiana riverboat casinos generated approximately $809.6 million in gross revenues. (See Table 4.9.) According to the Louisiana Gaming Control Board in *Report to the Louisiana State Legislature, 2011–2012* (2012, http://lgcb.dps.louisiana.gov/docs/2011-2012%20Annual%20Report.pdf), the state's riverboat casinos admitted nearly 21.7 million people during the fiscal year that ran from July 1, 2011, to June 30, 2012. The attendance figure was down from 28 million in FY 2005, possibly because of Hurricanes Katrina and Rita, which had severely damaged two riverboat casinos on Lake Charles (*Harrah's Pride* and *Harrah's Star*) and one on Lake Pontchartrain (*Bally's Belle of Orleans*). The total adjusted gross revenue for the riverboats in the period between July 1, 2011 and June 30, 2012 was approximately $1.7 billion. The Louisiana Gaming Control Board explains that the total gross

TABLE 4.8

Mississippi casino statistics, April–June 2012

Casino	Total employees*	Hotel employees	Gaming square foot	Other square foot	Total square foot	Avg # slot games	Avg # table games	Avg # poker games	Hotel rooms	Total parking	Activities in addition to gaming
Central											
Ameristar Casino Hotel	741	70	72,210	260,708	332,918	1,562	32	10	149	370,927	F&B (deli, buffet, steak house, & blues bar), entertainment, gift shop, convenience store with Subway, RV park, hotel with market, Star Club Lounge, and poker room
Diamondjacks Casino & Hotel	342	26	28,000	19,853	47,853	774	13	0	122	631	Legends Restaurant, Lucky Bean deli, DJ's Steakhouse
Harlow's Casino Resort	381	43	33,000	50,000	83,000	818	15	6	105	1,500	Hotel, 3 restaurants, entertainment arena
Isle of Capri Casino—Natchez	270	26	17,634	0	17,634	596	9	0	141	908	Buffet, deli, bar, hotel
Rainbow Casino	304	21	25,000	5,000	30,000	647	8	0	89	948	Hotel, 2 restaurants, gift shop, meeting room
Riverwalk Casino	392	26	25,000	95,000	120,000	715	17	0	80	748	
Trop Casino Greenville	239	0	22,218	0	22,218	577	5	0	0	386	
Region totals	**2,669**	**212**	**223,062**	**430,561**	**653,623**	**5,689**	**99**	**16**	**686**	**376,048**	
Coastal											
Beau Rivage Casino	2,367	459	75,744	2,103,583	2,179,327	2,058	85	16	1,735	3,959	Hotel, 3 fine dining restaurants, 4 casual dining restaurants, 4 miscellaneous shops/boutiques, retail promenade, Fallen Oak, arcade, convention center, spa, and showroom
Boomtown Casino—Biloxi	542	0	51,665	90,785	142,450	1,072	16	5	0	1,490	Steakhouse, 24-hour grill, buffet
Grand Casino Biloxi	712	96	31,275	453,520	484,795	750	32	0	494	2,705	Golf, hotel, buffet, LB's, Grand Cafe, lobby bar, pool, spa, Asian cafe
Hard Rock Casino—Biloxi	820	146	53,800	126,200	180,000	1,322	53	5	325	1,802	Restaurants, gift shops clothing boutique, entertainment showroom, lounges
Hollywood Casino Bay St. Louis	562	92	58,900	146,000	204,900	1,182	12	4	291	1,700	Golf course, RV park, ballrooms for conventions, 4 restaurants & Bay Tower Hotel
IP Casino Resort Spa	1,625	217	81,733	909,717	991,450	1,901	62	14	1,088	3,300	7 restaurants, 3 retail outlets, showroom, convention center, conference room, hotel, room service, 8 bars, banquet facilities, swimming pool, spa, fitness center, coffee shop, limo service, and valet parking
Island View Casino	1,160	177	82,935	659,406	742,341	1,912	45	0	565	4,200	Restaurants, hotel, pool, room service, retail, bars, limo service, valet parking, conference room, banquets, golf course
Isle of Capri Casino—Biloxi	651	37	57,819	618,700	676,519	1,133	29	9	710	0	Lava Bar, spa, Tradewinds, buffet, cafe, Farraddays'
Margaritaville Casino & Restaurant	960	0	25,300	40,000	65,300	820	18	0	0	900	Restaurants, gift shops, entertainment showroom, outdoor bar & marina
Palace Casino	660	103	38,000	62,000	100,000	1,047	26	0	234	1,556	Hotel, restaurants, swimming pool, bars, spa, gift shop
Silver Slipper Casino	547	0	36,826	63,174	100,000	963	25	5	0	1,700	Restaurants, live entertainment, general store, fishing
Treasure Bay Casino	564	27	24,557	715	25,272	811	26	0	179	1,096	Restaurants (3), ultra lounge/pool bar/gift shop/fitness room
Region totals	**11,170**	**1,354**	**618,554**	**5,273,800**	**5,892,354**	**14,971**	**429**	**58**	**5,621**	**24,408**	

TABLE 4.8

Mississippi casino statistics, April–June 2012 [CONTINUED]

Casino	Total employees*	Hotel employees	Gaming square foot	Other square foot	Total square foot	Avg # slot games	Avg # table games	Avg # poker games	Hotel rooms	Total parking	Activities in addition to gaming
Northern											
Bally's Tunica Casino	427	20	46,535	153,543	200,078	1,183	17	0	238	1,699	Dining at the steakhouse, Riverview buffet, and snack bar
Fitzgerald's Casino—Tunica	669	120	38,088	522,912	561,000	1,303	24	0	506	1,795	
Gold Strike Casino Resort	1,222	132	46,798	1,347,597	1,394,395	1,294	55	16	1,133	2,412	Bullion Stage Bar, Liquid Assets Bar / The Atrium Cafe / The Courtyard Buffet / The Chicago Steakhouse / The Millennium Theatre / The Food Court
Harrah's Casino Tunica	1,388	382	136,000	204,000	340,000	1,354	54	14	1,356	7,000	Health club, arcade, spa, swimming, gift shops, golf, car wash, RV park, bar/night club shooting range.
Hollywood Casino—Tunica	494	59	54,000	264,431	318,431	1,133	21	6	494	1,801	RV park, indoor pool
Horseshoe Casino and Hotel	1,227	48	63,000	222,500	285,500	1,470	73	16	507	1,776	Health club, swimming pool,gift shops, bar
Isle of Capri—Lula	524	39	63,500	65,000	128,500	1,025	18	5	485	1,500	
Resorts Tunica Hotel & Casino	459	37	42,902	331,311	374,213	1,047	13	0	201	2,738	
Sam's Town—Tunica	721	105	66,000	30,000	96,000	1,374	30	15	842	4,308	
Tunica Roadhouse Casino	432	39	32,800	0	32,800	754	24	2	135	4,265	Gift shop
Region totals	**7,563**	**981**	**589,623**	**3,141,294**	**3,730,917**	**11,937**	**329**	**74**	**5,897**	**29,294**	
State totals	**21,402**	**2,547**	**1,431,239**	**8,845,655**	**10,276,894**	**32,597**	**857**	**148**	**12,204**	**429,750**	

*Excludes hotel employees.

SOURCE: "Mississippi Gaming Commission Public Information: Quarterly Survey Information: April 1, 2012–June 30, 2012," in *Quarterly Reports—2nd Quarter 2012: Property Data,* Mississippi Gaming Commission, 2012, http://www.msgamingcommission.com/files/quarterly_reports/QRpt2Q12-Property.pdf (accessed August 22, 2012)

FIGURE 4.2

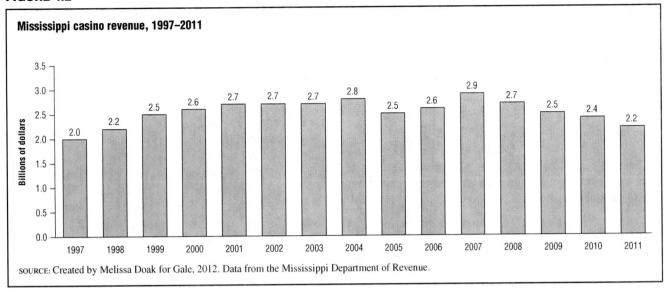

Mississippi casino revenue, 1997–2011

SOURCE: Created by Melissa Doak for Gale, 2012. Data from the Mississippi Department of Revenue.

TABLE 4.9

Louisiana riverboat gaming activity, July 1–December 31, 2011

Riverboat licensees	Opening date	Fiscal year to date admissions	Fiscal year to date total (adjusted gross revenue)	Fiscal year to date fee remittance
Boomtown Bossier	10/04/96	581,370	42,256,565	9,085,162
Eldorado Resort	12/20/00	1,571,186	78,047,649	16,780,244
Horseshoe	07/09/94	933,588	108,682,554	23,366,749
Diamondjacks	05/20/94	615,531	37,682,483	8,101,734
Sam's Town	05/20/04	914,119	56,594,951	12,167,914
Grand Palais	07/12/96	849,411	64,444,992	13,855,673
Isle- LC	07/29/95	197,305	6,490,200	1,395,393
L'auberge Du Lac	05/23/05	2,306,861	179,970,120	38,693,576
Amelia Belle	05/16/07	310,860	24,980,637	5,370,837
Boomtown N.O.	08/06/94	742,378	66,303,906	14,255,340
Treasure Chest	09/05/94	565,356	52,782,801	11,348,302
Belle of B.R.	09/30/94	438,319	32,928,107	7,079,543
Hollywood B.R.	12/28/94	589,609	58,454,322	12,567,679
Riverboat total		**10,615,893**	**$809,619,288**	**$174,068,147**

SOURCE: "Louisiana State Police Fiscal Year-to-Date Summary—Riverboats for the Period July 1, 2011–December 31, 2011," Louisiana State Police, August 2012, http://dpsweb.dps.louisiana.gov/lgcb.nsf/ddb20cf421af536586256e9b0049df46/d75a6c66c4ceb2218625798a005d08f7/$FILE/December%202011%20-%20Riverboat%20Revenue.pdf (accessed August 22, 2012)

casino revenue in Louisiana for FY 2012 was $2.4 billion, holding steady with FY 2011. (See Figure 4.3.) Revenues in FY 2012 were double that from FY 1998, when casinos started operating in Louisiana.

The state has four major casino markets: Shreveport–Bossier City, New Orleans, Lake Charles, and Baton Rouge. In 2011 the Shreveport market was the 12th-largest casino market in the United States, according to the AGA in *2012 State of the States*. A wide variety of games is allowed in Louisiana casinos, including baccarat, bingo, blackjack, craps, keno, poker, roulette, and slot machines. In "Louisiana State Police Video Gaming Division Revenue Report" (November 2012, http://dpsweb.dps.louisiana.gov/gsrr.nsf/f5b2cbf2a827c0198525624b00057d30/6ec7fb73e68ea7cb86257ad1005d34ce/$FILE/2012-11%20November%20Revenues%20-%20Video.xlsx),

the Louisiana Gaming Control Board indicates that the state also had 14,193 video gaming machines in truck stops, bars, restaurants, and other non-casino locations as of November 2012. The machines generated over $50 million in revenue that month.

INDIANA

In 1993 the state of Indiana legalized gambling on up to 11 riverboats in specific areas of the state: in the northwestern corner along Lake Michigan; at the southern border along the Ohio River; and around Patoka Lake in the southern part of the state. The Patoka Lake site initially received a riverboat license, but it was later vetoed by the U.S. Army Corps of Engineers.

The first riverboat began operation in December 1995 in Evansville. By December 1996 six riverboats were operating. In 2002 new legislation permitted dockside operation of the riverboats in counties that would accept it. Permanent mooring allows patrons to access the casinos anytime during operating hours rather than just during cruise boarding times. The measure was intended to make Indiana casinos more competitive with those in Illinois.

The new law also changed the wagering tax structure from a 22.5% flat tax on adjusted gross receipts to a graduated tax rate of 15% to 35%. A portion of the increased tax revenue is distributed to counties that do not have casinos. The admissions tax, which remained at $3 per person, is split among the state, county, and city: each gets $1 per person.

The Indiana Gaming Commission notes in *2012 Annual Report to Governor Mitch Daniels* (January 2013, http://www.in.gov/igc/files/FY2012-Annual.pdf)

that in 2012 there were 13 riverboat casinos, land-based casinos, and racinos operating in Indiana. Five of the casinos were situated along Lake Michigan and the outskirts of Chicago, and eight were located in the southern half of the state. Games allowed included baccarat, blackjack, craps, poker, and roulette.

According to the Indiana Gaming Commission, the total riverboat admission in Indiana was 25 million people during FY 2012. The total win during FY 2012 was more than $2.7 billion. (See Table 4.10.) In *2012 State of the States*, the AGA notes that in 2011 Indiana was the third-largest casino market in the United States in terms of gross revenue. In FY 2012 the state collected $754.1 million in wagering taxes, down 4.2% from FY 2011, and $74.9 million in admissions taxes, down 2.7% from FY 2011. (See Table 4.11.)

FIGURE 4.3

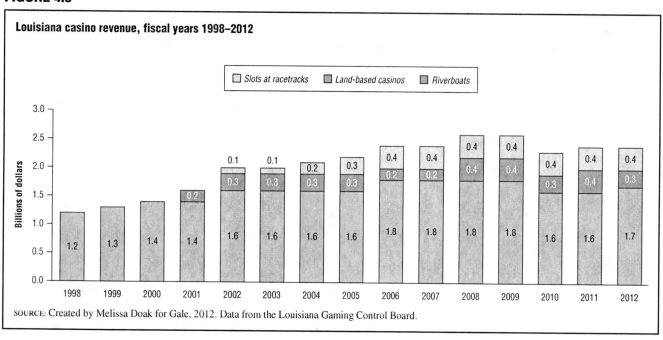

TABLE 4.10

Indiana gaming taxes, selected statistics, fiscal year 2012

Fiscal year 2012	Win total	Wagering tax	Admission tax	Total tax
Ameristar	$241,223,165	$68,868,494	$8,326,185	$77,194,679
Belterra	$149,681,356	$37,425,256	$4,998,222	$42,423,478
Blue Chip	$174,974,053	$46,292,859	$7,491,402	$53,784,261
Casino Aztar	$119,615,758	$28,414,279	$3,677,079	$32,091,358
French Lick	$86,485,021	$18,458,986	$2,973,354	$21,432,340
Hollywood	$429,110,433	$135,195,766	$10,831,911	$146,027,677
Hoosier Park	$222,463,973	$55,333,226	N/A	$55,333,226
Horseshoe Hammond	$499,526,314	$159,635,313	$17,297,628	$176,932,941
Horseshoe Southern Indiana	$259,876,086	$76,160,762	$6,718,542	$82,897,304
Indiana Grand	$246,404,943	$62,693,821	N/A	$62,693,821
Majestic Star	$110,862,839	$25,788,804	$4,371,984	$30,160,788
Majestic Star II	$90,539,012	$19,697,961	$4,371,984	$24,069,945
Rising Star	$92,612,865	$20,180,603	$3,850,674	$24,031,277
Total	**$2,723,375,818**	**$754,146,130**	**$74,908,965**	**$829,055,095**

SOURCE: "FY 2012 Tax Overview," in *2012 Annual Report to Governor Mitch Daniels*, Indiana Gaming Commission, 2012, http://www.in.gov/igc/files/FY2012-Annual.pdf (accessed August 22, 2012)

ILLINOIS

Illinois legalized riverboat gambling in 1990, the second state to do so. The Illinois Gaming Board was authorized to grant up to 10 casino licenses, each of which would allow up to two vessels to be operated at a single specific dock site. Each dock site could not have more than 1,200 gaming positions, and all wagering was to be cashless. Originally, riverboats were required to cruise during gambling, but they were later allowed to operate dockside.

Ten Illinois riverboat casinos generated $1.5 billion in adjusted gross revenue in 2011, up 7% from $1.4 billion in 2010. (See Figure 4.4.) As the AGA reports in *2012 State of the States*, these revenue increases were fueled in part by the new Rivers Casino in Des Plaines, which opened in July 2011. According to the Illinois Gaming Board, in *2011 Annual Report* (2012, http://www.igb.illinois.gov/annualreport/2011igb.pdf), the vast majority (about $1.3 billion, or 86%) of the 2011 revenue was from electronic gambling devices; the remainder was from table games. (See Figure 4.5.) Admissions totaled 14.8 million in 2011, up 7% from 13.8 million the year before.

Illinois levies an admissions tax and a wagering tax. In 2005 the admissions tax was set at $2 per person at Casino Rock Island and $3 per person for all other casinos. Wagering taxes start at 15% for casinos with adjusted gross revenue of less than or equal to $25 million and increase as revenue increases. The state and communities in which the casinos are located share casino taxes. The Illinois Gaming Board states that the casino industry paid $88.7 million in local taxes in 2011 (see Table 4.12) and $400.7 million in state taxes. The state received 82% of admissions and wagering taxes, and the cities and counties received 18%.

MISSOURI

The legalization of riverboat gambling in Missouri started in 1992 with a referendum that was approved by 64% of the voters. That was followed by a court case, a constitutional amendment (which was defeated by voters), and a wrangling over the definition of "games of skill." Eventually, in 1994 the general assembly passed a

TABLE 4.11

Indiana gaming taxes, fiscal years 2011 and 2012

	Fiscal year 2011	Fiscal year 2012	Difference	% Difference
Wagering tax				
July	43,954,217	42,878,602	(1,075,615)	−2.45%
August	49,722,369	45,972,067	(3,750,302)	−7.54%
September	54,903,758	53,373,763	(1,529,994)	−2.79%
October	63,353,293	56,312,298	(7,040,995)	−11.11%
November	62,315,996	58,181,231	(4,134,765)	−6.64%
December	63,325,568	64,656,271	1,330,703	2.10%
January	66,353,305	62,108,286	(4,245,019)	−6.40%
February	71,687,562	75,657,720	3,970,158	5.54%
March	81,161,415	77,982,021	(3,179,393)	−3.92%
April	77,503,089	72,349,041	(5,154,048)	−6.65%
May	78,306,533	72,513,859	(5,792,695)	−7.40%
June	74,865,428	72,160,970	(2,704,458)	−3.61%
Total	**$787,452,554**	**$754,146,130**	**($33,306,424)**	**−4.23%**
Admissions tax				
July	7,495,665	6,923,535	(572,130)	−7.63%
August	7,043,724	6,495,465	(548,259)	−7.78%
September	6,550,527	6,253,113	(297,414)	−4.54%
October	6,761,589	6,142,515	(619,074)	−9.16%
November	6,007,908	5,667,023	(330,885)	−5.51%
December	5,679,840	6,199,992	520,152	9.16%
January	5,833,407	5,764,842	(68,565)	−1.18%
February	6,037,776	6,440,490	402,714	6.67%
March	6,738,849	6,610,176	(128,673)	−1.91%
April	6,427,470	6,102,969	(324,501)	−5.05%
May	6,296,553	6,159,384	(137,169)	−2.18%
June	6,095,115	6,139,461	44,346	0.73%
Total	**$76,968,423**	**$74,908,965**	**($2,059,458)**	**−2.68%**

SOURCE: "FY 2011/2012 Tax Comparison," in *2012 Annual Report to Governor Mitch Daniels*, Indiana Gaming Commission, 2012, http://www.in.gov/igc/files/FY2012-Annual.pdf (accessed August 22, 2012)

FIGURE 4.4

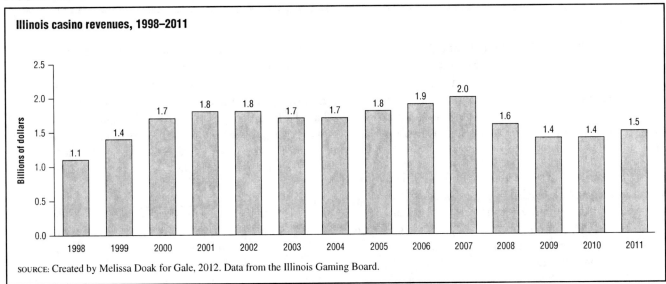

Illinois casino revenues, 1998–2011

SOURCE: Created by Melissa Doak for Gale, 2012. Data from the Illinois Gaming Board.

FIGURE 4.5

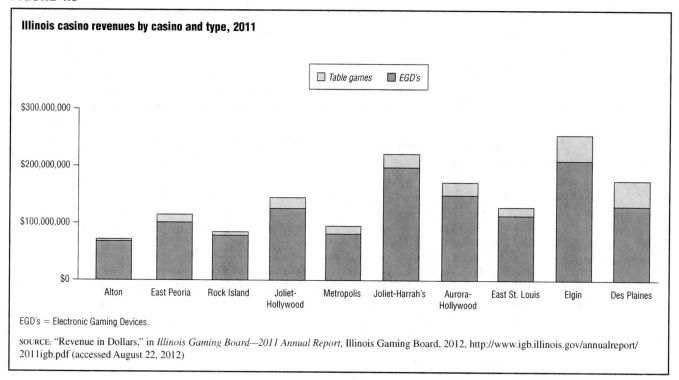

Illinois casino revenues by casino and type, 2011

□ Table games   ▨ EGD's

EGD's = Electronic Gaming Devices.

SOURCE: "Revenue in Dollars," in *Illinois Gaming Board—2011 Annual Report*, Illinois Gaming Board, 2012, http://www.igb.illinois.gov/annualreport/2011igb.pdf (accessed August 22, 2012)

TABLE 4.12

Local distribution of Illinois gaming taxes, 2007–11

	2007	2008	2009	2010	2011	% change 11 to '10
Alton	$7,724,803	$5,722,030	$5,369,552	$4,903,732	$4,598,774	−6.22%
East Peoria	8,011,938	7,188,723	7,087,935	7,073,458	6,984,630	−1.26%
Rock Island	2,411,087	2,387,351	4,779,745	5,354,352	5,625,633	5.07%
Joliet	36,168,333	28,335,882	23,573,344	22,975,414	21,810,944	−5.07%
Metropolis	9,921,866	7,407,894	6,964,396	6,621,939	5,559,086	−16.05%
Aurora	15,449,378	12,632,336	11,720,974	10,546,682	10,157,710	−3.69%
East St. Louis	11,738,204	10,292,397	9,623,667	8,596,621	8,455,040	−1.65%
Elgin	24,301,668	19,128,666	16,766,095	16,479,803	14,730,213	−10.62%
Des Plaines					10,819,591	
Total	**$115,727,277**	**$93,095,279**	**$85,885,708**	**$82,552,001**	**$88,741,621**	**7.50%**

SOURCE: "Distributions to Local Governments," in *Illinois Gaming Board—2011 Annual Report* Illinois Gaming Board, 2012, http://www.igb.illinois.gov/annualreport/2011igb.pdf (accessed August 22, 2012)

bill that defined games of skill and authorized riverboats to be located in artificial basins. The first two licenses for riverboat casinos were issued later that year. However, because the casinos could not offer games of chance, such as slot machines, competition from riverboats in Illinois kept customers away, and the casinos were not profitable.

After a petition drive, voters passed an initiative that allowed "only upon the Mississippi River and the Missouri River, lotteries, gift enterprises, and games of chance to be conducted on excursion gambling boats and floating facilities." The result was significant: revenues from casino riverboats during the first quarter of FY 1996 were more than twice what they had been during the first quarter of the previous year. Initially, the casinos were only allowed to hold two-hour gambling excursions. In 2000 the law was changed to allow continuous boarding. However, the original $500 loss limit per excursion that had been approved in 1992 still applies. Patrons are allowed to purchase only $500 worth of chips or tokens in any two-hour period, preventing them from losing more than that amount within the "excursion" period.

The AGA notes in *2012 State of the States* that in 2011, 12 riverboat casinos operated in six markets: Boonville, Caruthersville, Kansas City, LaGrange, St. Joseph, and St. Louis. All the riverboats remain dockside. Games allowed include blackjack, poker, and other card games, craps, roulette, slot machines, and several wheel games.

Gaming revenue topped $1 billion for the first time during FY 2001 and reached $1.8 billion in FY 2011. (See Figure 4.6.) Revenues at Missouri riverboats remained steady throughout the recession, although they did not grow as quickly as they had from 2000 to 2006.

MICHIGAN

Pari-mutuel horse racing (betting in which those who bet on the top competitors share the total amount bet and the house gets a percentage) was legalized in Michigan in 1933. During the 1970s the state lottery was legalized, and a concerted effort was made to allow casino gambling in Detroit. The casino effort was unsuccessful until 1994, when the Windsor Casino opened just across the river in Windsor, Ontario. By that time, more than a dozen tribal casinos were operating around the state of Michigan, and Detroit was in an economic downturn. Attitudes toward casino gambling changed, and in November 1996 Michigan voters narrowly approved ballot Proposal E, which authorized the operation of up to three casinos in any city that had a population of 800,000 people or more and was located within 100 miles (161 km) of any other state or country in which gaming was permitted. Casino gaming also had to be approved by a majority of voters in the city. Proposal E was subsequently modified and signed into law in 1997. Out of 11 casino proposals submitted, three were accepted: Atwater/Circus Circus Casino (later called MotorCity Casino), owned by Detroit Entertainment; Greektown Casino, owned by the Sault Ste. Marie Tribe of Chippewa Indians; and the MGM Grand, owned by MGM Grand Detroit Casino. The casinos were granted permission to open at temporary locations, with permanent facilities planned for a proposed waterfront casino district.

The first casino, MGM Grand, opened in July 1999 in a former Internal Revenue Service building. Later that year the MotorCity Casino started operations in a former bread factory. The Greektown Casino opened in November 2000 in the heart of the city. It was the first tribally owned casino to open off a reservation. Detroit became the largest city in the country to allow casino gambling.

The plan for a casino district was eventually abandoned because of rising real estate prices and local opposition, and the number of hotel rooms initially proposed was cut back after marketing studies showed that many casino customers were regional and did not need overnight lodging. The permanent casinos were also delayed by several lawsuits. However, work began on the permanent MGM Grand Detroit Casino and MotorCity Casino in the summer of 2006. The MGM Grand Detroit Casino opened in October 2007. The MotorCity Casino opened in stages throughout 2007, with a grand opening in June. The Greektown Casino filed for bankruptcy protection in May 2008. However, it opened an expanded casino in August 2008 and opened its hotel in February 2009.

The Michigan Gaming Control Board reports that the Detroit casinos grossed more than $1.4 billion in 2011, up very slightly from 2010. (See Figure 4.7.) Each casino paid 8.1% of adjusted gross receipts as a state wagering tax to be deposited in Michigan's School Aid Fund. Up until 2007 MGM Grand, MotorCity, and Greektown paid an additional 4%; 3.5% went to the state's general fund and 0.5% went to the Agriculture Equine Industry Development Fund. By 2008 MGM Grand and MotorCity were no longer required to pay the additional 4% because both had opened permanent casinos and hotels. According to the Michigan Gaming Control Board in *Annual Report to the Governor: Calendar Year 2011* (February 1, 2012, http://www.michigan.gov/documents/mgcb/annrep11_386483_7.pdf), the combined 8.1% state wagering taxes deposited in the School Aid Fund totaled $115.4 million in 2011.

FIGURE 4.6

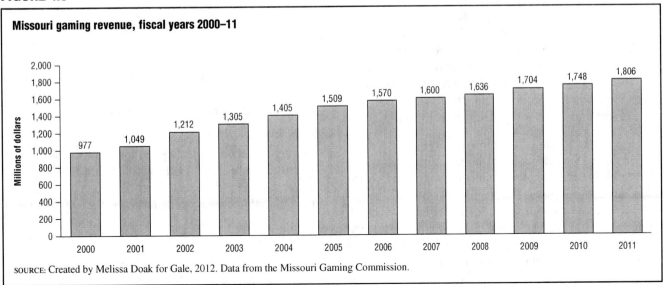

Missouri gaming revenue, fiscal years 2000–11

SOURCE: Created by Melissa Doak for Gale, 2012. Data from the Missouri Gaming Commission.

FIGURE 4.7

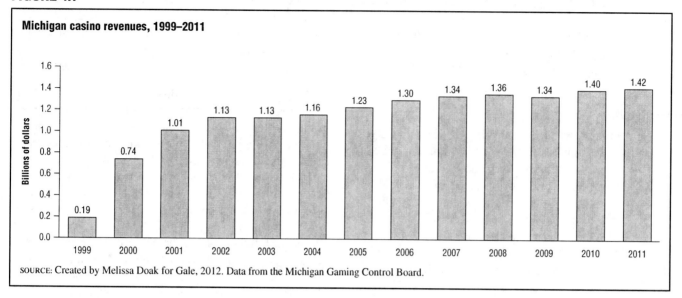

Michigan casino revenues, 1999–2011

SOURCE: Created by Melissa Doak for Gale, 2012. Data from the Michigan Gaming Control Board.

Unlike casinos in some other states, the Detroit casinos are not permitted under the Michigan Liquor Control Code to provide free alcoholic drinks. Games offered at the Detroit casinos include baccarat, blackjack, casino war, craps, keno, poker, roulette, slot machines, and video poker.

IOWA

Gambling was outlawed in the state of Iowa from the time of its statehood in 1846 until 1972, when a provision in the state constitution that prohibited lotteries was repealed. In 1973 the general assembly authorized bingo and raffles by specific parties. A decade later pari-mutuel wagering at dog and horse tracks was legalized, followed by a state lottery in 1985. In 1989 gambling aboard excursion boats was authorized for counties in which voters approved gambling referenda. Between 1989 and 1995 referenda authorizing riverboat gambling were approved in more than a dozen counties. The Iowa Racing and Gaming Commission granted licenses for riverboat gambling in 10 counties: Clarke, Clayton, Clinton, Des Moines, Dubuque, Lee, Polk, Pottawattamie, Scott, and Woodbury. By law, the residents of these counties vote every eight years on a county referendum that allows riverboat gambling to continue. In 1994 pari-mutuel racetracks gained approval to operate slot machines.

In 2011, 15 riverboat casinos and three racinos operated in Iowa. Games included bingo, blackjack, craps, keno, minibaccarat, poker, roulette, slots, and video poker. In *2011 Annual Report* (February 2012, http://www.iowa.gov/irgc/Annual%20Report%202011.pdf), the Iowa Racing and Gaming Commission indicates that in 2011 admissions to riverboat casinos totaled 16.3 million and to racinos totaled 5.9 million. The riverboats are required by law to meet space requirements for nongamblers and to provide shopping and tourism options. Slot machines are allowed at racinos only if a specific number of live races are held during each racing season.

In FY 2011 Iowa casino revenues totaled $1 billion and racino revenues totaled $457.9 million. (See Figure 4.8.) In other words, more than two-thirds (69%) of gambling revenues in Iowa were collected on riverboat casinos. The Iowa Racing and Gaming Commission notes that in 2011, $183.5 million in gaming taxes were collected by the state from the riverboat casinos, $9.4 million in taxes were collected by the cities and counties, and $7.5 million was deposited in an endowment fund. Iowa's gaming tax rate ranges from 5% to 24%, depending on revenue and the type of venue. In 2011 racinos paid $97.2 million in state taxes and $4.2 million in city and county taxes. They also made contributions to the gamblers' treatment and endowment funds and paid regulatory and daily licensing fees.

COLORADO

During the 1800s gambling halls and saloons with card games were prevalent throughout the mining towns of Colorado. However, gambling was outlawed in the state around the turn of the 20th century.

In November 1990 Colorado voters approved a constitutional amendment that permitted limited-stakes gaming in the towns of Black Hawk and Central City, near Denver, and Cripple Creek, near Colorado Springs. The first Colorado casinos opened in October 1991 and had gross revenues of nearly $8.4 million during their first month of operation.

According to the Colorado Division of Gaming in *2011 Annual Report* (2012, http://www.colorado.gov/cs/

FIGURE 4.8

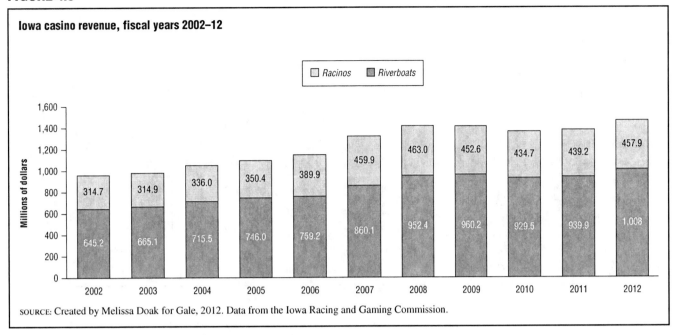

Iowa casino revenue, fiscal years 2002–12

SOURCE: Created by Melissa Doak for Gale, 2012. Data from the Iowa Racing and Gaming Commission.

Satellite?blobcol=urldata&blobheader=application%2F pdf&blobkey=id&blobtable=MungoBlobs&blobwhere= 1251778665479&ssbinary=true), before July 2009 only blackjack, poker, and slot machines were permitted in Colorado's casinos, and the maximum single bet was $5. However, in November 2008 Colorado voters approved Amendment 50, which gave voters in the locales where casinos were operating the option to add the games of craps and roulette and to raise the maximum single bet to $100. Voters in the three locales approved the changes, which went into effect on July 2, 2009.

The Colorado Division of Gaming notes that as of October 2011, 40 casinos operated in the state. They had gross revenues of $750.1 million in 2011. (See Figure 4.9.) Annual revenues grew steadily from 1997 to 2007, but then declined 12% between 2007 and 2008. Colorado gambling revenues subsequently increased to $734.6 million in 2009 and to $759.6 million in 2010, before falling slightly in 2011. In *Gaming in Colorado: Fact Book and 2011 Abstract* (2012, http://www.colorado.gov/cs/Satellite? blobcol=urldata&blobheader=application%2Fpdf&blob key=id&blobtable=MungoBlobs&blobwhere=125178 9371918&ssbinary=true), the Colorado Division of Gaming notes that the Black Hawk casinos have historically been the most successful in the state, accounting for between 70% and 74% of casino gambling revenue each year, followed by the Cripple Creek casinos (18% to 20% of the total) and the Central City casinos (7% to 10%). In 2011 the Black Hawk casinos took in $550.9 million, or just over 73.4% of the state's total casino revenues. The Cripple Creek casinos generated $131.4 million in revenues (roughly 17.5% of all casino earnings), while Central City casinos earned $67.8 million (9%).

From 2004 to 2009 Colorado's casinos had an adjusted gross revenue of $4.5 billion and paid $623.7 million in gaming taxes. The tax money was used to fund historical restoration projects and to offset the costs of casino gaming to state and local governments (including regulatory costs associated with the casino industry).

The gaming tax rate, which is set by the gaming commission annually, is based on each casino's adjusted gross proceeds (the amount of money wagered minus the amount paid out in prizes). In 2011 the tax ranged from approximately 0.24% for casinos with less than $2 million in adjusted gross proceeds to 19% for establishments with adjusted gross proceeds of more than $13 million.

In addition, the casinos pay annual device fees: $75 per slot machine and game table to the state and $750 to $1,265 to local jurisdictions. In *Gaming Update Newsletter* (January 2013, http://www.colorado.gov/cs/Satellite?blob col=urldata&blobheader=application%2Fpdf&blobkey= id&blobtable=MungoBlobs&blobwhere=12518432228 55&ssbinary=true), the Colorado Division of Gaming reports that in November 2012 there were 14,185 slot machines and 328 table games operating in the state.

SOUTH DAKOTA

Commercial casino gambling in South Dakota is restricted to the town of Deadwood in Lawrence County. A rustic mountain town about 60 miles (97 km) from Mount Rushmore, Deadwood was designated as a National Historic Landmark and is listed on both the National and South Dakota Registers of Historic Places. It had 35 casinos as of December 2011. The games allowed are blackjack, poker, and slot machines.

FIGURE 4.9

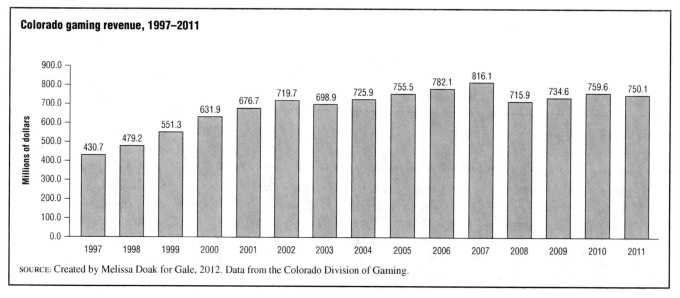

Colorado gaming revenue, 1997–2011

SOURCE: Created by Melissa Doak for Gale, 2012. Data from the Colorado Division of Gaming.

The rocky history of gambling in Deadwood is described by Katherine Jensen and Audie Blevins in *The Last Gamble: Betting on the Future in Four Rocky Mountain Mining Towns* (1998). The gold rush of 1876 brought large numbers of people into the town, and it soon became packed with saloons and gambling halls. The town became associated with notorious characters such as James Butler "Wild Bill" Hickok (1837–1876); Alice Ivers Tubbs (1851–1930), commonly called Poker Alice; and Martha Jane Cannary (1852–1903), better known as Calamity Jane.

Even though gambling was outlawed in the Dakota Territory in 1881, it continued quite openly in Deadwood with the apparent complicity of the local sheriff. According to Jensen and Blevins, gambling opponents complained in 1907 that the town's gambling halls "operated as openly as grocery stores, running twenty-four hours a day." However, on a busy Saturday night in 1947, the attorney general of South Dakota finally sent 16 raiders into the bars of Deadwood to show the town that the state meant business. The blatant days of gambling were over in Deadwood, although Jensen and Blevins note that the establishments continued to operate quietly for the next four decades.

In 1984 a group of Deadwood businessmen and community leaders began working to bring legalized gambling back to Deadwood, primarily to raise money to preserve the town's historic buildings. The group developed the slogan "Deadwood You Bet" and had it printed on hundreds of buttons. Despite widespread local support, the idea failed at the ballot box in 1984 and was voted down by the legislature in 1988. The measure made it onto the ballot in November 1988 following a massive petition effort. In 1989 South Dakota voters approved limited-stakes casino gambling for Deadwood. Originally, the

casinos could only offer a $5 maximum bet. This limit was raised to $100 in 2000.

In *Annual Report, Fiscal Year 2011* (2011, http://gaming.sd.gov/docs%20with%20links%20to%20website/FY11AnnualReport.pdf), the South Dakota Commission on Gaming indicates that Deadwood's casinos had a total combined gross revenue of $100.9 million in FY 2011, down from $106.2 million in FY 2010. (See Figure 4.10.) The casinos pay an 8% gaming tax on their adjusted gross revenue and an annual fee of $2,000 per card game or slot machine. According to the AGA in *2012 State of the States*, $16.4 million in gambling revenue taxes were collected in South Dakota in 2011.

PENNSYLVANIA

The Pennsylvania Race Horse Development and Gaming Act, also known as Act 71, was passed in 2004. The law made slot machines legal in the state as a way to raise revenues. The hope was that these revenues would provide Pennsylvania residents with property tax relief as well as fund economic development and attract tourists. The act also created the Pennsylvania Gaming Control Board, which would grant up to 14 gaming facility licenses, regulate and oversee casino gambling in the state, and provide a program for compulsive gamblers.

Act 71 indicated that slot machine licenses would be issued to seven racetracks, five nontrack stand-alone facilities, and two resort hotels. The maximum number of allowable slot machines in the state was set at 61,000. In 2006 the board issued casino licenses to six horse racing facilities: two were located near Philadelphia, one near Scranton, one near Harrisburg, one near Erie, and one near Pittsburgh. Permanent stand-alone casino licenses were issued to Foxwoods Casino in Philadelphia,

FIGURE 4.10

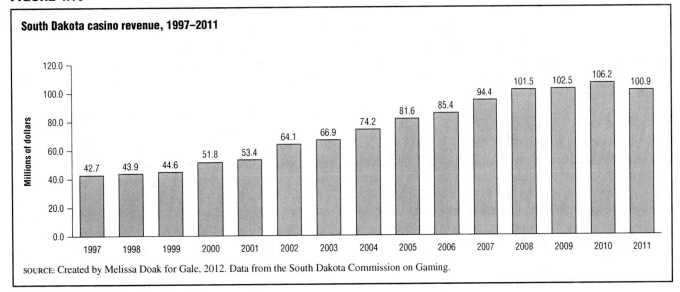

South Dakota casino revenue, 1997–2011

SOURCE: Created by Melissa Doak for Gale, 2012. Data from the South Dakota Commission on Gaming.

Mount Airy Casino Resort in Stroudsburg, Rivers Casino in Pittsburgh, Sands Casino Resort in Bethlehem, and SugarHouse Casino in Philadelphia.

The state's first licensed gaming facility opened in Wilkes-Barre in November 2006. The following month another facility opened its doors near Philadelphia. Several more casinos opened their doors in the following three years. In 2009 the Valley Forge Convention Center was granted a license to operate 500 slot machines as a resort hotel; a year later, the Sugarhouse Casino opened in Philadelphia. Act 71 was amended in 2010 to allow for table games. As the Pennsylvania Gaming Control Board reports in *2009–1010 Annual Report* (September 2010, http://www.pgcb.state.pa.us/files/communications/2009-2010_PGCB_Annual_Report.pdf), in FY 2010 the board issued 4,464 licenses, permits, and registrations for table games to facilitate the expansion at each casino in the state.

The additional revenues generated by the Sugarhouse Casino helped make Philadelphia the seventh-largest gambling market in the United States, while also raising the state's overall gambling earnings from less than $2.5 billion in 2010 to more than $3 billion in 2011, an increase of 21%, as reported by the AGA in *2012 State of the States*. In its *Annual Report 2011–2012* (September 2012, http://gamingcontrolboard.pa.gov/files/communications/2011-2012_PGCB_Annual_Report.pdf), the Pennsylvania Gaming Control Board states that in FY 2011–12 Pennsylvania casinos and racinos took in nearly $31.2 billion in wagers and $3 billion in gross revenue after payouts. The casino industry in Pennsylvania employed 16,406 people, and paid the state more than $1.5 billion in taxes. As of June 2012, 26,785 slot machines and 1,035 table games were operating at 11 locations around the state.

KANSAS

Stephanie Simon notes in "(State) House Rules in Kansas Casino" (*Wall Street Journal*, February 4, 2010) that Dodge City, Kansas, was known during the 1880s as "the wickedest little city in America." Among its attractions were casinos, saloons, and brothels. However, gambling was outlawed by 1900. More than a century later, in March 2007, it was reinstated when the Kansas legislature passed a bill allowing the Lottery Commission to establish up to four state-owned casinos as a way to raise revenue and provide jobs for thousands of workers. The law requires the state to own all the gambling equipment, although the buildings are owned by private companies.

The first casino to open was Boot Hill Casino and Resort in Dodge City. It opened in December 2009 with 584 slot machines and 10 table games. According to Simon, the Dodge City casino was expected to bring in $40 million each year, 27% of which would be collected by the state. Simon reports that despite opposition, business was brisk; in fact, lines formed to play slot machines and at times the manager had to close the doors to avoid exceeding allowed occupancy. The article "In First 8 Months, Returns Good for Kansas Casino" (ABC News, August 30, 2010) indicates that by August 2010 the casino was exceeding its revenue projections, having brought in $24.2 million since its opening and drawing tourists from throughout the Midwest. A second state-owned casino opened in Mulvane in December 2011. In *2012 State of the States*, the AGA reports that casino revenues in Kansas reached $48.5 million in 2011, a 28% increase over the $37.8 million generated in 2010.

MARYLAND

Maryland legalized casino gambling in 2008. As the Maryland State Lottery Agency reports in *Comprehensive*

Annual Financial Report for the Years Ended June 30, 2011 and 2010 (December 22, 2011, http://msa.maryland .gov/megafile/msa/speccol/sc5300/sc5339/000113/014 000/014711/unrestricted/20120547e.pdf), the state's first casino, the Hollywood Casino in Perryville, opened in September 2010; a second establishment, the Casino at Ocean Downs in Berlin, opened in January 2011. The casinos offer slot machines only, while providing customers with access to video-based lottery terminals. In *2012 State of the States*, the AGA reports that casino gambling revenue in Maryland topped $155.7 million in 2011, the first full year of operations at both casinos, while tax revenues exceeded $89.5 million. The AGA states that casino gambling provided an enormous boost to Maryland's overall gambling revenues, which rose more than 464% between 2010 and 2011.

WEST VIRGINIA

In 2007 the West Virginia Legislature passed the Racetrack Table Games Act, which opened the door for legalized casino table games at the state's horse and dog racing tracks. As the West Virginia Lottery reports in *Comprehensive Annual Financial Report for the Fiscal Year Ending June 30, 2012* (2012, http://www.wvlottery .com/pdf/WVL2012AR.pdf), two racing facilities, the Mountaineer Casino Racetrack & Resort and the Wheeling Island Hotel, Casino & Racetrack, began offering poker games to their customers in October 2007, and other table games in December of that year. In 2008 West Virginia voters approved a referendum allowing table games at the Greenbriar Resort in White Sulphur Springs, making the hotel the state's first casino not to be affiliated with a racing facility. That same year, the Mardi Gras Casino, a dog racing facility, began offering casino table games. In 2010 the state's fourth racing facility, Charles Town Races, launched a table game operation at its Hollywood Casino. According to the AGA in *2012 State of the States*, in 2011 these five casinos generated a combined $958.7 million in gross revenues.

CHAPTER 5

NATIVE AMERICAN TRIBAL CASINOS

Casinos operated by Native American tribes made $27.2 billion in 2011. (See Figure 5.1.) The American Gaming Association (AGA) reports in *2012 State of the States: The AGA Survey of Casino Entertainment* (2012, http://www.americangaming.org/files/aga/uploads/docs/sos/aga_sos_2012_web.pdf) that commercial casinos made $35.6 billion that same year. Therefore, in 2011 tribal casinos took in 43% of the total $62.8 billion in U.S. casino revenues.

According to the U.S. Census Bureau (March 2011, http://www.census.gov/newsroom/releases/archives/facts_for_features_special_editions/cb11-ff22.html), 5.2 million people in the United States (approximately 1.7% of the total U.S. population) identified themselves as Native American or Alaskan Native in the 2010 Census. The U.S. Bureau of Indian Affairs (BIA; http://www.bia.gov/), an agency of the U.S. Department of the Interior, indicates that there were 566 federally recognized tribes in the United States in 2013. The National Indian Gaming Association (NIGA), a trade organization for Native American casinos, reports in its *2010 Annual Report* (2011, http://www.indiangaming.org/info/2011_Annual_Report.PDF) that 237 tribes ran gaming facilities in 2010. As the AGA reports in *2012 State of the States*, there were a total of 459 tribal casinos in 29 states as of December 31, 2011.

HISTORY

The growth of tribal casinos can be traced to the late 1970s, when Native American tribes began operating bingo halls to raise funds for tribal purposes. Tribes in Florida and Wisconsin tried opening high-stakes bingo games on their reservations. Bingo games were legal in those states but subject to restrictions on the size of the jackpot and how often games could be held. The Seminole Tribe of Florida and the Oneida Tribe of Wisconsin took their respective states to court, arguing that they were sovereign nations and as such were not subject to state limitations on gambling.

In 1981 the U.S. Fifth Circuit Court of Appeals ruled in *Seminole Tribe of Florida v. Butterworth* (658 F.2d 310) that the Seminole Tribe could operate a high-stakes bingo parlor because the state of Florida did not have regulatory power over the tribe, which was a sovereign governing entity. A similar ruling was issued in *Oneida Tribe of Indians v. State of Wisconsin* (518 F.Supp. 712 [1981]). Both cases concluded that the states' gambling laws were regulatory, or civil, in nature rather than criminal because the states already allowed bingo games to take place.

Other tribes also initiated lawsuits, and the issue eventually reached the U.S. Supreme Court. In *California v. Cabazon Band of Mission Indians* (480 U.S. 202 [1987]), the court ruled that California could not prohibit a tribe from conducting activities (in this case, high-stakes bingo and poker games) that were legal elsewhere in the state. In 1989 the Bay Mills Indian Community opened the King's Club in Brimley, Michigan, the first Native American gambling hall to offer slot machines and blackjack.

GAMBLING CLASSES

In 1988 Congress passed the Indian Gaming Regulatory Act in response to the court decisions. The act allows federally recognized tribes to open gambling establishments on their reservations if the state in which they are located already permits legalized gambling. It set up a regulatory system and three classes of gambling activities:

- Class I—social gaming for minimal prizes and traditional gaming (e.g., in tribal ceremonies or celebrations)

- Class II—bingo and bingolike games, lotto, pull tabs (paper tickets that have tabs concealing symbols or numbers), tip jars (lotterylike games played with

FIGURE 5.1

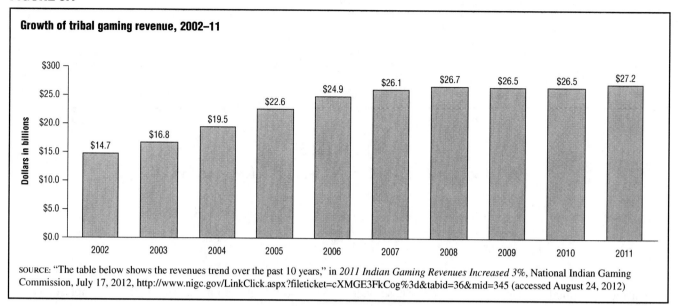

Growth of tribal gaming revenue, 2002–11

SOURCE: "The table below shows the revenues trend over the past 10 years," in *2011 Indian Gaming Revenues Increased 3%*, National Indian Gaming Commission, July 17, 2012, http://www.nigc.gov/LinkClick.aspx?fileticket=cXMGE3FkCog%3d&tabid=36&mid=345 (accessed August 24, 2012)

preprinted tickets), punch boards (thick cardboard with symbols or numbers concealed behind foil), and nonbanking card games (such as the type of poker that is played against other players instead of the house)

- Class III—banking card games (card games in which the player bets against the house), casino games, slot machines, pari-mutuel betting (in which those who bet on the top competitors share the total amount bet and the house gets a percentage) on horse and greyhound racing and on jai alai, electronic facsimiles of any game of chance, and any other forms of gaming not included in Class I or II

Class I games are regulated exclusively by the tribes and require no financial reporting to other authorities. Class II and III games are allowed only if such games are already permitted in the state where the tribe is located. According to the U.S. Government Accountability Office (GAO), the investigatory branch of Congress, court rulings have maintained that tribes can operate casinos where state-run lotteries exist and charitable casino nights are permitted.

Class II and III operations require that the tribe adopt a gaming ordinance that is approved by the National Indian Gaming Commission (NIGC), a government body that was established to regulate gaming on tribal lands. In addition, Class III gaming requires that the tribe and state have an agreement, called a tribal-state compact (or treaty), that is approved by the U.S. secretary of the interior. A compact is supposed to balance the interests of the state and the tribe in regard to standards for operation and maintenance, the applicability of state and tribal laws and regulations, and the amount needed by the state to defray its regulatory costs. Tribes may have

compacts with more than one state and may have different compacts for different types of gambling operations.

REGULATION

Native American casinos are regulated at three levels of government: federal, state, and tribal. Federal regulation is performed by the NIGC, which oversees the licensing of gaming employees and management and reviews tribal gaming ordinances. The NIGC also has enforcement powers, with penalties ranging from fines to the closure of operations. Most violations do not result in closure, but in notification followed by fines. For example, Jay Weaver reports in "Seminole Tribe Accused of Violating Federal Laws" (*Miami Herald*, June 8, 2010) that in June 2010 the NIGC charged the Seminole Tribe in Florida with violating gaming laws by spending hundreds of thousands of dollars in gambling profits on six members. The case was resolved in October 2010, with the Seminole Tribe admitting to the violations. In an Agreed To Civil Fine Assessment (October 27, 2010, http://www.nigc.gov/LinkClick. aspx?link=NIGC+Uploads%2freadingroom%2fenforcementactions%2fseminolefl%2fCFA-10-01.pdf&tabid=124&mid=774), the tribe agreed to pay a fine of $500,000 and to establish stricter auditing procedures.

Most violations concern tribes' failure to submit annual audits or mandatory paperwork by the required deadlines. In July 2006 the Santa Rosa Rancheria Tachi-Yokut Tribe was found in violation for failing to conduct proper background checks on casino employees. The tribe had 90 days to check the backgrounds of the employees in question or face fines of up to $25,000 per day. The tribe took immediate action to begin completing the required documentation, and a settlement was reached (September 6, 2006, http://www.nigc.gov/Link Click.aspx?link=NIGC+Uploads%2freadingroom%2fen forcementactions%2fsantarosarancheria%2fsa0615.pdf& tabid=124&mid=774) wherein the tribe was fined $40,000, with half of the fine suspended if documentation was completed by October 30, 2006.

The federal government also has criminal jurisdiction over cases involving embezzlement, cheating, and fraud at tribal gaming operations because these crimes are federal offenses.

State regulation is spelled out in the tribal-state compacts. They cover matters such as the number of slot machines that may be operated; limits on the types and quantities of card games that can be offered; minimum gambling ages in the casinos; authorization for casino workers to unionize; public health and safety issues; compulsive gambling issues; the effects of tribal gaming on other state enterprises; and how much revenue should be paid to the state and how often.

The tribes themselves are the primary regulators of tribal gaming. The NIGA reports in *Economic Impact of Indian Gaming* (March 2010, http://www.indiangaming .org/info/NIGA_2009_Economic_Impact_Report.pdf) that $260 million was spent by the tribes on the regulation of their industry in 2009.

FEDERAL RECOGNITION

Native American casinos must be a tribal endeavor, not an individual endeavor—that is, a random group of Native Americans cannot start a tribal casino. Only a tribe's status as a sovereign entity, which is granted by the federal government, allows it to conduct gaming.

The list of federally recognized tribes is maintained by the BIA. As of January 2013, the most current list was published in "Indian Entities Recognized and Eligible to Receive Services from the United States Bureau of Indian Affairs" (*Federal Register*, vol. 77, no. 155, August 10, 2012).

Throughout U.S. history tribes have received federal recognition through treaties with the U.S. government, via congressional actions, or through BIA decisions. Most tribes were officially recognized during the 18th and 19th centuries. In the 21st century recognition can be achieved either through an act of Congress or through a series of actions, known as the "federal acknowledgment process," that can take many years. Under the Code of Federal Regulations, Title 25, Part 83 (January 2013, http://www.bia.gov/idc/groups/public/documents/text/idc-001219.pdf), a group of Native Americans must meet seven criteria to be federally recognized as a tribe:

- The group must have been identified as a Native American entity on a substantially continuous basis since 1900.

- A predominant portion of the group must make up a distinct community and have existed as a community from historical times to the present.

- The group must have maintained political influence or authority over its members as an autonomous entity from historical times until the present.

- The group must submit a copy of its current governing documents, including membership criteria.

- The group's membership must consist of individuals who descended from a historical Native American tribe or from historical Native American tribes that combined and functioned as a single autonomous political entity.

- The membership of the group must be composed primarily of people who are not members of an existing acknowledged Native American tribe.

- The tribe must not be the subject of congressional legislation that has terminated or forbidden a federal relationship.

Federal recognition is important to Native American tribes if they are to be eligible for billions of dollars in federal assistance. According to the BIA, in "What We Do" (January 2013, http://www.bia.gov/WhatWeDo/index .htm), in 2013 the federal government held about 55 million acres (22.3 million ha) of land in trust for federally recognized Native American tribes and their members. If a tribe does not have a land base, the federal government can take land in trust for the tribe once it receives recognition. That land is no longer subject to local jurisdiction, including property taxes and zoning ordinances.

Most tribes require that a person have a particular degree of Native American heritage (usually 25%) to be an enrolled member. Some tribes require proof of lineage. The BIA states that in 2012 federally recognized tribes had approximately 1.9 million members.

One of the most contentious issues related to tribal casinos is the authenticity of the tribes themselves. Critics charge that some Native American groups want federal recognition only as a means to enter the lucrative gambling business. The GAO examines this issue in *Indian Issues: Improvements Needed in Tribal Recognition Process* (November 2001, http://www.gao.gov/new.items/d0249 .pdf). There were 193 tribes with gambling facilities in 2001. According to the GAO, 170 (88%) of the tribes could trace their federal recognition to the time of the Indian Reorganization Act of 1934 or similar legislation from the 1930s. About 59% of those tribes were engaged in gambling operations in 2001. By contrast, 45% of the tribes recognized since 1960 were engaged in gambling operations.

The GAO indicates that the procedures established by the BIA in 1978 to ensure that the recognition of tribes be uniform and objective had become too long and inconsistent. Backlogs became constant because the number of petitions for recognition began to climb during the 1990s. However, the GAO explains in *Indian Issues: Timeliness of the Tribal Recognition Process Has Improved, but It Will Take Years to Clear the Existing Backlog of Petitions* (February 10, 2005, http://www .gao.gov/new.items/d05347t.pdf) that by 2005 the backlog of cases had been steadily reduced and could potentially be completed by 2008. Regardless, other sources, such as the article "Landless Tribe Waits Federal Recognition" (Associated Press, January 5, 2008), report waits of as long as 15 years. As of January 2013, the most recent tribe to receive recognition was the Shinnecock Indian Nation of Southampton, New York. As Danny Hakim reports in "U.S. Recognizes an Indian Tribe on Long Island, Clearing the Way for a Casino" (June 15, 2010, http://www .nytimes.com/2010/06/16/nyregion/16shinnecock.html?hp& _r=0), the Obama administration approved the tribe's petition in June 2010, ending a 32-year legal battle.

REVENUES

Because tribes are sovereign governments, they are not required by law to make public statements of their revenues, so financial information on individual tribal casinos is not publicly released. Each year the NIGC announces total gaming revenue from the previous year for all tribal gaming facilities combined. It also breaks down the revenue by U.S. region and revenue class. The NIGC indicates in "2011 Indian Gaming Revenues Increased 3%" (July 17, 2012, http://www.nigc.gov/Link Click.aspx?fileticket=cXMGE3FkCog%3d&tabid=36& mid=345) that in FY 2011 tribal casinos made $27.2 billion, up 3% from $26.5 billion in FY 2010. This revenue is broken down by region in Figure 5.2.

Tribal casinos in the Sacramento Region (or Region II, comprising California and northern Nevada) were the most profitable in FY 2011, earning $6.9 billion. (See Figure 5.2.) Because tribal casinos do not exist in northern Nevada, all of this revenue was actually from California tribal casinos. Tribes with gaming facilities in Region II accounted for approximately one-quarter (25.4%) of all tribal casino revenue nationwide.

The second-most profitable region for tribes with gaming operations in FY 2011 was Washington, D.C., or Region VI, which encompasses the states of Alabama, Connecticut, Florida, Louisiana, Mississippi, New York, and North Carolina. The region took in $6.7 billion in casino revenues, or 24.6% of all tribal casino revenue nationwide. (See Figure 5.2.) Casinos operating in Connecticut, especially Foxwoods Casino and Resort, are thought to be the largest source of the region's revenue.

Several tribal gaming regions experienced financial growth between 2010 and 2011. (See Figure 5.3.) The region with the largest percentage increase in revenues during that span was Oklahoma City (also known as the western part of Region V, an area comprising western Oklahoma and Texas), where earnings rose 8% in 2011. The region with the second highest increase that year was Tulsa (the eastern part of Region V, consisting of eastern Oklahoma and Kansas), where revenues increased 7%.

The GAO reports in *Indian Issues: Improvements Needed in Tribal Recognition Process* that in 1988, the year the Indian Gaming Regulatory Act was passed, tribal casino revenues totaled $171 million. That amount grew to $9.8 billion in 1999. Revenues reported by the NIGC from 2002 to 2011 are shown in Figure 5.1. Over this period, tribal casino revenues grew from $14.7 billion to $27.2 billion, an increase of more than 85%. By contrast, the AGA indicates in *2012 State of the States* that consumer spending at commercial casinos grew from $28.1 billion in 2002 to $35.7 billion in 2011, an increase of just 27%. According to the article "Success amidst the Storm" (*Indian Country Today*, September 5, 2010), economic strategies that were put in place at tribal casinos before the recession began, such as installing top-notch golf courses and other amenities, helped maintain steady growth in the midst of the general economic downturn.

Tribal gaming revenues reported by the NIGC for 2011 are broken down by revenue class in Table 5.1. Approximately 56% of tribal gambling operations reported revenues of less than $25 million each and took in just under 8% of all gaming revenues. In contrast, 5.5% of tribal gambling operations earned $250 million or more and took in a little more than 38% of all gaming revenues, and 13% of all operations earned between $100 million and $250 million and took in about one-third (33.4%) of all gaming revenues.

The Indian Gaming Regulatory Act requires that net revenues from tribal gaming be used to fund tribal government operations or programs, to provide for the general welfare of the tribe and its members, to promote tribal economic development, and to help fund operations of local government agencies. In fact, revenues from tribal gaming often make significant contributions to social services on reservations. For example, In "Native Americans Can't Always Cash in on Casinos" (*Guardian* [London], August 9, 2010), Barbara Wells indicates that the Muckleshoot Tribe casino profits have provided seed money for unrelated businesses and funded a medical facility that offers medical and dental care for all tribe members. The profits have also helped the tribe build homes for its elders and provide funds for 200 Washington state charities through the Muckleshoot Charity Fund.

The NIGA reports in *Economic Impact of Indian Gaming* how tribes spent the net revenues of tribal casinos in 2009: 20% was used for education, child/elderly care, and charitable contributions; 19% was used for economic development; 17% was used for health care; 17% was used

FIGURE 5.2

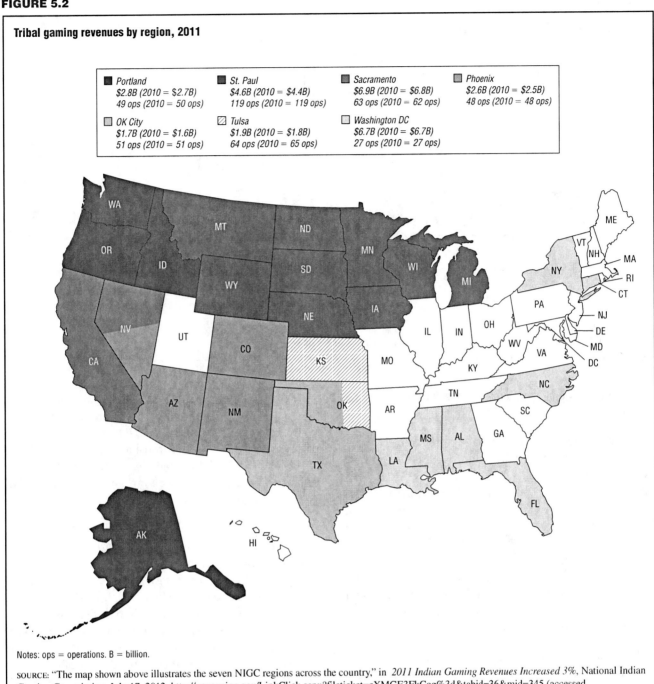

Tribal gaming revenues by region, 2011

- ■ Portland
  $2.8B (2010 = $2.7B)
  49 ops (2010 = 50 ops)
- ■ St. Paul
  $4.6B (2010 = $4.4B)
  119 ops (2010 = 119 ops)
- ■ Sacramento
  $6.9B (2010 = $6.8B)
  63 ops (2010 = 62 ops)
- ■ Phoenix
  $2.6B (2010 = $2.5B)
  48 ops (2010 = 48 ops)
- □ OK City
  $1.7B (2010 = $1.6B)
  51 ops (2010 = 51 ops)
- ▨ Tulsa
  $1.9B (2010 = $1.8B)
  64 ops (2010 = 65 ops)
- □ Washington DC
  $6.7B (2010 = $6.7B)
  27 ops (2010 = 27 ops)

Notes: ops = operations. B = billion.

SOURCE: "The map shown above illustrates the seven NIGC regions across the country," in *2011 Indian Gaming Revenues Increased 3%*, National Indian Gaming Commission, July 17, 2012, http://www.nigc.gov/LinkClick.aspx?fileticket=cXMGE3FkCog%3d&tabid=36&mid=345 (accessed August 24, 2012)

for police and fire protection; 16% was used for infrastructure; and 11% was used for housing. (See Figure 5.4.) Tribes with gaming operations may distribute gaming revenues to individual tribe members through per capita payments but are not required to do so. Such payments must be approved by the U.S. secretary of the interior as part of the tribe's Revenue Allocation Plan and are subject to federal income tax.

TRIBAL-COMMERCIAL CASINO VENTURES

Building casinos can be expensive. Tribes that have built them have had to borrow large sums of money and/or obtain investors to do so. In general, the Indian Gaming Regulatory Act requires that tribes partner with companies for no more than five years at a time and limits the companies' take to 30% of the total revenue. Under some circumstances, the partnership can last seven years and the companies' portion can be as much as 40% of the total revenue. These five- to seven-year contracts can also be renewed if both parties and the state government agree to the renewal. The NIGC notes in "Approved Management Contracts" (http://www.nigc.gov/Reading_Room/Management_Contracts/Approved_Management_Contracts.aspx) that as of January 2013, 54 tribes

FIGURE 5.3

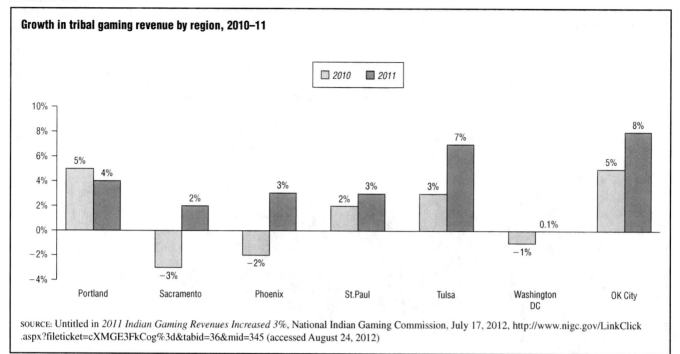

Growth in tribal gaming revenue by region, 2010–11

SOURCE: Untitled in *2011 Indian Gaming Revenues Increased 3%*, National Indian Gaming Commission, July 17, 2012, http://www.nigc.gov/LinkClick .aspx?fileticket=cXMGE3FkCog%3d&tabid=36&mid=345 (accessed August 24, 2012)

had 64 management contracts in place with commercial companies.

Native American casinos have often faced fierce opposition from commercial casino operators hoping to thwart competition. For example, tribal casinos in California could cut deeply into the Nevada casino business because California residents, who have long provided a large share of Nevada's gambling revenue, could gamble closer to home. However, some commercial casino operators have seen increased opportunities for revenue through partnerships with Native American tribes, and some tribes—especially small tribes—have welcomed the investment capital and management experience offered by commercial partners.

For example, Thunder Valley Casino is a Native American gaming venture located about 30 miles (48 km) northeast of Sacramento, California. The casino, which opened in June 2003, is owned by the United Auburn Indian Community, which has about 300 members. The casino was financially backed and managed by Station Casinos of Las Vegas. The tribe selected the company because it was willing to provide $200 million to build the casino and agreed to manage the casino for the tribe; in return, Station Casinos receives 24% of Thunder Valley Casino's net revenues. Before the casino opened, tribe members lived in poverty on a 3-acre (1.2-ha) reservation. However, with the casino came full health, dental, and vision insurance for each tribe member. Gaming revenues also funded the United Auburn Indian Community Tribal School, which has a teacher-student ratio of 1 to 7. In June 2010 the tribe opened a new expansion to the casino: a 297-room hotel

that had a spa and 14 restaurants and bars. As Dale Kasler reports in "Red Hawk Casino's Fortunes Have Disappointed So Far" (December 11, 2011, http://www.modbee .com/2011/12/11/1982905/red-hawk-casinos-fortunes-have.html), by 2011 each member of the United Auburn Indian Community was receiving an estimated $30,000 per month in profits generated by the casino.

Casino ventures between companies and small tribes are particularly controversial. According to Timothy Egan in "Lawsuit in California Asks, Whose Tribe Is It, Anyway?" (*New York Times*, April 10, 2002), critics suggest that small tribes are being manipulated by outside investors who only want to cash in on tribal casinos. The California Nations Indian Gaming Association (CNIGA) insists that small tribes should not be denied the tremendous economic opportunities offered by casinos. Egan notes that Susan Jensen, a spokesperson for the CNIGA, said, "The reason some of these tribes have only one or two people left is because Indians were exterminated."

Tribal Casinos off the Reservation

Another aspect of tribal gaming is the construction of tribal casinos on land outside reservations. Brad Knickerbocker reports in "Tribal Casinos Push beyond the Reservations" (*Christian Science Monitor*, October 14, 2005) that by 2005 three dozen tribes had applied to the BIA to build casinos outside their reservations. Many of these tribes had casinos on their reservations and were looking to expand into different markets, many closer to major cities. To build a new casino on nonreservation land, tribes must convince the BIA that they have claim to a parcel of

TABLE 5.1

Tribal gaming revenues by size of gaming operations, 2007–11

Gaming revenue range	Number of operations	Revenues (in thousands)	Percentage of operations	Percentage of revenues	Mean (in thousands)	Median (in thousands)
Gaming operations with fiscal years ending in 2011						
$250 million and over	23	$10,421,992	5.5%	38.4%	$453,130	$378,397
$100 million to $250 million	55	$9,065,678	13.1%	33.4%	$164,831	$156,252
$50 million to $100 million	52	$3,639,595	12.4%	13.4%	$69,992	$66,151
$25 million to $50 million	55	$1,902,860	13.1%	7.0%	$34,597	$32,784
$10 million to $25 million	98	$1,629,551	23.3%	6.0%	$16,628	$15,753
$3 million to $10 million	70	$413,441	16.6%	1.5%	$5,906	$5,525
Under $3 million	68	$80,691	16.2%	0.3%	$1,187	$1,010
Total	**421**	**$27,153,807**				
Gaming operations with fiscal years ending in 2010						
$250 million and over	21	$10,009,379	5.0%	37.8%	$476,637	$377,728
$100 million to $250 million	53	$8,685,402	12.6%	32.8%	$163,876	$156,824
$50 million to $100 million	53	$3,756,504	12.6%	14.2%	$70,877	$65,898
$25 million to $50 million	61	$2,091,904	14.5%	7.9%	$34,294	$32,550
$10 million to $25 million	88	$1,435,762	20.9%	5.4%	$16,315	$15,641
$3 million to $10 million	72	$444,384	17.1%	1.7%	$6,172	$6,102
Under $3 million	74	$79,198	17.5%	0.3%	$1,070	$839
Total	**422**	**$26,502,533**				
Gaming operations with fiscal years ending in 2009						
$250 million and over	21	$10,256,700	5.0%	38.7%	$488,414	$387,003
$100 million to $250 million	50	$8,167,831	11.9%	30.8%	$163,357	$158,652
$50 million to $100 million	52	$3,707,540	12.4%	14.0%	$71,299	$70,729
$25 million to $50 million	67	$2,384,381	16.0%	9.0%	$35,588	$33,474
$10 million to $25 million	90	$1,473,178	21.5%	5.6%	$16,369	$15,900
$3 million to $10 million	68	$415,275	16.2%	1.6%	$6,107	$6,174
Under $3 million	71	$77,542	16.9%	0.3%	$1,092	$779
Total	**419**	**$26,482,447**				
Gaming operations with fiscal years ending in 2008						
$250 million and over	23	$11,197,566	5.7%	41.9%	$486,851	$415,966
$100 million to $250 million	47	$7,764,163	11.6%	29.0%	$165,195	$164,918
$50 million to $100 million	52	$3,605,181	12.8%	13.5%	$69,330	$67,054
$25 million to $50 million	66	$2,286,574	16.3%	8.6%	$34,645	$32,179
$10 million to $25 million	85	$1,409,292	21.0%	5.3%	$16,580	$16,214
$3 million to $10 million	69	$408,109	17.0%	1.5%	$5,915	$5,867
Under $3 million	63	$67,941	15.6%	0.3%	$1,078	$908
Total	**405**	**$26,738,826**				
Gaming operations with fiscal years ending in 2007						
$250 million and over	22	$10,999,559	5.6%	42.1%	$499,980	$417,707
$100 million to $250 million	47	$7,807,413	12.0%	29.9%	$166,115	$158,777
$50 million to $100 million	46	$3,281,581	11.8%	12.6%	$71,339	$71,113
$25 million to $50 million	58	$2,070,824	14.8%	7.9%	$35,704	$33,423
$10 million to $25 million	90	$1,529,902	23.0%	5.9%	$16,999	$16,192
$3 million to $10 million	67	$396,957	17.1%	1.5%	$5,925	$5,699
Under $3 million	61	$57,236	15.6%	0.2%	$938	$755
Total	**391**	**$26,143,472**				

SOURCE: "NIGC Tribal Gaming Revenues," National Indian Gaming Commission, 2012, http://www.nigc.gov/Portals/0/NIGC%20Uploads/Tribal%20Data/GamingRevenues20072011.pdf (accessed August 24, 2012)

land where they would like to build the new casino. The BIA can then put the land into a trust for the tribe.

In 2008 the U.S. House of Representatives considered two bills, H.R. 2176: To Provide for and Approve the Settlement of Certain Land Claims of the Bay Mills Indian Community (http://judiciary.house.gov/hearings/printers/110th/41419.PDF) and H.R. 4115: To Provide for and Approve the Settlement of Certain Land Claims of the Sault Ste. Marie Tribe of Chippewa Indians (http://www.gpo.gov/fdsys/pkg/BILLS-110hr4115ih/pdf/BILLS-110hr4115ih.pdf), that would have authorized the construction of casinos in Michigan hundreds of miles from the reservation

lands of the Bay Mills Indian Community and the Sault Ste. Marie Tribe of Chippewa Indians. These would have been the first such off-reservation casinos. In June 2008 the House failed to pass the bills, effectively preventing the expansion of off-reservation gambling at that time.

In addition, in November 2008 the U.S. Supreme Court heard arguments for *Carcieri v. Kempthorne* (129 S. Ct. 338 [2009]), a case in which the state of Rhode Island challenged the authority of the federal government to take land into trust for the Narragansett Tribe. In February 2009 the court ruled in Rhode Island's favor, deciding that the federal government could no longer put

FIGURE 5.4

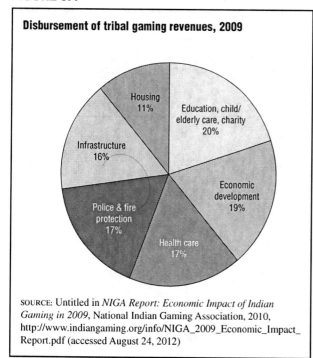

Disbursement of tribal gaming revenues, 2009

SOURCE: Untitled in *NIGA Report: Economic Impact of Indian Gaming in 2009*, National Indian Gaming Association, 2010, http://www.indiangaming.org/info/NIGA_2009_Economic_Impact_Report.pdf (accessed August 24, 2012)

land into trust for newly recognized tribes. Matt Viser explains in "Supreme Court Ruling May Torpedo Tribe's Casino Plans" (*Boston Globe*, February 24, 2009) that unless Congress takes action, tribes will no longer be able to use the federal recognition process as a way to put land into trust to build a casino.

Still, Native American groups continued to explore legal avenues for expanding casino holdings onto off-reservation land. In 2010 the Bay Mills Indian Community used funds from a tribal land trust to purchase a 40-acre plot in Vanderbilt, Michigan, a small town 100 miles south of the Bay Mills reservation. As Melissa Anders reports in "Michigan's Casino Landscape Could Expand as Tribes Seek 'Off-Reservation' Gaming Operations" (August 23, 2012, http://www.mlive.com/business/index.ssf/2012/08/michigan_casinos_tribal_off-re.html), the tribe opened a casino on its Vanderbilt property in November of that year, citing a state law stating that land acquired with tribal land trust funds was subject to the same regulations as those governing reservations. Although a federal judge ordered the casino closed in March 2011, the tribe won an appeal a year later, when the Sixth Circuit Court of Appeals reversed the ruling. As Anders further notes, during this time the Sault Ste. Marie Tribe of Chippewa Indians was in negotiations to build an off-reservation casino in the city of Lansing. By late 2012, Native American groups in Washington, California, and other states were pursuing similar off-reservation casino projects, taking advantage of a process through which the U.S. Department of Interior has the power to establish land trusts with newly-acquired Native American properties.

THE STORY OF NATIVE AMERICAN CASINOS IN TWO STATES

Connecticut

Tribal casinos are not required by law to make their financial records public. Even though exact figures are not known, various reports indicate that the tribal casinos operating in Connecticut are extremely profitable. As of January 2013, only two tribal casinos were operating in Connecticut. Foxwoods Casino and Resort is operated by the Mashantucket Pequot Tribe in Ledyard, and the Mohegan Sun is operated by the Mohegan Tribe in nearby Uncasville. Both are located in a rural area of eastern Connecticut.

In "About Foxwoods" (2013, http://www.foxwoods.com/aboutus.aspx), Foxwoods describes itself as being "one of the premier entertainment destinations in the Northeast." In 2013 it had six casinos and five hotels, several large conference rooms, a spa, a golf and country club, a shopping mall, dozens of restaurants, and a theater. Foxwoods had over 6,300 slot machines and 350 gaming tables, as well as one of the world's largest bingo halls.

The Mohegan Sun indicates in "About Mohegan Sun" (http://www.mohegansun.com/common/) that it had 1,200 hotel rooms, 40 restaurants and bars, and three casinos in 2013. The complex also included a 10,000-seat arena, a showroom, an extensive retail complex, meeting and function space, and its own gas station.

Foxwoods in particular has an interesting history. According to Kim Isaac Eisler, in *Revenge of the Pequots: How a Small Native American Tribe Created the World's Most Profitable Casino* (2002), during the 1980s the Connecticut legislature passed a law that allowed the wagering of "play money" on casino games such as blackjack, roulette, craps, and poker. The Mothers against Drunk Driving organization championed the law to encourage high schools to hold casino-type events following proms to reduce drunk driving by teenagers. Under this law, the Mashantucket Pequot Tribe was able to get a license for a "charity" gambling casino. It also procured $60 million from the resort developer Sol Kerzner (1935–) to begin construction.

Foxwoods opened in 1992. At that time, slot machines were not permitted. In 1994 the tribe negotiated a deal with Lowell P. Weicker (1931–; A Connecticut Party), the governor of Connecticut, that provided the tribe with exclusive rights to operate slot machines within the state. In return, the tribe agreed to make yearly payments to the state of $100 million or 25% of the revenue from the casino's slot machines, whichever was greater. By 1997 Foxwoods was considered the largest and most profitable casino in the United States.

In 1994 the Mohegan Tribe also signed a compact with Weicker to operate a casino. The Mashantucket

Pequot Tribe granted the Mohegan Tribe permission to include slot machines in its new casino. In return, the state set the annual payment required from each tribe at $80 million or 25% of their slot revenue, whichever was greater. The Mohegan Sun opened in 1996 after receiving financing from Kerzner.

The Mashantucket Pequots' standing as a tribe is not without controversy. In *Without Reservation: How a Controversial Indian Tribe Rose to Power and Built the World's Largest Casino* (2001), Jeff Benedict claims that the Mashantucket Pequots never should have been legally recognized as a tribe by the federal government because some members are not actually descendants of the historic Pequot tribe. The tribe achieved its recognition by an act of Congress. Benedict made his allegations a major part of his unsuccessful bid for Congress during the summer of 2002. He later helped found the Connecticut Alliance against Casino Expansion (CAACE), a nonprofit coalition that lobbied against additional casinos in Connecticut. The CAACE also sought federal legislation to reform the tribal recognition process.

Legalized gambling in Connecticut is regulated by the Division of Special Revenue, which conducts licensing, permitting, monitoring, and education. It also ensures that the correct revenues are transferred to the state's general fund and to each municipality that hosts a gaming facility or charitable game. The Division of Special Revenue indicates that Connecticut collected $3.4 billion from Foxwoods between 1993 and fiscal year 2013 and $2.8 billion from Mohegan Sun. (See Table 5.2.) These casino revenues represented more than 42% of all gaming payments to the state general fund from 1972 to 2012. (See Figure 5.5.)

However, the economic benefits of the casinos in Connecticut reach far beyond payments to the state general fund. In *Gambling in Connecticut: Analyzing the Economic and Social Impacts* (June 22, 2009, http://www.ct.gov/dosr/lib/dosr/june_24_2009_spectrum_final_final_report_to_the_state_of_connecticut.pdf), the Division of Special Revenue analyzes the economic impact of Foxwoods and Mohegan Sun and finds that in addition to direct tax revenue (slot machine revenue contributions, regulatory levies, personal income tax, and local property tax), the state also earned approximately $556.4 million in 2007 in indirect taxes, which include personal income taxes from employees in and sales tax from businesses that cater to the casino industry. (See Table 5.3.) In addition, Foxwoods and Mohegan Sun generated a combined 32,510 direct, indirect, and induced jobs in Connecticut in 2007. (See Table 5.4.) The total gross regional product contributed by the two casinos was estimated at $1.9 billion in 2007, and personal income generation for state residents was estimated at $1.2 billion.

California

In *Gaming Tribe Report* (January 4, 2013, http://www.nigc.gov/Portals/0/NIGC%20Uploads/readingroom/listandlocationoftribalgamingops/statea.pdf), the NIGC indicates that in 2013, 62 tribes in California had gaming operations, by far the most of any state. According to the NIGC, the state's tribal casinos earned nearly $7 billion in FY 2011, which was about 25% of the nationwide tribal total of $27.2 billion. Industry analysts predict that this percentage will continue to grow as the California market matures. The National Conference of State Legislatures notes in "Federal and State Recognized Tribes" (January 2013, http://www.ncsl.org/IssuesResearch/StateTribal/ListofFederalandStateRecognizedTribes/tabid/13278/Default.aspx) that the state had 115 federally recognized tribes in 2013, which was 20% of the national total. Most are described as small extended family groups living on a few acres of federal trust property called *rancherias*. Some tribes have only a handful of members.

Before 2000 the gambling operations of California tribes were largely limited to bingo halls because state law prohibited the operation of slot machines and other gambling devices, certain card games, banked games, and games where the house collects a share of the amount wagered. In 2000 California voters passed Proposition 1A, which amended the state constitution to permit Native American tribes to operate lottery games, slot machines, and banking and percentage card games on tribal lands. The constitutionality of the measure was immediately challenged in court.

In January 2002 Joseph Graham "Gray" Davis Jr. (1942–; Democrat), the governor of California, signed 62 gambling compacts with California tribes. The compacts allowed each tribe to have a maximum of 2,000 slot machines. The governor also announced plans to cap the number of slot machines in the state at 45,000. At the time, there were already 40,000 slot machines in operation and dozens of tribal casinos in the planning stages. The governor put a moratorium on new compacts while Proposition 1A made its way through the courts. In August 2002 a U.S. district court ruled that tribal casinos were entitled to operate under the provisions of the state gaming compacts and Proposition 1A.

In 2003 the state of California suffered a severe budget crisis. Davis was ultimately forced out of office through a special recall election in which Arnold Schwarzenegger (1947–; Republican) became the governor. In the press release "Schwarzenegger Far off the Mark on Tribal Governments" (September 23, 2003, http://www.cniga.com/media/pressrelease_detail.php?id=40), the CNIGA states that in televised campaign ads Schwarzenegger promised voters to make tribal casinos "pay their fair share," arguing that "their casinos make billions, yet pay no taxes and virtually nothing to the state." The

TABLE 5.2

Connecticut tribal gaming payments to state general fund, 1993–July 2012

Fiscal year end 6/30	Lottery	Parimutuel						Charitable games	Casino			Grand total
		Plainfield Greyhound	Bridgeport Shoreline Star	Hartford Jai Alai	Milford Jai Alai	Subtotal	Off-track betting		Foxwoods	Mohegan Sun	Subtotal	
1993	221,700,000	2,578,114	2,632,772	2,962,939	3,138,557	11,312,382	16,200,000	1,735,931	$30,000,000		$30,000,000	280,948,313
1994	217,250,000	682,389	446,604	519,205	713,048	2,361,246	5,788,175	1,805,800	113,000,000		113,000,000	340,205,221
1995	249,650,000	592,446	350,990	421,212	639,706	2,004,354	6,129,150	1,748,657	135,724,017		135,724,017	395,256,178
1996	262,050,000	490,421	210,335	141,034	858,996	1,700,786	6,610,554	1,723,649	148,702,765		148,702,765	420,787,754
1997	251,520,868	308,935	47,231	0	521,138	877,304	6,874,079	1,491,772	145,957,933	$57,643,836	203,601,769	464,365,792
1998	264,274,830	281,153	38,816	0	401,319	721,288	5,441,570	1,423,223	165,067,994	91,007,858	256,075,852	527,936,763
1999	271,308,022	255,094	37,090	0	341,630	633,814	5,472,648	1,258,380	173,581,104	113,450,294	287,031,398	565,704,262
2000	253,598,047	210,483	35,425	0	324,365	570,273	5,616,495	1,205,865	189,235,039	129,750,030	318,985,069	579,975,749
2001	252,002,987	167,740	40,930	0	294,562	503,232	5,674,281	1,162,360	190,683,773	141,734,541	332,418,314	591,761,174
2002	271,509,680	162,945	41,969	0	137,764	342,678	5,736,901	1,284,454	199,038,210	169,915,956	368,954,166	647,827,879
2003	256,814,859	134,743	43,222	0	0	177,965	5,783,231	1,230,391	196,300,528	190,953,944	387,254,472	651,260,918
2004	280,763,074	109,394	43,116	0	0	152,510	5,783,041	1,398,295	196,883,096	205,850,884	402,733,980	690,830,900
2005	268,515,000	64,837	39,462	0	0	104,299	5,275,182	1,431,054	204,953,050	212,884,444	417,837,494	693,163,029
2006	284,864,998	0	25,757	0	0	25,757	5,055,057	1,305,163	204,505,785	223,020,826	427,526,611	718,777,586
2007	279,000,000	0	0	0	0	0	4,808,425	1,297,756	201,380,257	229,095,455	430,475,712	715,581,893
2008	283,000,000	0	0	0	0	0	4,603,607	1,211,178	190,037,675	221,373,298	411,410,973	700,225,758
2009	283,000,000	0	0	0	0	0	4,195,243	1,063,435	177,153,485	200,651,400	377,804,885	666,063,563
2010	285,500,000	0	0	0	0	0	3,816,676	945,375	169,408,149	189,845,097	359,253,246	649,515,297
2011	289,300,161	0	0	0	0	0	3,699,415	876,064	174,092,415	185,488,712	359,581,127	653,456,767
2012	310,000,000	0	0	0	0	0	3,766,758	683,627	165,547,090	178,783,321	344,330,411	658,780,796
2013	20,922,500	0	0	0	0	0	302,039	61,287	12,800,086	15,030,324	27,830,410	49,116,236
	$7,599,406,946	$141,970,035	$77,420,591	$76,296,801	$75,884,044	$371,571,471	$364,132,527	$32,331,402	$3,384,052,451	$2,756,480,220	$6,140,532,671	$14,507,975,017

Notes:
Revenue transferred on cash basis per fiscal year.
The above transfers represent:
  a) actual lottery transfers through July 31, 2012 as reported by the Connecticut Lottery Corporation.
  b) collection of parimutuel taxes, net of payments to municipalities and other entities, for the former jai alai and greyhound facilities.
  c) collection of parimutuel taxes, net of payments to municipalities and other entities, for races conducted through July 31, 2012 for Off-Track Betting (OTB).
  d) estimated sealed ticket and bingo revenue through July 31, 2012.
  e) actual casino contributions through August 15, 2012, based on reported video facsimile/slot machine revenue through July 31, 2012.

From its inception in 1976 through June 30, 1993, the OTB system was state operated. For that period, transfers represented the fund balance in excess of division needs. The OTB systems was sold to a private operator effective July 1, 1993 and since then transfers are based on a statutory parimutuel tax rate.

SOURCE: Adapted from "Transfers to the General Fund," in *Gaming Revenue and Statistics*, State of Connecticut, Division of Special Revenue, August 17, 2012, http://www.ct.gov/dcp/lib/dcp/pdf/gaming/stmt2012.pdf (accessed August 24, 2012)

FIGURE 5.5

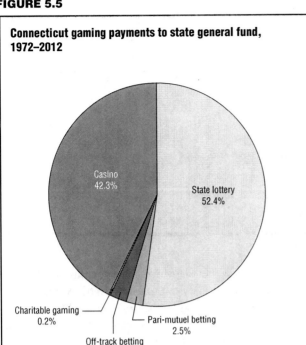

Connecticut gaming payments to state general fund, 1972–2012

- Casino 42.3%
- State lottery 52.4%
- Charitable gaming 0.2%
- Pari-mutuel betting 2.5%
- Off-track betting 2.5%

SOURCE: Adapted from "Transfers to the General Fund," in *Gaming Revenue and Statistics*, State of Connecticut, Division of Special Revenue, August 17, 2012, http://www.ct.gov/dcp/lib/dcp/pdf/gaming/stmt2012.pdf (accessed August 24, 2012)

TABLE 5.3

Operational impact for Foxwoods and Mohegan Sun, 2007

Tax/fee	Revenue to state	Revenue to local govt.	Total revenue to govt.
Direct			
Slot revenue contribution	$339,553,712	$90,922,000	$430,475,712
Regulatory levy	$9,964,629		$9,964,629
Personal income tax (direct)	$31,217,846		$31,217,846
Local property tax		$48,850,000	
Indirect and induced			
Personal income tax (indirect & induced)	$22,633,633		$22,633,633
Sales tax (indirect & induced)	$13,306,921		$13,306,921
Total direct	$380,736,187	$139,772,000	$520,508,187
Total indirect & induced	$35,940,554	$0	$35,940,554
Total direct, indirect, & induced	$416,676,742	$139,772,000	$556,448,742

SOURCE: "Figure 61. Operational Impact for Foxwoods and Mohegan Sun, 2007," in *Gambling in Connecticut: Analyzing the Economic and Social Impacts*, State of Connecticut, Division of Special Revenue, June 2009, http://www.ct.gov/dosr/lib/dosr/june_24_2009_spectrum_final_final_report_to_the_state_of_connecticut.pdf (accessed August 24, 2012). Data from Spectrum Gaming Group Research.

CNIGA was outraged, calling the remarks "hurtful" and accusing Schwarzenegger of having "a complete and almost frightening lack of understanding of the legal status of Indians and tribal governments." The CNIGA also reminded voters that the tribal casinos paid more than $100 million per year into a special fund that was designated to pay for the effects of tribal gaming on local communities.

In June 2004 Schwarzenegger signed new compacts that preserved the exclusive gaming rights of five California tribes: the Pala Band of Mission Indians, the Pauma Band of Mission Indians, the Rumsey Band of Wintun Indians, the United Auburn Indian Community, and the Viejas Band of Kumeyaay Indians. The slot machine cap was also raised above 2,000 machines per tribe. In exchange, the tribes agreed to pay the state $1 billion up front and a licensing fee for each new slot machine that was added above the current limit. Payments were expected to total between $150 million and $275 million per year through 2030, when the compacts are set to expire.

The state continued to form tribal compacts that permitted casino expansion in exchange for higher taxes. One of the more notable deals was made with the Agua Caliente Band of Cahuilla Indians. The tribe owned two casinos in Palm Springs. In August 2006 the state agreed to let the tribe open a third casino with 5,000 slot machines if the tribe paid an estimated $1.9 billion in taxes over the following 23 years. Many Californians were concerned that if such deal making were allowed to continue, casinos could be as prevalent as shopping malls and lead to higher instances of gambling addiction.

In 2007 four referenda petitions were proposed to overturn compacts that had recently been negotiated between four tribes—the Agua Caliente Band of Cahuilla Indians, the Morongo Band of Mission Indians, the Pechanga Band of Luiseño Indians, and the Sycuan Band of the Kumeyaay Nation—and the state. Even though the compacts had already been signed by Schwarzenegger and ratified by the legislature, a petition campaign that was supported by the California Federation of Teachers, the American Indian Rights and Resource Organization, the California Tax Report Association, and the United Farm Workers succeeded in getting approval of the new compacts on the ballot in February 2008. California voters were asked to approve or disapprove of the four new compacts with a "yes" or "no" vote on Propositions 94, 95, 96, and 97. Collectively, the compacts allowed the four tribes to operate an extra 17,000 slot machines with an additional payment of $9 million per year to the Revenue Sharing Trust Fund. Voters approved the four compacts. In October 2009 the CNIGA reported in the press release "California Tribes Draw Much Needed Gaming Device Licenses" (http://www.cniga.com/media/pressrelease_detail.php?id=98) that the Ninth Circuit Court of Appeals in California had cleared the way for the issuing of 3,547 new gaming device licenses to 11 other tribes in the state.

Onell R. Soto notes in "Rincon Tribe Wins Slot Suit against State" (*San Diego Union-Tribune*, March 27,

TABLE 5.4

Economic impact of Foxwoods and Mohegan Sun, 2007

	Foxwoods	Mohegan Sun	Total
Employment (direct, indirect and induced)	16,490	16,020	32,510
Private sector employment	14,015	13,714	27,729
State and local government employment*	2,475	2,306	4,781
Gross regional product	$974,351,000	$902,328,200	$1,876,679,200
Personal income (by place of residence)	$611,100,000	$585,600,000	$1,196,700,000

Note: 2007 figures have been adjusted to reflect 2008 dollars.

*Includes municipal government employees throughout the state along with all state employees. The Regional Economic Models, Inc. (REMI) model calculations are based on inputs of state and local government spending resulting from tax revenues generated at the casinos. The model does not differentiate between full- and part-time jobs. Only public-sector jobs are included in this category.

SOURCE: "Figure 60. Economic Impact of Operations Foxwoods and Mohegan Sun, 2007," in *Gambling in Connecticut: Analyzing the Economic and Social Impacts*, State of Connecticut, Division of Special Revenue, June 2009, http://www.ct.gov/dosr/lib/dosr/june_24_2009_spectrum_final_final_report_to_the_state_of_connecticut.pdf (accessed August 24, 2012). Data from Spectrum Gaming Group Research.

2010) that in March 2010 the Rincon Band of Luiseño Indians won their lawsuit against the state over the number of slot machines they could operate at their casino in North County. A federal judge ruled that the state should permit 56,000 slot machines under compacts signed with Governor Davis in 1999. However, because some tribes had renegotiated with California and received additional slot machines in exchange for a larger payment to the state, there were already approximately 65,000 machines in tribal casinos throughout California in March 2010. According to the 500 Nations website (http://500nations.com/California_Casinos.asp), as of January 2013 there were 63,835 slot machines at 68 tribal casinos throughout the state.

CHAPTER 6
THE ECONOMIC AND SOCIAL EFFECTS OF CASINOS

Assessing the effects of casinos on society is complicated because many factors have to be considered. Most relate to economics, but some address quality of life and moral issues. Proponents of casino gambling consider it part of the leisure and entertainment sector—like amusement parks or movie theaters. In a casino, participants exchange their money for a good time. Those who support casino gambling generally do not see it as a moral issue.

Furthermore, proponents of casinos consider them to be a vital part of the tourism industry. The American Gaming Association (AGA) indicates in *2012 State of the States: The AGA Survey of Casino Entertainment* (2012, http://www.americangaming.org/files/aga/uploads/docs/sos/aga_sos_2012_web.pdf) that in 2012, 60% of Americans viewed casino gambling as either somewhat important or very important to the tourist industry as a whole.

Opponents provide a variety of reasons for their disapproval of casino gambling. Some disapprove of gambling on religious grounds because they believe it contradicts moral principles of thrift, hard work, and sober living. Others are wary of an industry that was associated with mobsters, swindlers, and corrupt politicians throughout much of its history in the United States. Still others point out that casinos provide a place for those who are prone to problem gambling to act on those urges. Easy accessibility to casinos, they suggest, encourages some people to gamble who otherwise would not and should not. Outlawing casinos is one way to protect people from their own bad judgment.

NATIONAL PUBLIC OPINION

According to Paul Taylor, Cary Funk, and Peyton Craighill of the Pew Research Center, in *Gambling: As the Take Rises, So Does Public Concern* (May 23, 2006, http://www.pewsocialtrends.org/files/2010/10/Gambling.pdf),

42% of the people surveyed in 2006 said casinos are detrimental to their communities, whereas 34% said casinos have a positive impact. However, a smaller percentage of people who lived near a casino (38%) had a negative view of the casino's influence on their community than those who did not live near a casino (45%). The AGA reports in *2012 State of the States* that more than four out of five Americans (81%) viewed casino gambling as an acceptable activity for either themselves or others. Furthermore, the AGA survey finds that most Americans participate in activities other than gambling while visiting a casino. More than three-quarters (76%) of respondents dined at a fine restaurant while visiting a casino, and nearly two-thirds (62%) attended a concert or other performance. More than one-quarter (27%) of people who visited casinos stated that they never or rarely gambled, and fewer than half (47%) reported gambling either most of the time or always when visiting a casino.

Elected officials and civic leaders tend to have an even more positive view of casinos in their communities. In *2012 State of the States* the AGA asked 210 elected officials and civic leaders about the effects of casinos in their communities. Of those surveyed, 83% said the casinos have a positive impact. Approximately 76% praised casinos as helping other businesses, and 74% touted casinos as being responsible corporate citizens.

THE EFFECTS OF NATIVE AMERICAN CASINOS

Native American tribes that encounter opposition to their casino plans attribute opposition to the same issues that commercial casinos face, although some also see racism as a factor.

The Cons

Critics contend that tribal casinos:

- Unfairly compete against local hotels, restaurants, and pari-mutuel operators

- Hurt state lottery sales

- Place an increased burden on states to address problems resulting from pathological gambling

- Introduce opportunities for money laundering (the act of engaging in transactions that are designed to hide or obscure the origin of illegally obtained money) and organized crime

Some critics suggest that casinos encourage and perpetuate a cycle of dependence: tribe members who were formerly dependent on the federal government are now dependent on their tribal government. They believe that, ultimately, casinos will hurt the culture and political stability of the tribes.

Donald L. Barlett and James B. Steele argue in "Indian Casinos: Wheel of Misfortune" (*Time*, December 16, 2002), a high-profile criticism of Native American casinos, that government regulations provide little oversight, breed corruption, and have led to few real economic benefits for the majority of Native Americans. They also assert that "while most Indians continue to live in poverty, many non-Indian investors are extracting hundreds of millions of dollars—sometimes in violation of legal limits—from casinos they helped establish, either by taking advantage of regulatory loopholes or cutting backroom deals."

In *Gambling in the Golden State: 1998 Forward* (May 2006, http://www.library.ca.gov/crb/06/04/06-004 .pdf), Charlene W. Simmons of the California State Library catalogs all the known positive and negative effects that Native American casinos have on California communities. According to Simmons, Native American casinos have slightly higher incidences of bankruptcy and crime, particularly violent crimes such as aggravated assault. The casinos have also strained the local infrastructure. Most of the casinos bring many people into rural areas with narrow two-lane roads and limited sewage systems. Even though casinos help the economies of their immediate communities, they often siphon money away from adjacent communities because people spend their money at casinos rather than at stores and eating establishments in their own neighborhoods.

The Pros

The National Indian Gaming Association (NIGA) notes in *The Economic Impact of Indian Gaming* (March 2010, http://www.indiangaming.org/info/NIGA_2009 _Economic_Impact_Report.pdf) that in 2009 tribal gaming and associated businesses had:

- Generated revenues of $26.2 billion from Native American gaming

- Generated another $3.2 billion in gross revenue from related hospitality and entertainment services

- Provided jobs for 628,000 Americans

- Paid $8.4 billion in wages

- Paid $9.4 billion in federal taxes and revenue savings

- Paid $2.4 billion in state taxes, revenue sharing, and regulatory payments

- Paid $100 million in local taxes and government services agreements

- Funded essential tribal programs, such as schools, hospitals, water and sewer systems, roads, police and firefighting programs, and cultural and social projects

In *The American Indians on Reservations: A Databook of Socioeconomic Change between the 1990 and 2000 Censuses* (2005), Jonathan B. Taylor and Joseph P. Kalt find that income increased by 35% between 1990 and 2000 on non-Navajo gaming reservations, whereas income only grew by 14% on non-Navajo nongaming reservations. The Navajo did not have casinos until 2008, when the Navajo Nation approved its first casino, the Fire Rock Navajo Casino, in Church Rock, New Mexico.

Most tribal lands are located in areas of the country that have limited natural resources and industry, so tribal casinos often bring much needed wealth to the tribes and their neighbors. James I. Schaap points out in "The Growth of the Native American Gaming Industry: What Has the Past Provided, and What Does the Future Hold?" (*American Indian Quarterly*, vol. 34, no. 3, Summer 2010) that Native American gaming has been able to do "what no other antipoverty program has been able to accomplish in reversing the cycle of displacement and impoverishment of Native Americans: tribal gaming has been hailed as the 'new buffalo' for Indians and has been credited with wrestling once-destitute reservations from the grip of poverty, unemployment, and welfare dependency." He notes that revenues from tribal casinos have been invested in infrastructure, schools, social service programs, and medical facilities. Other tribal businesses that cater to the casinos have also become major employers. These socioeconomic changes have helped reduce domestic violence, crime, and suicide rates.

Nevertheless, Schaap indicates that casinos have not solved all the socioeconomic problems that beset the Native American community. The Native American median household income (half of all households earned more and half earned less) was just 73% of the U.S. median household income in 2005, and the poverty rate of Native Americans, at 25.3%, was twice that of the national poverty rate of 12.6%. Unemployment, violent crime, homicide, and infant mortality rates remain higher in native communities than in U.S. communities nationwide. The high school dropout rate remains 50% higher in native communities, and only 13.6% of Native

Americans have attained a bachelor's degree, compared with 27.2% of Americans nationwide.

ECONOMICS

The AGA indicates in *2012 State of the States* that in 2011 commercial casinos took in more than $35.6 billion. In *2011 Indian Gaming Revenues Increased 3%* (July 17, 2012, http://www.nigc.gov/LinkClick.aspx?fileticket= cXMGE3FkCog%3d&tabid=36&mid=345), the National Indian Gaming Commission (NIGC) notes that tribal casinos took in $27.2 billion that same year. Therefore, U.S. commercial and tribal casinos together took in $62.8 billion in 2011, making the casino industry an extremely big business in the United States. Most casinos have been huge successes for their investors, who range from middle-class stockholders in major corporations to billionaires such as Donald Trump (1946–) and Stephen A. Wynn (1942–). Most tribal casinos have been economically successful as well, bringing unimagined wealth to Native Americans, many of whom were at the very bottom of the U.S. economic ladder only a decade ago. Casinos are also labor-intensive businesses that employ hundreds of thousands of people, who support their families, pay taxes, and buy goods and services—factors that contribute to the economic health of their communities.

The economic effects of casinos on local and state governments are also significant. Commercial casinos pay billions of dollars every year to government agencies in the form of application fees, regulatory fees, wagering taxes, and admission taxes. Even though governments incur increased costs for more police, roads, and sewers, casino taxes and fees help fund programs that improve the quality of life in the immediate vicinity or state. Tribal casinos, though exempt from state and local taxation, pay billions of dollars each year to compensate states and municipalities for regulatory and public service expenses.

Direct Government Revenue from Casinos

In *2012 State of the States*, the AGA reports that commercial casinos generated tax revenues of $7.9 billion in 2011, a 4.5% increase over tax revenues from 2010. Pennsylvania generated the most gambling tax revenue in 2011 ($1.5 billion), followed by Nevada ($865.3 million), Indiana ($846.4 million), and New York ($593.4 million).

According to the AGA, the nation's top 10 racetrack casino (racino) markets generated $4.4 billion in revenues in 2011. Philadelphia led the way, earning $842.1 million; the racino business in Yonkers, New York, earned $577.1 million, and the racetrack casino in Charles Town, West Virginia, earned $541.2 million.

Direct Government Revenue from Native American Casinos

The Indian Gaming Regulatory Act of 1988 requires that net revenues from tribal gaming be used to fund tribal government operations and programs, to promote tribal economic development, to donate to charitable organizations, and to help fund operations of local government agencies.

The revenues earned by tribal casinos are not taxable because the casinos are operated by tribal governments: just as the U.S. government does not tax the states for revenue earned from lottery tickets, it does not tax tribal governments for revenue earned from casinos. Therefore, tribal casinos generate less tax revenue than commercial casinos. Tribe members who live on reservations and who are employed at tribal enterprises, such as casinos, are not subject to state income taxes. However, tribe members do pay federal income tax, Federal Insurance Contributions Act tax, and Social Security tax on their wages, even if those wages are earned at tribal enterprises. Wages paid to tribe members living off reservations and to nontribe employees are subject to state income taxes.

The NIGA reports in *Economic Impact of Indian Gaming* (March 2010, http://www.indiangaming.org/info/NIGA_2009_Economic_Impact_Report.pdf) that Class II and III Native American gaming paid $9 billion in federal taxes and $2.4 billion in state and local taxes in 2009. (See Figure 6.1.) Class II and III gaming includes bingo, card and table games, lotto, slot machines, and pari-mutuel gambling (gambling in which those who bet on the top competitors share the total amount bet and the house gets a percentage). These tax revenues also include employer and employee Social Security taxes, personal and corporate income taxes, and excise taxes. In addition, Native American gaming produced an estimated $3.1 billion in federal revenue savings through reduced welfare and unemployment payments.

EMPLOYMENT AND CAREERS

According to the AGA in *2012 State of the States*, 339,098 people were employed in commercial casinos in 2011. Tribal casinos employed more than 204,000 people in 2009. (See Figure 6.2.) Because gaming workers are employed in the entertainment and hospitality industry, they need excellent communication and customer-service skills, but the financial aspect of casino activities also requires personal integrity and the ability to maintain composure when dealing with angry or emotional patrons. A high school diploma or the equivalent is usually preferred for all entry-level jobs. Table 6.1 describes the duties, qualifications, training requirements, and earnings of several categories of casino workers.

All casino employees—from managers to dealers to slot repair technicians—must be at least 21 years old and have licenses from the appropriate regulatory agency. Obtaining a license requires a background investigation—applicants can be disqualified from casino employment for a variety of reasons, including links to organized crime, a felony record, and gambling-related offenses. Requirements for education, training, and experience are up to individual casinos. The Bureau of Labor Statistics (March 29, 2012, http://www.bls.gov/ooh/personal-care-and-service/gaming-services-occupations.htm) considers the overall employment outlook for the industry on par with the average of all occupations, with gaming services job opportunities projected to grow at a rate of 13% between 2010 and 2020.

The growth of the casino employment market has spurred a related increase in vocational and professional training for casino workers. The University of Nevada, Las Vegas, which is only 1.5 miles (2.4 km) from the Strip, offers a major in gaming management that includes instruction in gaming operations, marketing, hospitality, security, and regulations. At Tulane University's School of Continuing Studies in New Orleans, students can choose from several programs that last between one and four years, including a bachelor's degree in casino resort management. Students pursuing a degree in hospitality and tourism management at the University of Massachusetts can specialize in casino management. Central Michigan University, which is located near the Soaring Eagle Casino and Resort operated by the Saginaw Chippewa Tribe, offers a business degree in gaming and entertainment management that includes coursework in the protection of casino table games, gaming regulations and control, the mathematics of casino games, and the sociology of gambling. The Casino Career Institute, which includes a large mock casino, is a division of Atlantic Cape Community College in downtown Atlantic City, New Jersey. When it opened in 1978, it was the first gaming school in the country to be affiliated with a community college.

Employment at Commercial Casinos

As the AGA reports in *2012 State of the States*, in 2011 commercial casinos employed 339,098 people, who earned a total of $12.9 billion in wages, benefits, and tips. Nevada was far and away the largest provider of commercial casino jobs in 2011, with 174,381 casino employees; by comparison, the next biggest casino employer,

FIGURE 6.1

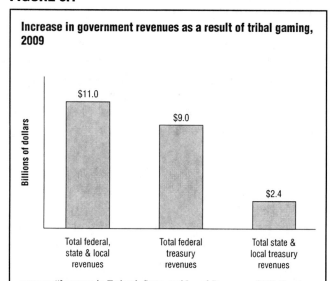

Increase in government revenues as a result of tribal gaming, 2009

SOURCE: "Increase in Federal, State, and Local Revenues, 2009 Due to Class II & III Indian Gaming," in *NIGA Report: Economic Impact of Indian Gaming in 2009*, National Indian Gaming Association, 2010, http://www.indiangaming.org/info/NIGA_2009_Economic_Impact_Report.pdf (accessed August 24, 2012)

FIGURE 6.2

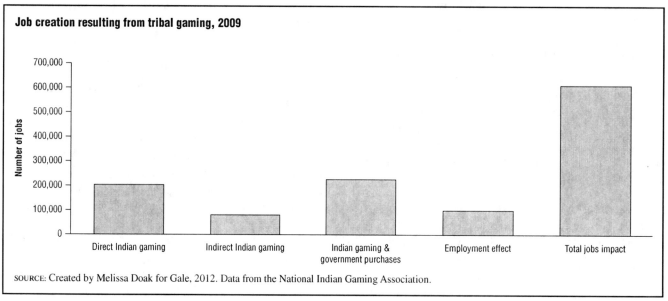

Job creation resulting from tribal gaming, 2009

SOURCE: Created by Melissa Doak for Gale, 2012. Data from the National Indian Gaming Association.

TABLE 6.1

Casino occupations, 2012

Title	Responsibilities	Education training	Median salary
Gaming managers	Plan, organize, direct, control, or coordinate gaming operations in a casino. Formulate gaming policies. Interview, hire, train, and evaluate new workers and create work schedules and station assignments.	Associates or Bachelor's degree. Hands-on experience may be substituted for formal education. Most managers gain experience in other casino jobs, typically as dealers, and have a broad knowledge of casino rules, regulations, procedures, and games.	$62,820
Gaming supervisors	Oversee gaming operations and personnel in an assigned area. Circulate among the tables to ensure that all stations and games are attended to each shift. Interperet the casino's operating rules for patrons. Plan and organize activities for guests staying at a casino hotels. Address service complaints.	Associates or Bachelor's degree. Hands-on experience may be substituted for formal education. Most supervisors gain experience in other gaming jobs before moving into supervisory positions.	41,160
Slot key persons (also called slot attendants or slot technicians)	Coordinate and supervise the slot department and its workers. Verify and handle payoff winnings to patrons, reset slot machines after payoffs, refill slot machines with money, make minor repairs and adjustments to the machines, enforce safety rules and report hazards.	No formal eduation requirements, but completion of technical training helpful. Most positions are entry-level and provide on-the-job training.	22,720
Gaming and sports book writers and runners	Assist in the operation of games such as bingo. Scan tickets presented by patrons and calculate and distribute winnings. May operate equipment that randomly selects the numbers, announce numbers selected, pick up tickets from patrons, collect bets, or receive, verify, and record patrons' cash wagers.	High school diploma or GED. Usually trained on the job.	18,800
Gaming dealers	Operate casino table games such as craps, baccarat, blackjack, or roulette. Determine winners of game, calculate and pay winning bets, and collect losing bets. May be required to monitor patrons to determine if they are following the rules of the game.	Completion of a training program at a vocational or technical school. An in-depth knowledge of casino games may be substituted for formal education. Most casinos require employees to audition for such jobs.	14,730

SOURCE: Adapted from "Gaming Services Occupations," in *2012–2013 Occupational Outlook Handbook*, U.S. Department of Labor, Bureau of Labor Statistics, March 2012, http://www.bls.gov/oco/ocos275.htm (accessed August 24, 2012)

New Jersey, supported 32,823 commercial gaming jobs that same year. Between 2010 and 2011, the highest percentage growth in the number of commercial casino jobs occurred in New York, where the number of casino jobs rose from 3,465 to 5,082, an increase of nearly 47%.

Overall, the number of commercial casino jobs fell slightly between 2010 and 2011, from 340,564 to 339,098, a decline of 0.4%. Total industry wages also dropped during this period, from $13.3 billion to $12.9 billion.

Employment at Native American Casinos

In *Economic Impact of Indian Gaming*, the NIGA reports that tribal gaming directly employed 204,000 people in 2009. Another 101,000 were attributed to the indirect effects of tribal casinos, such as businesses at which casino workers spent their wages, while 80,000 restaurant and hotel jobs were attributed to the continued expansion of Native American gaming operations. The NIGA estimates that tribal casinos were indirectly responsible for 224,000 other jobs by purchasing goods and services from businesses around the country. Capital construction projects (e.g., casino building) were associated with the creation of 19,000 other jobs. In total, the NIGA credits tribal gaming for the employment of approximately 628,000 people in 2009.

Historically, employees at tribal casinos have not been covered by the federal labor laws that protect workers at commercial casinos. As sovereign entities, tribes were considered excluded from Title VII of the Civil Rights Act of 1964 and Title I of the Americans with Disabilities Act of 1990, which prohibit discrimination in employment on the basis of race, sex, physical impairment, and other criteria. In addition, the National Labor Relations Act exempts government entities from the requirement that they allow employees to form unions. Tribes, having been ruled to be sovereign governments by both the National Labor Relations Board (NLRB) and a federal court, operated under their own laws and blocked unions if they chose to do so.

However, some court cases have held that Occupational Safety and Health Administration requirements, the Fair Labor Standards Act, and the Employee Retirement Income Security Act do apply to tribal businesses conducted on reservations. Furthermore, the NLRB, after a 2004 challenge by UNITE HERE, a union that represents hotel and restaurant employees, overturned 30 years of precedent and ruled in *San Manuel Indian Bingo and Casino* (341 NLRB 1055 [2004] aff'd. 475 F.3d 1306 [D.C. Cir. 2007]) that the San Manuel Indian Bingo and Casino in Southern California could not stop the formation of a union.

The NLRB (May 2, 2008, http://mynlrb.nlrb.gov/link/document.aspx/09031d458011aadc) explains that *San Manuel Indian Bingo and Casino* was used as a precedent to rule against the Mashantucket Pequot Tribe's contention that employment at Foxwoods Casino and Resort could not be regulated by federal law because of the tribe's status as a sovereign nation. In October 2007 a Decision and Direction of Election was issued to allow the United Auto Workers (UAW) and the American Federation of Labor and Congress of Industrial Organizations (AFL-CIO) to organize dealers at Foxwoods. The election was held in November 2007, and most employees voted in favor of the union. The union was officially certified in June 2008. Although the Mashantucket Pequot Tribe contested the legitimacy of the union in subsequent appeals, as of 2013 the NLRB had repeatedly struck down the tribe's petitions, and the union remained intact. As Stephen Singer reports in "Auto Union Eyes Conn. Mohegan Sun Casino Workers" (July 18, 2012, http://www.businessweek.com/ap/2012-07-18/auto-union-eyes-conn-dot-mohegan-sun-casino-workers), in July 2012 the UAW, inspired by the success of labor group efforts at Foxwoods, launched a campaign to unionize 1,400 table game workers at the nearby Mohegan Sun Casino in Montville.

TOURISM

According to the AGA in *2012 State of the States*, 59.7 million Americans, or more than one-quarter (27%) of the nation's adult population, visited a casino in 2011. Among all forms of gambling, casino gaming was second only to playing the lottery (44%) in popularity among American adults. In addition, in 2011 more than three-quarters (79%) of adults who visited a casino in 2011 expected to visit a casino again at least once in the coming year.

Las Vegas

No destination better represents the marriage between gambling and tourism than Las Vegas. Regardless, it has had its ups and downs. During the early 1990s the city experienced a steep decline in revenues because of competition from legal gambling on riverboats and tribal casinos in other states. To counteract this development, the city began a drive to shift its focus from an adult playground to a family destination. As part of the campaign, $12 billion was spent to refurbish almost every hotel on the Strip and to add entertainment facilities. Theme hotels became a big draw. Adult entertainment along the Strip, such as topless shows, gave way to magic shows, circus events, and carnival rides. The Las Vegas Convention and Visitors Authority (LVCVA) focused advertising on families. The result was a huge increase in visitors.

However, children distracted their parents from gambling. Casino owners noticed that the changes did not bring in more gambling revenue, so during the late 1990s the city began to change its image again. Adult entertainment made a comeback along the Strip: casino hotels began offering more topless and nude shows, although managers insisted that the nudity presented at their casinos would always be tasteful and artistic. They were careful not to offend shareholders of their parent corporations or to alienate women, who were potential gamblers that made up nearly 60% of Las Vegas visitors. In 2001 MGM Grand shut down its family theme park.

Theresa Howard reports in "Vegas Goes for Edgier Ads" (*USA Today*, August 3, 2003) that in early 2003 the LVCVA launched a somewhat risqué ad campaign with the slogan "What Happens Here, Stays Here." It may have been part of the reason that Las Vegas tourism and casino revenue increased substantially during 2005 and 2006. The focus on adults continued throughout the recession of 2008 and 2009, with MGM Grand launching the "Get Rewarded for Your Sins" promotion in October 2009. Amanda Finnegan explains in "Vegas Tourism Companies Embrace Social Media Strategies" (*Las Vegas Sun*, November 11, 2009) that the promotion encouraged visitors to recount their Vegas mishaps on Twitter and possibly win free hotel accommodations.

However, the picture of Las Vegas as a frivolous adult playground backfired somewhat during the recession. Las Vegas tourism was hit hard in February 2009, when President Barack Obama (1961–; Democrat) publicly remarked that companies taking federal bailout monies should not hold conventions in Las Vegas using taxpayers' money. In the wake of these comments, both Wells Fargo and Goldman Sachs canceled Las Vegas meetings, and many lower profile companies followed suit. In "Signs Go South for LV" (*Las Vegas Review-Journal*, March 11, 2009), Benjamin Spillman notes that between December 2008 and March 2009, 340 conventions scheduled for the city had been canceled. As the LVCVA reports in "2011 Las Vegas Year-to-Date Executive Summary" (2012, http://www.lvcva.com/includes/content/images/media/docs/Year-end-2011.pdf), in 2011 Las Vegas hosted more than 19,000 conventions, an increase of 5.7% over 2010.

Atlantic City

Tourism in Atlantic City increased following the introduction of casino gambling, but not as fast or as much as many had hoped. From the 1880s to the 1940s Atlantic City was a major tourist destination, particularly for people living in the Northeast. Visitors went for the beaches and to walk along the town's boardwalk and piers, which featured carnival-like entertainment. However, during the 1960s the city fell into an economic depression as tourists ventured farther south to beaches in Florida and the Caribbean.

Casino gambling was legalized in 1976 in the hopes that the city would recapture its former glory and rival Las Vegas as a tourist destination. Progress was slow through the 1980s and early 1990s. Even though visitors began to go to Atlantic City, they mostly arrived by bus or car and stayed only for a day or two. In 1984 the state established the Casino Reinvestment Development Authority (CRDA) to revitalize the city using the funds from a 1.3% tax on casino revenues.

The economic troubles that had ravaged the city's businesses before gambling was legalized were not easily overcome. Vacant lots, dilapidated buildings, and housing projects surrounded the casinos. The overall atmosphere was not particularly appealing to vacationers or convention-goers. Mike Kelly notes in "Gambling with Our Future: City Poised to Hit Jackpot, or Lose Everything" (*Record* [West Paterson, New Jersey], July 1, 1993) that in 1993 the city was "trapped in a web of poverty and blight." At that time, the typical visitor was a retiree who arrived by bus and stayed only for the day. According to Kelly, Atlantic City's 30 million annual visitors actually represented about 5 million people making multiple trips.

During the late 1990s initiatives by the CRDA and other groups began to pay off. Hundreds of new homes were built and commercial businesses were established. One of the largest convention centers in the country opened in May 1997. The city's image began to improve, and tourism showed a moderate surge.

Nevertheless, the first decade of the 21st century was extremely challenging for Atlantic City. The city's casinos experienced a decrease in attendance because of two major events: the recession and smoking restrictions on the casino floor, which went into effect in 2008. Even though the casino market nationwide was hit hard by the recession, Atlantic City's revenues went down the most. According to the article "Atlantic City Casino Revenue Declines 11.3 Percent in August" (*Press of Atlantic City*, September 10, 2010), in August 2010 casino revenues tumbled for the 24th straight month. That month was the first full month of table games in Pennsylvania's nine casinos, and in September 2010 a new casino was due to open in Philadelphia, which was just an hour's drive away from Atlantic City.

In 2010 city officials hoped that *Boardwalk Empire*, a new HBO television series that featured Atlantic City during the Prohibition Era (1920–1933), would beef up tourism in the declining city. Wayne Parry reports in "Atlantic City Hopes 'Boardwalk Empire' Brings the Tourists" (Associated Press, September 25, 2010) that the city unveiled a variety of 1920s-themed promotions in the hopes of capitalizing on the free publicity, including meals and hotel rooms that were priced at $19.20, straight-razor shaves, and special whiskey cocktails. In spite of these inventive promotional efforts, however, the city continued to struggle in 2012. As the AGA reports in *2012 State of the States*, casino revenues in New Jersey fell 7% between 2010 and 2011, in the face of increased competition from gaming facilities in nearby Pennsylvania and Delaware.

CRIME

Officials must realize that legal gambling will attract an unsavory element that can jeopardize the safety and well-being of the city's residents and the many visitors who come to gamble.

—Federal Bureau of Investigation, *FBI Law Enforcement Bulletin* (January 2001)

When gambling was legalized in Nevada in 1931, the law kept corporations out of the casino business by requiring that every shareholder obtain a gaming license. This law, which was designed to safeguard the integrity of the casinos, unintentionally gave organized crime a huge advantage. The nation was in the midst of the Great Depression (1929–1939), and building a flashy casino hotel was expensive. Few legitimate businesspeople had the cash to finance a casino, and banks were reluctant to lend money for something they considered to be a bad investment. Organized crime groups had made fortunes selling bootleg liquor during Prohibition, so they were able to make the capital investments needed to build and operate lavish casino hotels that attracted visitors.

The marriage between casinos and organized crime in Nevada lasted for decades but was eventually ended by gaming officials and law enforcement. In the 21st century there is little evidence of organized crime activity in the casino industry. Regulatory agencies keep a watchful eye on casinos to make sure mobsters and their associates do not gain a new foothold.

Casinos keep an equally watchful eye on their patrons and employees. For example, a host of security guards and cameras constantly monitors the casino floor. Observers watch dealers and patrons at the gaming tables and all money-counting areas. Some casinos use high-tech facial recognition programs to scan incoming patrons and quickly identify any known felons or other undesirables. Even though the industry does not release data on crimes committed by casino employees, analysts believe employee theft and embezzlement account for millions of dollars in losses each year.

Vice crimes, particularly prostitution, as well as weapons crimes also occur. Details of the types of crimes found around casinos are illustrated by the Missouri Gaming Commission in *Annual Report 2011* (2011, http://www.mgc.dps.mo.gov/annual%20reports/2011_ar/00_FullReport.pdf). Commission agents oversaw 3,300 arrests at Missouri casinos between July 2010 and June 2011. (See Table 6.2.) This total includes charges for acts that were committed both on and off casino property. January and April 2011 experienced the highest crime rates of the year, with 321 arrests made in each month. As Figure 6.3 shows, 2,925 of these arrests, or nearly 89%, were for misdemeanor infractions.

TABLE 6.2

Arrests made at Missouri casinos, fiscal year 2011

Boat	Jul	Aug	Sep	Oct	Nov	Dec	Jan	Feb	Mar	Apr	May	Jun	Total
Ameristar KC	17	26	14	37	12	19	13	43	29	37	54	45	346
Ameristar SC	25	29	36	25	12	22	32	28	36	42	42	21	350
Argosy	32	20	16	19	27	25	22	27	27	29	6	24	274
Harrah's MH	39	17	26	29	16	11	21	16	17	8	25	9	234
Harrah's NKC	2	27	16	7	14	18	21	22	5	29	9	5	195
IOC-BN	4	6	3	4	7	4	7	12	12	6	1	4	70
IOC-KC	22	36	24	37	40	19	67	20	18	42	37	31	393
Lady Luck/IOC	1	2	0	2	6	1	1	3	7	2	1	3	29
Lumiere Place	6	90	87	71	91	132	109	65	100	80	97	96	1094
Mark Twain	0	8	2	2	1	4	5	4	2	4	0	2	34
River City	22	12	22	16	15	17	20	23	26	41	8	26	248
St. Jo	1	3	1	3	4	6	3	4	3	1	2	2	33
	61	**276**	**247**	**252**	**245**	**278**	**321**	**267**	**282**	**321**	**282**	**268**	**3300**

Note: Totals obtained from the Missouri State Highway Patrol (MSHP) Gaming Division Districts. Fiscal year: July 1, 2010–June 30, 2011

SOURCE: "2011 MGC Fiscal Year: Casino Arrest Totals," in *Missouri Gaming Commission Annual Report 2011*, Missouri Gaming Commission, 2011, http://www .mgc.dps.mo.gov/annual%20reports/2011_ar/00_FullReport.pdf (accessed August 24, 2012)

FIGURE 6.3

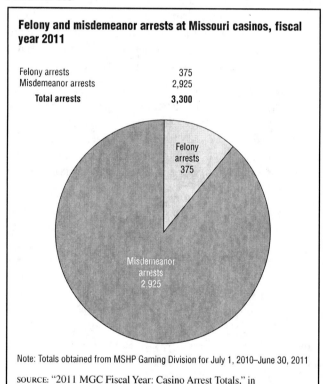

Felony and misdemeanor arrests at Missouri casinos, fiscal year 2011

Felony arrests	375
Misdemeanor arrests	2,925
Total arrests	**3,300**

Felony arrests 375

Misdemeanor arrests 2,925

Note: Totals obtained from MSHP Gaming Division for July 1, 2010–June 30, 2011

SOURCE: "2011 MGC Fiscal Year: Casino Arrest Totals," in *Missouri Gaming Commission Annual Report 2011*, Missouri Gaming Commission, 2011, http://www.mgc.dps.mo.gov/annual%20reports/ 2011_ar/00_FullReport.pdf (accessed August 24, 2012)

According to Earl L. Grinols and David B. Mustard in "Casinos, Crime, and Community Costs" (*Review of Economics and Statistics*, vol. 88, no. 1, February 2006), the amount of crime in a community with a casino has a direct relationship to the maturity of the casino. The researchers collected crime data from all 3,165 counties in the United States with and without casinos between 1977 and 1996. Their analysis shows that when a casino first opened in a county, crime changed very little, but slowly rose and then grew steadily in subsequent years. Even though increased employment and expanded law enforcement reduced crime initially, over time these effects were overtaken by factors that were related to casinos. Grinols and Mustard note, "Specifically, problem and pathological gamblers commit crimes as they deplete their resources, nonresidents who visit casinos may both commit and be victims of crime, and casino-induced changes in the population start small but grow." The researchers also note that "overall, 8.6% of property crime and 12.6% of violent crime [which includes robberies] in counties with casinos was due to the presence of the casino." Furthermore, they find "mixed evidence about whether casino openings increase neighbor-county crime rates."

Douglas M. Walker of the College of Charleston responds to Grinols and Mustard's study in "Do Casinos Really Cause Crime?" (*Econ Journal Watch*, vol. 5, no. 1, January 2008). He argues that Grinols and Mustard failed to address the effects of tourism on the crime rate, that the source of their data (the Uniform Crime Reports) is not appropriate for investigating longitudinal changes in local crime, and that they do not consider that casinos are sometimes introduced in high-crime areas. He concludes, "My point is not to suggest that casinos do not cause crime. They might.... However, the errors in the Grinols and Mustard study deserve attention because of the influence their study seems to be having among researchers, policymakers, the media, and voters."

SUICIDE

The possible link between casino gambling and suicide rates has been the subject of much investigation. For example, in December 1997 David P. Phillips, Ward R.

Welty, and Marisa M. Smith concluded in "Elevated Suicide Levels Associated with Legalized Gambling" (*Suicide and Life-Threatening Behavior*, vol. 27, no. 4) that "visitors to and residents of major gaming communities experience significantly elevated suicide levels." The researchers found that in Atlantic City "abnormally high suicide levels" for visitors and residents appeared only after casinos opened.

However, five years later Richard McCleary et al. found in "Does Legalized Gambling Elevate the Risk of Suicide?" (*Suicide and Life-Threatening Behavior*, vol. 32, no. 2, Summer 2002) little to no correlation between suicide rates and the presence of casino gambling in U.S. communities. After comparing the 1990 suicide rates of 148 metropolitan areas in different regions of the country, the researchers found that the presence of casinos could account for only 1% of the regional differences in suicide rates. They also compared "before and after" suicide rates for cities in which gambling had been legalized. Even though increased suicide rates were noted in Atlantic County, New Jersey, and Harrison County, Mississippi, after the advent of gambling, the increases were not considered statistically significant. McCleary et al. noted that suicide rates dropped significantly in Lawrence County, South Dakota, after casino gambling was introduced in the town of Deadwood.

In "Risk Factors for Suicide Ideation and Attempts among Pathological Gamblers" (*American Journal on Addictions*, vol. 15, no. 4, July–August 2006), David C. Hodgins, Chrystal Mansley, and Kylie Thygesen find that suicidal ideation and suicide attempts are more likely among pathological gamblers. However, the history of suicidal thoughts generally preceded problem gambling behavior by an average of more than 10 years. The researchers conclude that previous mental health disorders, such as clinical depression, put individuals more at risk for both suicide and gambling problems. In other words, gambling itself does not cause suicide attempts. Paul W. C. Wong et al. find in "A Psychological Autopsy Study of Pathological Gamblers Who Died by Suicide" (*Journal of Affective Disorders*, vol. 120, no. 1, January 2010) that a high proportion of suicide cases in which pathological gambling was present had a comorbid (an additional or coexisting disease) psychiatric illness, most often depression, at the time of death.

According to the American Foundation for Suicide Prevention (2013, http://www.afsp.org/index.cfm?fuseaction=home.viewpage&page_id=05114FBE-E445-7831-F0C1494E2FADB8EA), Nevada, a state in which gambling is widely practiced, had the fourth-highest suicide rate in the nation in 2010. The Centers for Disease Control and Prevention indicates in *WISQARS Injury Mortality Reports, 1999–2010* (September 30, 2011, http://www.cdc.gov/injury/wisqars/fatal_injury_reports.html) that the suicide rate in Nevada was 20.3 suicides per 100,000 population in 2010, which was significantly higher than the national average of 12.4 per 100,000 population. Many mental health experts attribute Nevada's high suicide rate to the huge inflow of new residents who lack a support system of family and friends. Loneliness and despair are more likely to overwhelm such people than those who have an emotional safety net in place. In general, suicide rates are higher in the western states than in any other region. For example, both Wyoming (23.2 per 100,000) and Montana (22.9 per 100,000) had higher suicide rates than Nevada in 2010. Even Utah, which does not allow legal gambling, had a rate of 17.1 suicides per 100,000 population.

BANKRUPTCY

Establishing a definitive link between gambling habits and bankruptcy is difficult. The Council on Compulsive Gambling of New Jersey notes in the press release "Correlation between Gambling and Bankruptcy Holding Strong" (August 22, 2001, http://www.800gambler.org/ArticleDetails.aspx?ContentID=90) that a 2001 study by SMR Research Corporation of Hackettstown, New Jersey, attributes 14.2% of U.S. bankruptcy filings to gambling problems. The researchers compare bankruptcy filing rates for 3,109 counties in 2000. They find that the 244 counties in which casinos operated had a bankruptcy rate that was 13.7% higher than counties without a casino. The AGA disputes the researchers' findings by pointing out that other factors were not considered, such as liberal bankruptcy laws and the ease with which credit cards can be obtained.

Ernest Goss and Edward A. Morse of Creighton University examine in *The Impact of Casino Gambling on Individual Bankruptcy Rates from 1990–2002* (August 25, 2005, http://papers.ssrn.com/sol3/papers.cfm?abstract_id=801185) the bankruptcy rates between 1990 and 2002 in 253 counties with casinos. According to their analysis, these counties actually saw a drop in bankruptcies when the casinos first opened. The researchers reason that the revenue and jobs brought in by a casino likely helped the residents' financial situation. However, after a casino was open for nine years bankruptcies trended the other way. Eventually, the bankruptcy rate in a county with a casino was 2.3% higher on average than a county without a casino.

In "Pathologic Gambling and Bankruptcy" (*Comprehensive Psychiatry*, vol. 51, no. 2, March–April 2010), Jon E. Grant et al. of the University of Minnesota School of Medicine study 517 pathological gamblers and find that there were specific clinical differences between those who declared bankruptcy and those who did not. The researchers report that gamblers who declared bankruptcy were more likely to be single and to have work, marital, or legal problems secondary to gambling. These gamblers also tended to have an earlier age of onset problem gambling and were more likely to have comorbid depressive disorders or substance use disorders than were gamblers who did not declare bankruptcy.

COMPULSIVE GAMBLING

Even though compulsive and pathological gambling are real problems, most gamblers play for recreation and practice healthy gambling behaviors. In *2012 State of the States*, the AGA explains that in 2011 more than eight out of 10 casino gamblers (84%) set a budget before they began gambling and that nearly half (48%) of gamblers allowed themselves to lose no more than $100 per day.

Self-Exclusion Programs

Many casinos operate self-exclusion programs in which people can voluntarily ban themselves from casinos. A number of states also offer self-exclusion programs for all casinos within their borders. For example, Missouri's Voluntary Exclusion Program (http://www.mgc.dps.mo.gov/DAP/FAQ_DAP.html) was created in 1996 after a citizen requested that he be banned from the riverboat casinos because he was unable to control his gambling. The Missouri Gaming Commission requires that the casinos remove self-excluded people from their direct marketing lists, deny them check-cashing privileges and membership in players' clubs, and cross-check for their names on the self-exclusion list before paying out any jackpots of $1,200 or more. The casinos are not responsible for barring listed people, but anyone listed is to be arrested for trespassing if he or she violates the ban and is discovered in a casino. However, self-excluded people can enter the casino for employment purposes.

Sara E. Nelson et al. study the effectiveness of Missouri's Voluntary Exclusion Program in "One Decade of Self Exclusion: Missouri Casino Self-Excluders Four to Ten Years after Enrollment" (*Journal of Gambling Studies*, vol. 26, no. 1, March 2010). The researchers find that most gamblers who enrolled in the self-exclusion program had been able to reduce their gambling. However, half of the self-excluders who had attempted to enter Missouri casinos after they enrolled in the program were still able to do so. Nelson et al. conclude that the benefits of the program are more attributable to the act of enrollment than in the casinos' actual enforcement of the ban. In addition, the researchers suggest that self-excluders who sought additional mental health treatment were better able to control their gambling problem and that self-exclusion programs should provide information about additional help and treatment options at the time of enrollment.

Programs in other states are similar. If a self-excluded person is discovered in an Illinois casino, his or her chips and tokens are taken away and their value is donated to charity. The Illinois self-exclusion program runs for a minimum of five years. After that time, people can be removed from the program if they provide written documentation from a licensed mental health professional that they are no longer problem gamblers. Self-exclusion in Michigan is permanent; a person who chooses to be on the Disassociated Persons List is banned for life from Detroit casinos. In New Jersey the Casino Control Commission allows people to voluntarily suspend their credit privileges at all Atlantic City casinos. The commission maintains a list of those who have joined the program and shares the list with the casinos.

Besides casinos and states, companies that provide the ATMs and cash-advance services for casinos have put self-exclusion programs into place. For example, Global Payments provides self-exclusion and even self-limit services for people with gambling problems. Those who put their names on the self-exclusion list are denied money or cash advances, whereas the self-limit program restricts how much money patrons can withdraw during a specified period.

Hotlines and Treatment

All the states operate gambling hotlines that either refer callers to other groups for help or provide counseling over the phone. According to the Mississippi Council on Problem and Compulsive Gambling (2013, http://www.msgambler.org/), 58% of the callers to its hotline in 2011 obtained the number through a casino. In *Governor's Report on Compulsive Gambling* (February 2011, https://edocs.dhs.state.mn.us/lfserver/Public/DHS-6341-ENG), the Minnesota governor's office reports that the state received 1,054 calls to its Problem Gambling Hotline in 2010, compared with 1,302 calls in 2009, a 19% decrease. In 2009 and 2010 combined, the state of Minnesota provided outpatient treatment to 1,620 problem gamblers; an additional 329 individuals received inpatient treatment during the same period. According to the governor's report, there were 52 state-approved outpatient providers for problem gamblers in 2010.

Each year, the Minnesota state budget allocates funds to address the problem of compulsive gambling, providing Helpline assistance, outpatient and inpatient treatment, and public awareness initiatives. According to the *Governor's Report on Compulsive Gambling*, funding for problem gambling programs in Minnesota totaled $1.8 million in 2010. Roughly 41% of this total, or $746,741, was allocated to outpatient treatment programs, while an additional $515,000 was designated for inpatient treatment.

The Iowa Department of Public Health tracks statistics on clients who are admitted to its gambling treatment program. In "Profile of Gamblers Admitted to Treatment for State Fiscal Year 2012" (2013, http://www.idph.state .ia.us/IGTP/common/pdf/reports/profile_of_gamblers.pdf), the department indicates that 46.6% reported gambling debts of greater than $5,000. Nearly two-thirds (63.9%) of the clients said their primary wagering in the past six months had been done on slot machines, while another 14.3% said their primary wagering had been at table games in casinos. As Table 6.3 shows, 44% of Iowans treated for problem gambling in 2010 had attained only a high school diploma or general equivalency diploma (commonly known as a GED), while 18% had graduated with at least a four-year college degree. More than half (56%) of problem gamblers receiving treatment were female; more than one-third (38%) were married, and 70% had one or more children living in their household. Fewer than half of problem gamblers in Iowa (44%) had full-time jobs in 2010. As Table 6.4 indicates, about 80% of all problem gamblers who entered the Iowa Gambling Treatment Program in 2010 owed some amount of gambling-related debt at the time of their admission; 5% owed $100,000 or more in gambling-related debts. Nearly three-quarters (72%) of problem gamblers in the Iowa Gambling Treatment Program admitted to playing slot machines in 2010; by comparison, only 26% reported playing scratch tickets, 22% played casino table games, and 19% played the lottery. (See Figure 6.4.)

Industry Educational Efforts

In "Code of Conduct for Responsible Gaming" (September 15, 2003, http://www.americangaming.org/files/aga/ uploads/docs/aga_code_brochure.pdf), the AGA describes the actions that its members pledge to take to ensure that responsible gambling is conducted and encouraged at casinos. These actions include the proper training of employees and the promotion of responsible gambling on company websites and through brochures and signs that are posted at the casinos. AGA members also agree to provide opportunities for patrons to self-exclude themselves from casino play. Each year the AGA sponsors Responsible Gaming Education Week. The theme of the 15th annual event held from July 30 to August 3, 2012, was "All in for Responsible Gaming" (2012, http://www.ncrg.org/public-education-and-outreach/ events/rgew).

UNDERAGE GAMBLING

The legal gambling age in all commercial casinos in the United States is 21 years; in tribal casinos it varies from 18 to 21 years.

The Nevada Gaming Commission reports in *Nevada Gaming Control Act and Ancillary Statutes* (January 2013, http://gaming.nv.gov/index.aspx?page=51) that as of January 2000, Regulation 14 banned slot machines with themes that were "derived from or based on a product that is currently and primarily intended or marketed for use by

TABLE 6.3

Clients admitted to the Iowa Gambling Treatment Program, by selected characteristics, 2010

Gender	44%	Male
	56%	Female
Children	70%	Children in household/financially responsible for one or more children
	30%	No children in household or not financially responsible for any children
Marital status	38%	Married
	29%	Single
	19%	Divorced
	08%	Cohabitating
	03%	Separated
	04%	Widowed
Education	18%	College graduate (bachelor's degree or higher)
	32%	Some college
	44%	High school/GED (General Education Diploma)
	06%	Less than high school
Employment	44%	Employed full-time
	12%	Employed part-time
	19%	Unemployed in past 30 days and looking for work
	25%	Not in labor force
Health	54%	Have private health insurance (not including Medicare or Medicaid)
insurance	46%	No private health insurance (may be covered by Medicare or Medicaid)
Hispanic/Latino	98%	Non-Hispanic
	02%	Hispanic/Latino
Race	94%	White-Caucasian
	04%	African-American
	01%	American Indian
	02%	Asian
Primary source	91%	State unit reimbursement
of payment for	07%	Self pay or other private pay
treatment	<1%	Other government (e.g., Medicaid, Medicare, State non-unit reimbursement)
	<1%	Private health insurance
	1%	No charge

Note: This corresponds to an *unemployment rate* of 25% using a formula of (unemployed/(employed + unemployed))*100. Among those who were not in the labor force, there were 8 homemakers, 7 students, 32 retired persons, and 47 persons on disability.

Sample size for demographics:
Gender (sample size = 486), Children (sample size = 488), Marital Status (sample size = 488), Education (sample size = 488), Employment (sample size = 488), Health insurance (sample size = 488), Hispanic/Latino (sample size = 487), Race (sample size = 476), and Primary source of payment (sample size = 488).

SOURCE: Melvin E. Gonnerman, Jr., et al., "Background Characteristics of Clients Admitted in 2010 for Treatment," in *Iowa Gambling Treatment Outcomes System: Year 6*, University of Northern Iowa, Center for Social and Behavioral Research, October 2011, http://www.idph.state.ia.us/IGTP/ common/pdf/reports/igto_report_year6.pdf (accessed August 24, 2012)

persons under 21 years of age." The so-called slots-for-tots regulation is supposed to prevent the introduction of slot machines displaying cartoon characters that might appeal to children. The issue receives particular attention in Nevada because the state's casinos allow escorted children to walk through the casino. Most states prohibit the passage of minors through the gambling area.

The AGA lists in "Code of Conduct for Responsible Gaming" a number of rules that member casinos should follow to ensure that minors do not gamble in casinos. For example, they should not display cartoon figures, pictures of underage people, or pictures of collegiate sports athletes on the casino floor. They are also supposed to stop any minor from loitering on the casino floor, and casino employees are to be trained to deal with minors who attempt to buy alcohol or gamble.

Casinos appear to be successful in following the guidelines. For example, data compiled by the Michigan Gaming Control Board are shown in Table 6.5. A total of 3,324 minors who tried to enter the three Detroit casinos in 2011 were denied entry. Thirty-six minors were physically escorted from the premises, and 58 were taken into custody by law enforcement officers.

POLITICS

Gambling and politics have always been linked, largely because casinos and other gaming establishments are so heavily regulated, the number of licenses available is often limited, and a great deal of money can be made by the people who hold those licenses. Lobbying (a common

TABLE 6.4

Debt of clients at admission to the Iowa Gambling Treatment Program, 2010

	Gambling-related debt	Total debt	Credit card debt	Overdue bills
None	22%	10%	39%	42%
$1–$1,999	11%	07%	15%	15%
$2,000–$4,999	13%	08%	12%	11%
$5,000–$9,999	14%	09%	09%	09%
$10,000–$19,999	17%	18%	11%	09%
$20,000–$49,999	14%	17%	09%	07%
$50,000–$99,999	06%	12%	03%	04%
$100,000 or more	05%	18%	01%	03%
Median	$6,000	$17,900	$1,000	$950
Mean	$19,354	$56,742	$8,848	$10,552

Note: Sample sizes: Gambling-related (sample size = 488), Total (sample size = 488), Credit card (sample size = 488), and Overdue bills (sample size = 488).

SOURCE: Melvin E. Gonnerman, Jr., et al., "Table A2. Debt at Admission," in *Iowa Gambling Treatment Outcomes System: Year 6*, University of Northern Iowa, Center for Social and Behavioral Research, October 2011, http://www.idph.state.ia.us/IGTP/common/pdf/reports/igto_report_year6.pdf (accessed August 24, 2012)

TABLE 6.5

Contacts with minors in casinos in Detroit, Michigan, selected statistics, 2011

	MGM Grand	MotorCity	Greektown
1. The number of minors who were denied entry into the casino.	792	1,587	845
2. The number of minors who were physically escorted from the casino premises.	18	0	18
3. The number of minors who were detected participating in gambling games other than slot machines.	2	7	6
4. The number of minors who were detected using slot machines.	0	8	12
5. The number of minors who were taken into custody by a law enforcement agency on the casino premises.	18	22	18
6. The number of minors who were detected illegally consuming alcohol on the casino premises.	3	6	0

SOURCE: "Casino Licensees' Reported Contacts with Minors on Licensed Casino Premises during Calendar Year 2011," in *Annual Report to the Governor, Calendar Year 2011*, Michigan Gaming Control Board, April 2012, http://michigan.gov/documents/mgcb/annrep11_386483_7.pdf (accessed August 26, 2012)

FIGURE 6.4

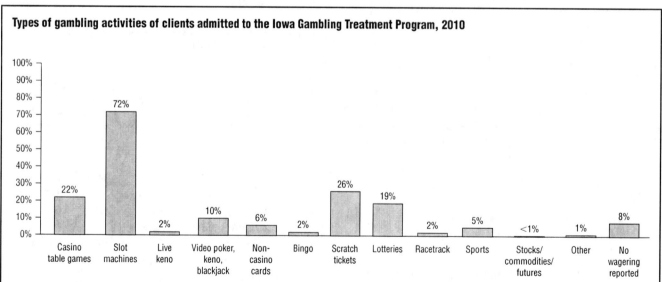

Types of gambling activities of clients admitted to the Iowa Gambling Treatment Program, 2010

Note: Clients were asked to assign the percentage of all money wagered for each activity. The values above show the percentage of clients who said at least 1% of their money was wagered on a particular activity.

SOURCE: Melvin E. Gonnerman, Jr., et al., "Types of Gambling Activities (Past 6 Months)," in *Iowa Gambling Treatment Outcomes System: Year 6*, University of Northern Iowa, Center for Social and Behavioral Research, October 2011, http://www.idph.state.ia.us/IGTP/common/pdf/reports/igto_report_year6.pdf (accessed August 24, 2012)

factor in the political system) can easily turn into influence peddling and bribery at all levels of government.

Some jurisdictions have become so concerned about the confluence of political pressure and money that they prohibit casino license applicants from making contributions to political candidates. Mississippi decided to prevent this temptation by not setting a limit on the number of casinos that can be built. State officials claimed their policy would prevent the bribery, extortion, and favoritism that had plagued neighboring Louisiana, where the number of licenses available for riverboat casinos was set at 15. Those licenses were so highly prized that Governor Edwin Edwards (1927–; Democrat) extorted $3 million from people who wanted them. In May 2000 he was convicted of racketeering, extortion, and fraud and sentenced to 10 years in prison.

On the federal level, politics and gambling intersect on issues that affect more than one state or Native American tribe. At that intersection, some people see opportunities to make a lot of money. One such operator was Jack Abramoff (1958–), a prominent lobbyist in the District of Columbia, who pleaded guilty to fraud, tax evasion, and conspiracy to bribe public officials in January 2006. He was sentenced to five years and 10 months in prison and ordered to pay $21 million in restitution.

Many credit Abramoff and his colleagues with securing the defeat of the Internet Gambling Prohibition Act of 1999. The bill was one of the first anti–Internet gambling bills proposed in Congress. It was passed in the U.S. Senate in 1999 and was put forth in the U.S. House of Representatives the following year. At the time, Abramoff was working for eLottery, an Internet site that wanted to sell state lottery tickets online. Their business was threatened by the legislation, so Abramoff sent money to conservative special interest groups to get them to pressure conservative House members to drop the bill because it contained exceptions for horse racing and jai alai. Through procedural maneuvering, a two-thirds majority was needed to pass the bill; it failed. When the bill's original supporters demanded that it be revived, Abramoff targeted 10 Republican House members in vulnerable districts with media and direct-mail campaigns that accused them of being "soft on gambling" if they voted for the bill. The representatives received so much pressure from their constituents that the House Republican leadership, fearing that the party might lose four seats in the 2000 election, decided not to bring the bill up for another vote.

Later in his career Abramoff and his team defrauded Native American tribes out of millions of dollars. Typically he promised that, as their lobbyist, he could secure funding from the government for special projects, such as wider roads or new schools, and that he could keep the government from interfering in their operations, including casinos. In return, the tribes paid his lobbying firm and a public relations company more than $85 million.

In some instances Abramoff worked against a tribe behind the scenes and then offered to help it out for huge sums of money. For example, in 2002 he and his colleagues were instrumental in shutting down the Speaking Rock Casino in El Paso, Texas. He then went to the Tigua Tribe, which operated the casino, and claimed that he and his colleagues could convince Congress to reopen the casino. The tribe paid $4.2 million in lobbying fees, but the casino remained closed. After years of legal battling, the facility reopened in 2010 as the Speaking Rock Entertainment Center, offering free concerts to attract patrons to its restaurant, bar, and limited video gaming machines.

Atlantic City and its local government have also been implicated in corruption. The article "Gov. Christie Pledges to Turn Atlantic City Casino District into 'Las Vegas East'" (*Newark Star-Ledger*, July 21, 2010) reports on the findings of a governor's commission that the Atlantic City local government had mismanaged—possibly criminally—hundreds of millions of dollars in tax revenues from the casinos. As a result of the commission's findings, Chris Christie (1962–; Republican), the governor of New Jersey, pledged in July 2010 that the state would take over the management of Atlantic City's casino district. As Duane Morris writes in "New Jersey's Bill S-12 Redesigns the Regulatory System for the Gaming Industry" (February 11, 2011, http://www.lexology.com/library/detail.aspx?g=66411faa-30e9-48cb-949c-b22ec5e75a45), in February 2011 Christie signed a new law granting the state greater authority to regulate the gaming industry, while also transferring authority over all gambling operations from the Casino Control Commission to the Division of Gaming Enforcement.

CHAPTER 7
LOTTERIES

A lottery is a game of chance in which people pay for the opportunity to win prizes. Part of the money taken in by a lottery is used to award the winners and to pay the costs of administering the lottery. The money left over is profit. Lotteries are extremely popular and legal in more than 100 countries.

In the United States all lotteries are operated by state governments, which have granted themselves the sole right to do so. In other words, they are monopolies that do not allow any commercial lotteries to compete against them. The profits from U.S. lotteries are used solely to fund government programs. As of 2013, lotteries operated in 43 states and the District of Columbia. In addition, lottery tickets could be legally purchased by any adult physically present in a lottery state, even if that adult did not reside in the state.

According to the North American Association of State and Provincial Lotteries (NASPL), Americans wagered $68.8 billion in lotteries in fiscal year (FY) 2012. (See Table 7.1.) U.S. lottery sales were up from $63.1 billion in FY 2012, an increase of 9%.

LOTTERY HISTORY

Early History

The drawing of lots to determine ownership or other rights is recorded in many ancient documents. The practice became common in Europe in the late 15th and early 16th centuries. Lotteries were first tied directly to the United States in 1612, when King James I (1566–1625) of England created a lottery to provide funds to Jamestown, Virginia, the first permanent British settlement in North America. Lotteries were used by public and private organizations after that time to raise money for towns, wars, colleges, and public works projects.

During the 1760s George Washington (1732–1799) conducted a lottery to finance the construction of the Mountain Road in Virginia. Benjamin Franklin (1706–1790) supported lotteries to pay for cannons during the American Revolution (1775–1783). John Hancock (1737–1793) ran a lottery to finance the rebuilding of Faneuil Hall in Boston, Massachusetts, after it was nearly destroyed by fire in 1761. Lotteries fell into disfavor during the 1820s because of concerns that they were harmful to the public. New York was the first state to pass a constitutional prohibition against them.

The Rise and Fall of Lotteries

The southern states relied on lotteries after the Civil War (1861–1865) to finance Reconstruction (1865–1877). The Louisiana lottery, in particular, became widely popular. According to the Louisiana Lottery Corporation, in "History of Lotteries" (January 2013, http://www.louisianalottery.com/assets/docs/fact%20sheets/HistoryofLotteries.pdf), in 1868 the Louisiana Lottery Company was granted permission by the state legislature to operate as the state's only lottery provider. In exchange, the company agreed to pay $40,000 per year for 25 years to the Charity Hospital of New Orleans. The company was allowed to keep all other lottery revenues and to pay no taxes on those revenues. The Louisiana lottery was popular nationwide.

In 1890 Congress banned the mailing of lottery materials. The Louisiana lottery was abolished in 1895 after Congress passed a law against the transport of lottery tickets across state lines. Following its closure the public learned that the lottery had been operated by a northern crime syndicate that regularly bribed legislators and committed widespread deception and fraud. The resulting scandal was widely publicized. Public opinion turned against lotteries, and by the end of the 19th century lotteries were outlawed across the country.

Negative attitudes about gambling began to soften during the early 20th century, particularly after the failure of Prohibition (1920–1933). The state of Nevada legalized

TABLE 7.1

State lottery sales and profits, fiscal years 2011 and 2012

	Fiscal year 2011		Fiscal year 2012	
Lottery jurisdiction	**Sales (millions)**	**Profit (millions)**	**Sales (millions)**	**Profit (millions)**
Arizona	$583.53	$146.30	$646.68	$164.70
Arkansas	$464.00	$94.20	$473.10	$97.50
California	$3,438.57	$1,129.00	$4,371.49	$1,320.00
Colorado	$518.90	$113.40	$545.30	$123.20
Connecticut	$1,016.60	$289.30	$1,081.70	$310.00
Delaware	$710.40	$287.00	$686.76	$271.33
D.C.	$231.46	$62.17	$252.15	$65.50
Florida	$4,008.72	$1,191.82	$4,449.90	$1,321.60
Georgia	$3,597.90	$846.10	$3,834.70	$901.30
Idaho	$147.05	$37.50	$175.84	$41.50
Illinois	$2,278.76	$689.97	$2,680.14	$708.50
Indiana	$791.45	$230.20	$855.59	$210.84
Iowa	$271.39	$68.00	$310.85	$78.73
Kansas	$243.70	$71.50	$246.14	$72.00
Kentucky	$772.35	$212.30	$823.55	$216.40
Louisiana	$383.60	$136.40	$429.60	$156.90
Maine	$216.40	$50.20	$228.30	$54.30
Maryland	$1,817.54	$586.62	$1,989.91	$683.07
Massachusetts	$4,427.90	$802.20	$4,741.40	$833.90
Michigan	$2,339.95	$727.32	$2,413.46	$770.00
Minnesota	$504.44	$121.89	$520.03	$123.65
Missouri	$1,000.70	$265.20	$1,097.40	$280.00
Montana	$46.00	$10.80	$52.60	$13.10
Nebraska	$131.92	$32.06	$150.61	$36.08
New Hampshire	$229.15	$62.21	$254.92	$66.77
New Jersey	$2,636.40	$930.00	$2,758.80	$950.00
New Mexico	$135.54	$41.30	$133.79	$41.30
New York	$7,868.21	$3,049.15	$8,439.47	$2,887.99
North Carolina	$1,461.11	$436.24	$1,596.69	$456.76
North Dakota	$23.00	$5.92	$26.00	$7.62
Ohio	$2,601.00	$738.80	$2,750.00	$771.03
Oklahoma	$198.27	$69.40	$199.97	$69.99
Oregon	$1,036.30	$525.30	$1,051.50	$526.60
Pennsylvania	$3,207.91	$960.61	$3,480.90	$1,060.89
Rhode Island	$3,125.60	$354.80	$3,532.18	$377.70
South Carolina	$1,047.06	$271.13	$1,135.65	$297.74
South Dakota	$583.42	$107.98	$603.19	$100.40
Tennessee	$1,187.00	$293.40	$1,311.00	$323.40
Texas	$3,811.27	$1,025.09	$4,190.82	$1,156.56
Vermont	$95.54	$21.40	$100.93	$22.30
Virginia	$1,482.69	$444.21	$1,616.00	$487.06
Washington	$510.50	$150.10	$535.20	$138.00
West Virginia	$1,392.45	$558.12	$1,457.53	$662.98
Wisconsin	$502.00	$144.80	$547.00	$149.90
Total U.S. ($US)	**$63,077.65**	**$18,391.41**	**$68,778.74**	**$19,409.08**

Note: At the time of publication, some data may be unaudited.

SOURCE: Adapted from "Lottery Sales and Profits," North American Association of State and Provincial Lotteries, 2013, http://www.naspl.org/index.cfm?fuseaction=content&menuid=17&pageid=1025 (accessed January 14, 2013)

casino gambling during the early 1930s, and gambling for charitable purposes slowly became more commonplace across the country. Still, lingering fears about fraud kept public sentiment against lotteries for two more decades.

Rebirth in the 1960s

In "History of the New Hampshire Lottery" (2009, http://www.nhlottery.org/AboutUs/History.aspx), the New Hampshire Lottery Commission notes that in 1963 the New Hampshire legislature authorized a sweepstakes to raise revenue. The state did not have a sales tax or state income tax at that time, and it desperately needed money for education programs. Patterned after the popular Irish Sweepstakes, the game was much different from the lotteries of the 21st

century. Tickets were sold for $3, and drawings were held infrequently. The biggest prizes were tied to the outcomes of particular horse races at the Rockingham Park racetrack in Salem, New Hampshire. Nearly $5.7 million was wagered during the lottery's first year.

The New York Lottery indicates in "New York Lottery Mission Statement" (2013, http://nylottery.ny.gov/wps/portal?PC_7_SPTFTVI4188AC0IKIA9Q6K0QS0_WCM_CONTEXT=/wps/wcm/connect/NYSL+Content+Library/NYSL+Internet+Site/About+Us/Mission+for+Education/) that New York introduced a lottery in 1967. It was particularly successful, grossing $53.6 million during its first year. It also enticed residents from neighboring states to cross state lines and buy tickets. Twelve other states established lotteries during the 1970s (Connecticut, Delaware, Illinois, Maine, Maryland, Massachusetts, Michigan, New Jersey, Ohio, Pennsylvania, Rhode Island, and Vermont). Analysts suggest that lotteries became so firmly entrenched throughout the Northeast for three reasons: each state needed to raise money for public projects without increasing taxes, each state had a large Catholic population that was generally tolerant of gambling, and history shows that states are more likely to start a lottery if one is already offered in a nearby state. For example, Ron Stodghill and Ron Nixon report in "For Schools, Lottery Payoffs Fall Short of Promises" (*New York Times*, October 7, 2007) that Michael F. Easley (1950–; Democrat), the former governor of North Carolina, said before his state established a lottery, "Our people are playing the lottery. We just need to decide which schools we should fund, other states' or ours."

During the 1980s lottery fever spread south and west. Seventeen states (Arizona, California, Colorado, Florida, Idaho, Indiana, Iowa, Kansas, Kentucky, Missouri, Montana, Oregon, South Dakota, Virginia, Washington, West Virginia, and Wisconsin) plus the District of Columbia started lotteries. Six more states (Georgia, Louisiana, Minnesota, Nebraska, New Mexico, and Texas) started lotteries during the 1990s. They were joined after 2000 by Arkansas, North Carolina, North Dakota, Oklahoma, South Carolina, and Tennessee.

LOTTERY GAMES

Early lottery games were simple raffles in which a person purchased a ticket that was preprinted with a number. The player typically had to wait for weeks for a drawing to determine if the ticket was a winner. These types of games, called passive drawing games, were the dominant lottery games in 1973. By 1997 they had ceased to exist, as consumers demanded more exciting games that provided quicker payoffs and more betting options.

Nearly all states that operate lotteries offer cash lotto and scratch-off instant games. Players of lotto games select a group of numbers from a large set and are then awarded prizes based on how many of their numbers are picked in a random drawing. Most lotto tickets sell for $1, and drawings are held once or twice per week to determine the winning numbers. Scratch-off instant games are paper tickets on which certain spaces have been coated with a scratch-off substance that when removed reveals numbers or text underneath that must match posted sequences to win.

Most states offer other numbers games, such as three- and four-digit games. Pull tabs, spiel, keno, and video lottery games are much less common. Pull tabs are two-ply paper tickets that must be separated to reveal symbols or numbers underneath that must match posted sequences

to win. Spiel is an add-on feature to a lotto game that provides an extra set of numbers for a fee that must be matched to numbers selected in the random drawing to win. Keno is a lotto game in which a set of numbers is selected from a large field of numbers; players select a smaller set of numbers and are awarded prizes based on how many of their numbers match those in the drawn set. Video lottery terminals are electronic games of chance played on video screens that simulate popular casino games such as poker and blackjack. Keno and video lottery games are considered by many to be casino-type games, especially because they can be played every few minutes (in the case of fast keno) or at will (in the case of video lottery terminals), which makes them more controversial and generally less acceptable than more traditional lottery games.

As of January 2013, many lottery games were conducted using computer networks. Retail outlets have computer terminals that are linked by phone lines to a central computer at the lottery commission, which records wagers as they are made. The computer network is a private, dedicated network that can be accessed only by lottery officials and retailers. Players can either choose their numbers themselves or allow the computer to select numbers randomly, an option known as Quick Pick. The computer link allows retailers to validate winning tickets.

Most lotto drawings are televised live. Some states also air lottery game shows in which contestants compete for money and prizes. For example, *The Big Spin*, the California State Lottery's 30-minute game show, was broadcast from 1985 to 2009. Michigan Lottery began airing the quarterly game show *Make Me Rich!* in October 2009. Contestants must mail in an instant lotto ticket to win a chance to compete in the show. Several games give contestants the chance to win a new car or up to $2 million.

Lottery winners generally have six months to one year to collect their prizes, depending on state rules. If the top prize, typically called the jackpot, is not won, the amount of the jackpot usually rolls over to the next drawing, increasing the jackpot. Lotteries are often most popular when the jackpot has rolled over several times and grown to an unusually large amount.

Most states allow players to choose in advance how a jackpot will be paid to them—either all at once (the cash lump-sum prize) or in installments (an annuity, usually paid out over 20 or 25 years). Either way, in most states taxes are subtracted from the prize.

Scratch Games

In 1974 Massachusetts became the first state to offer an instant lottery game using scratch-off tickets. By 2013 games involving scratch-off tickets (or "scratchers," as they are called in some states) were extremely popular. Lottery organizations offer many different scratch games with various themes.

Scratch games run for a specified period, usually for several months to a year. Many scratch-off tickets allow a player to win multiple times on each ticket. The top prize amounts are often hundreds of thousands of dollars. However, some of the games offer prizes besides money, including merchandise, trips, vehicles, and tickets to sporting events or concerts. For example, in 2006 a Missouri scratch game gave away a seat at a table at the World Poker Tour tournament. In 2010 the Illinois Lottery unveiled a scratch game in which the top-five prizes were full tuition and fees for four years at the college or university of the winner's choice. The total winnings for such prizes often include payment by the lottery commission of federal and state income taxes on the value of the prizes.

Many lotteries have teamed with sports franchises and other companies to provide popular products as prizes. For example, in June 2008 the New Jersey Lottery announced a scratch game in which a Harley-Davidson motorcycle was the top prize. Many brand-name promotions feature famous celebrities, sports figures and teams, or cartoon characters. These merchandising deals benefit the companies through product exposure and advertising; the lotteries benefit because the companies share advertising costs.

In 2013 most states offered "high-profit point tickets"—scratch-off tickets priced as high as $30, which are often part of a holiday or themed promotion. (Traditional scratch-off tickets sell for $1 to $5.) The higher-priced tickets appeal to many scratch players because they offer more valuable prizes and payouts than regular-priced tickets. However, in "'Zero' Chance Lottery Tickets Stun Some Players" (CNN.com, July 7, 2008), Jason Carroll and Susan Chun report that in 2008 state lotteries came under fire for continuing to sell the high-priced scratch-off tickets even after the top prize had been won. In fact, Scott Hoover of Washington and Lee University sued the state of Virginia for a breach of contract after he bought a scratch-off ticket called "Beginner's Luck" and later learned that the top prizes had already been won. Dennis Cauchon notes in "Scratcher Lottery Tickets under Fire" (*USA Today*, June 29, 2008) that even though lawsuits such as Hoover's were unsuccessful in the courts, the bad publicity they engendered led many states, including Virginia, to stop selling scratch-off tickets after the top prizes were gone.

Most lotteries operate toll-free numbers or websites that provide information on scratch-game prizes. Patrons can find out which prizes have been awarded and which remain to be claimed.

Second-Chance Games

Sometimes even nonwinning lottery tickets have value. Most state lotteries run occasional second-chance drawings—and even third-chance drawings—in which holders of nonwinning tickets for particular games can still win cash or prizes. For example, in "Miami Dolphins, Florida Lottery Launch Scratch-Off Game" (*Sun-Sentinel* [Fort Lauderdale, Florida], July 30, 2010), Sarah Talalay notes that in 2010 the state of Florida partnered with the Miami Dolphins to sell Dolphins scratch-off tickets. Losing tickets could be entered into the lottery's website to win Dolphins tickets, VIP passes, sports gear, and stadium tours. According to the Maryland State Lottery Agency, in "2nd Chance Contests" (2013, http://mdlottery.com/games/2nd-chance-contests/), Ravens Cash Fantasy players could enter losing tickets for a chance to win $250,000, "Season Tickets for Life" to Baltimore Ravens football games, or other prizes. The Nebraska Lottery explains in "Truck$ and Buck$ Second-Chance Giveaway" (2012, http://www.nelottery.com/article.xsp?aid=2701) that its Truck$ and Buck$ tickets could be entered for a chance to win a new pickup truck.

Video Lottery Games

Video lottery games are highly profitable computer games that are played on video lottery terminals (VLTs). They are monitored and controlled by a central computer system that is overseen by a state's lottery agency. In 2013 VLTs were operated in eight states: Delaware, Maryland, Montana, New York, Oregon, Rhode Island, South Dakota, and West Virginia. In 2006 three of these states, Delaware, Rhode Island, and West Virginia, launched the first multistate, progressive video lottery game (a progressive jackpot is one that increases with each game played). Known as Ca$hola, the game begins with a $250,000 jackpot.

VLTs in Rhode Island are leased by the state to private operators. VLTs in the other states are owned and operated by state lottery commissions. In Delaware, New York, and Rhode Island, VLTs are only allowed at racetracks. Except in New York, profits from the VLTs are split between the racetracks and the state lotteries. The VLTs in New York were challenged in court because the state's constitution requires that lottery proceeds benefit education programs. Some VLT revenue was going to racetracks, so the courts declared the diversion of lottery revenue unconstitutional. In 2005 the state legislature amended the law. Under the new legislation the money for the racetrack owners comes out of the state's general fund and all the money gathered from the VLTs goes to education.

VLTs were introduced in Iowa in 2003, and eventually nearly 6,000 VLTs were bringing in over $1.1 billion in revenue. However, calls to the state's hotline for gambling problems rose in 2005, largely because of VLTs, so the state legislature decided to shut down the VLT program in 2006.

Video lottery games have become controversial because many people consider them hard-core gambling. They allow continuous gambling for large sums of money, as opposed to lotto play, which features drawings only once or twice per week. Opponents of video lottery games contend that they are much more addictive than traditional lottery games because of their availability and instant payoffs. They also contend that the games have a special appeal to young people, who are accustomed to playing video games.

Powerball and Mega Millions

During the 1980s lottery officials realized that multistate lotteries could offer higher payoffs than single-state lotteries because the costs of running one game could be shared. The Multi-State Lottery Association (MUSL) was formed in 1987 as a nonprofit association of states offering lotteries. It administers a variety of games, the best known of which is Powerball. In this lotto game each ticket has six numbers: five numbers are selected out of 55 numbers, and then a separate number, the Powerball, is selected out of 42 numbers. The odds of winning the jackpot are about 195 million to 1. Drawings have been held twice weekly since the first drawing in April 1992. As of January 2013, the largest jackpot ever paid out was $587.5 million in November 2012. It was split evenly between two winners in Arizona and Missouri.

Mega Millions is a popular multistate game that is offered in 42 states and the District of Columbia. Players choose six numbers from two separate number pools: five numbers from 1 to 56, and one number from 1 to 46. All six numbers must be chosen in the drawing to win the jackpot. The Texas Lottery Commission and the Center for Public Policy at the University of Houston find in *Demographic Survey of Texas Lottery Players 2011* (December 2011, http://www.uh.edu/hcpp/Texas-Lottery-Report-2011%20%28FINAL%29.pdf) that more than half of Texas Mega Millions players, or 52.9%, purchased Mega Millions tickets "a few times" in 2011; more than a quarter (26.9%) played Mega Millions at least once a week. (See Figure 7.1.) As of January 2013, the biggest Mega Millions jackpot was won in March 2012—$640 million was split between three winners in Illinois, Kansas, and Maryland.

In 2013 MUSL (http://www.powerball.com/pb_about .asp) had 33 members. Each member state offered at least one MUSL game. In January 2010 most states offering Mega Millions began offering Powerball as well. As of January 2013, 41 states, the U.S. Virgin Islands, and the District of Columbia offered Powerball. Only two U.S.

FIGURE 7.1

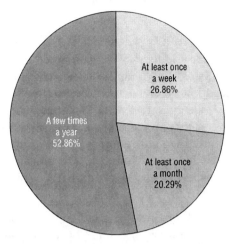

Percentage of Texas respondents playing Mega Millions, by frequency, 2011

[Sample size = 350]

At least once a week 26.86%

A few times a year 52.86%

At least once a month 20.29%

SOURCE: "Figure 18. Frequency of Purchasing Mega Millions Tickets," in *Demographic Study of Texas Lottery Players 2011*, University of Houston, Hobby Center for Public Policy, December 2011, http://www .txlottery.org/export/sites/lottery/Documents/Texas-Lottery-Report-2011.pdf (accessed August 25, 2012). Courtesy of the Texas Lottery Commission.

jurisdictions with lotteries did not offer Powerball: California and Puerto Rico. However, according to the news report "Commission Unanimously Approves Adding Powerball to California Lottery" (November 29, 2012, http://sacramento .cbslocal.com/2012/11/29/commission-unanimously-approves-adding-powerball-to-california-lottery/), in November 2012 the California State Lottery Commission voted to begin selling Powerball tickets in April 2013. Industry analysts believe that Mega Millions and Powerball will eventually be merged into a single "national" game.

Even though Powerball and Mega Millions are the most widely available multistate lottery games, other games are also available. Players of Hot Lotto compete for a $1 million jackpot by picking five white numbers from 1 to 30 and one orange number from 1 to 19. Numbers are drawn twice per week; if no one wins, the jackpot continues to grow. The game is available in 15 locations: Delaware, Idaho, Iowa, Kansas, Maine, Minnesota, Montana, New Hampshire, New Mexico, North Dakota, Oklahoma, South Dakota, Vermont, West Virginia, and the District of Columbia.

Other games are offered regionally. Wild Card 2 is offered in four states: Idaho, Montana, North Dakota, and South Dakota. Players pick five numbers between 1 and 31 and one of 16 different "wild cards." Drawings are held twice per week. 2by2 is played daily in Kansas, Nebraska, and North Dakota; players pick two red numbers and two white numbers from 1 to 26, giving them eight ways to win the $22,000 jackpot. Win for Life is played in Georgia, Kentucky, Oregon, and Virginia; players choose six numbers from 1 to 42. Drawings are held twice per week. Grand prize winners receive $1,000 per week for life.

HOW LOTTERIES OPERATE

In 2013 most lotteries were administered directly by state lottery boards or commissions. Quasi-governmental or privatized lottery corporations operate the lotteries in Connecticut, Georgia, Kentucky, Louisiana, and Tennessee. In most states enforcement authority regarding fraud and abuse rested with the attorney general's office, state police, or the lottery commission. The amount of oversight and control that each legislature has over its lottery agency differs from state to state.

Even though lotteries are a multimillion-dollar business, lottery commissions employ only a few thousand people nationwide. Lottery commissions set up, monitor, and run the games that are offered in their state, but the vast majority of lottery sales are by retail outlets that contract to sell the games.

Retailers

According to the NASPL in "Did You Know" (2013, http://www.naspl.org/index.cfm?fuseaction=content &menuid=14&pageid=1020), lottery tickets were sold at approximately 240,000 locations throughout North America in 2013. Most lottery ticket retailers were located in convenience stores, supermarkets, and gas stations.

Retailers get commissions on lottery sales and bonuses when they sell winning tickets. They also get increased store traffic and media attention, especially if they become known as "lucky" places to purchase lottery tickets. Some state lottery websites list the stores where winners purchased their tickets. For example, in "Lucky Retailers" (2013, http://www.calottery.com/lucky-retailers), the California State Lottery notes that one retailer in San Lorenzo, California, had sold four winning million-dollar-plus tickets as of 2013.

Lottery tickets are often impulse purchases, so retailers sell them near the checkout. This also allows store operators to keep an eye on ticket vending machines to prevent play by underage customers. Because convenience stores increasingly offer pay-at-the-pump gasoline sales—transactions that are likely to decrease in-store traffic—lottery officials in Minnesota and several other states are contemplating ways to sell and print tickets at the gas pumps. In fact, a patent (U.S. Patent 6364206, http://www.patentstorm.us/patents/6364206.html) was issued in 2002 that would enable lottery ticket transactions at gas pumps.

In "Q&A with *The Lottery Wars* Author Matthew Sweeney" (*Time*, June 16, 2009), Brad Tuttle notes that Matthew Sweeney, the author of *The Lottery Wars: Long Odds, Fast Money, and the Battle over an American Institution* (2009), suggests that state lotteries are increasingly selling lottery tickets through vending machines in an effort to eliminate long lines in convenience stores and as a way to draw younger players into the stores. John Lyon reports in "Family Council Wants Ban on Lottery Vending Machines" (*Arkansas News* [Little Rock, Arkansas], April 22, 2010) that in 2010 Arkansas installed 100 lottery ticket vending machines throughout the state. In "Lawmakers Hear from Opponents of Lottery Vending Machines" (*Arkansas News*, August 26, 2010), Lyon notes that as of August 2010, 36 states sold lottery tickets through vending machines.

LOTTERY PLAYER DEMOGRAPHICS

In *2012 State of the States: The AGA Survey of Casino Entertainment* (2012, http://www.americangaming.org/files/aga/uploads/docs/sos/aga_sos_2012_web.pdf), the American Gaming Association (AGA) indicates that 44% of adults purchased a lottery ticket in 2011, which was by far the most common form of gambling surveyed. Many state lottery commissions conduct demographic studies of lottery players, largely because they want to better target them in marketing campaigns. The findings in two states provide some insight into lottery players.

Texas

In *Demographic Survey of Texas Lottery Players 2011*, the Texas Lottery Commission and the Hobby Center for Public Policy state that 40.5% of state residents played some form of lottery game in 2011, up from 33.8% in 2010. (See Figure 7.2.) In general, lottery players in Texas were slightly more likely than non-lottery players to be employed full time. (See Table 7.2.) Respondents between the ages of 45 and 54 were the most likely to play the lottery, with nearly half (47.3%) of that age group purchasing lottery tickets in 2011; by comparison, fewer than one in five residents (19.4%) between the ages of 18 and 24 played the lottery that year. (See Table 7.3.)

The amount of money various demographic groups spent on the lottery differed greatly, however. In Texas, minorities, males, and individuals without college degrees were likely to spend the most on the lottery in 2011. (See Table 7.3.) According to the Texas Lottery Commission and the Hobby Center for Public Policy, the most popular game was Lotto Texas: 71.5% of people who played lottery games played Lotto Texas, and over one-third (34.8%) of these people purchased tickets at least once per week.

FIGURE 7.2

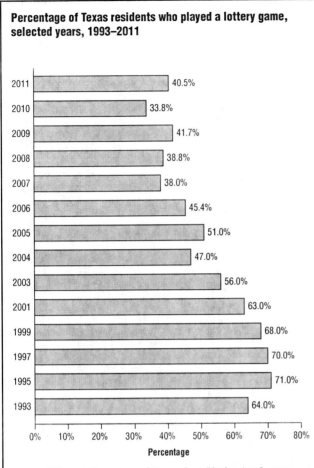

Percentage of Texas residents who played a lottery game, selected years, 1993–2011

Year	Percentage
2011	40.5%
2010	33.8%
2009	41.7%
2008	38.8%
2007	38.0%
2006	45.4%
2005	51.0%
2004	47.0%
2003	56.0%
2001	63.0%
1999	68.0%
1997	70.0%
1995	71.0%
1993	64.0%

Percentage

SOURCE: "Figure 1. Percentage of Respondents Playing Any Lottery Game," in *Demographic Study of Texas Lottery Players 2011*, University of Houston, Hobby Center for Public Policy, December 2011, http://www.txlottery.org/export/sites/lottery/Documents/Texas-Lottery-Report-2011.pdf (accessed August 25, 2012). Courtesy of the Texas Lottery Commission.

South Carolina

According to the South Carolina Education Lottery in *Player Profile Study 2006* (September 2006, http://www.statelibrary.sc.gov/scedocs/L917/000391.ppt), 54% of those polled had played the South Carolina lottery. About 51% of females surveyed had played the lottery, as opposed to 49% of males. A higher percentage of African-Americans (62%) had played the lottery than whites (50%). Of all age groups, a higher percentage of people between 35 and 54 years had played the lottery (58%) than any other age group.

Seventeen percent of players in the South Carolina survey said they played the lottery more than once per week during the past year ("frequent players"), 13% said they played about once per week ("regular players"), and the rest said they played one to three times per month ("occasional players") or less ("infrequent players"). In South Carolina, high school educated, middle-aged men in the middle of the economic spectrum were more likely to be "frequent players" than any other demographic group.

The South Carolina Education Lottery also reports where and when South Carolinians purchased their tickets. In 2006 people usually purchased tickets at a gas station or convenience store that sold gas (91%), as opposed to a grocery store (12%) or a convenience store without gas (8%). Most players purchased their tickets on the weekdays (44%), versus the weekend (32%), or both (18%). Sixty percent reported purchasing their tickets after four o'clock in the afternoon. The most popular game was Powerball, which was played by 43% of those polled. Another 41% played scratch-off tickets.

GROUP PLAY

Groups of people frequently pool their money to buy lottery tickets, particularly for large jackpots. Group wins are beneficial to the lotteries because they generate more media coverage than solo wins and expose a wider group of friends, relatives, and coworkers to the idea that lotteries are winnable. However, pooling arrangements, even those between only two people, can lead to disagreements if a group actually wins a jackpot. Several such groups have ended up in court, but given the number of winners every year, such cases are relatively rare.

Some states have formalized group play. For example, the California State Lottery started the Jackpot Captain program in 2001 to help "group leaders" manage lotto pools. Lotto captains have access to a special website that gives them tips on organizing and running group play. They can download and print forms that help them track players, games, dates, and jackpots. Lotto captains can also participate in special drawings for cash and prizes. As of January 2013, the Rhode Island Lottery established the most recent captains program in April 2008. The state lottery offers the PowerBall and Mega Millions Group Play Program, which allows group play captains access to a special group play page and a group play tool kit.

WHY DO PEOPLE PLAY LOTTERIES?

A lottery is a unique gambling event because it costs only a small amount of money for a chance to win a large jackpot. Even though the odds are extremely long, the huge jackpot is the main selling feature. Rollover jackpots spur ticket sales. As more people buy tickets, the jackpot grows, whereas the odds of winning decrease. However, this does not deter people from buying tickets—sales actually increase under these circumstances.

Mark D. Griffiths and Richard T. A. Wood of Nottingham Trent University examine in *Lottery Gambling and Addiction: An Overview of European Research* (April 28, 2000, https://www.european-lotteries.org/data/info_130/Wood.pdf) why people continue to play the lottery despite the long odds. Among the most common reasons are the lure of a large jackpot in exchange for a small investment;

TABLE 7.2

Demographic characteristics of Texas lottery players and non-players, 2009–11

	All (Sample size = 1,697)		Past-year players (Sample size = 687)		Non-players (Sample size = 1,010)	
Demographic factors	Number and percentage responding					
Year*						
2011	1,697	(100%)	687	(40.48%)	1,010	(59.52%)
2010	1,691	(100%)	572	(33.83%)	1,119	(66.17%)
2009	1,678	(100%)	699	(41.66%)	979	(58.34%)
Income	**Sample size = 1,067 (100%)**		**Sample size = 450 (100%)**		**Sample size = 617 (100%)**	
Less than $12,000	75	(7.03%)	19	(4.22%)	56	(9.08%)
Between $12,000 and $19,999	96	(9.00%)	32	(7.11%)	64	(10.37%)
Between $20,000 and $29,999	119	(11.15%)	58	(12.89%)	61	(9.89%)
Between $30,000 and $39,999	105	(9.84%)	38	(8.44%)	67	(10.86%)
Between $40,000 and $49,999	94	(8.81%)	43	(9.56%)	51	(8.27%)
Between $50,000 and $59,999	88	(8.25%)	39	(8.67%)	49	(7.94%)
Between $60,000 and $74,999	91	(8.53%)	48	(10.67%)	43	(6.97%)
Between $75,000 and $100,000	133	(12.46%)	65	(14.44%)	68	(11.02%)
More than $100,000	266	(24.93%)	108	(24.00%)	158	(25.61%)
Employment status	**Sample size = 1,679 (100%)**		**Sample size = 680 (100%)**		**Sample size = 999 (100%)**	
Employed full-time	751	(44.73%)	321	(47.21%)	430	(43.04%)
Employed part-time	107	(6.37%)	41	(6.03%)	66	(6.61%)
Unemployed/looking for work	137	(8.16%)	56	(8.24%)	81	(8.11%)
Not in labor force	94	(5.60%)	38	(5.59%)	56	(5.61%)
Retired	590	(35.14%)	224	(32.94%)	366	(36.64%)
Own or rent home	**Sample size = 1,671 (100%)**		**Sample size = 675 (100%)**		**Sample size = 996 (100%)**	
Own	1,344	(80.43%)	551	(81.63%)	793	(79.62%)
Rent	296	(17.71%)	113	(16.74%)	183	(18.37%)
Occupied without payment	31	(1.86%)	11	(1.63%)	20	(2.01%)
Age of respondent	**Sample size = 1,556 (100%)**		**Sample size = 630 (100%)**		**Sample size = 926 (100%)**	
18 to 24	103	(6.62%)	20	(3.17%)	83	(8.96%)
25 to 34	115	(7.39%)	43	(6.83%)	72	(7.78%)
35 to 44	210	(13.50%)	90	(14.29%)	120	(12.96%)
45 to 54	275	(17.67%)	130	(20.63%)	145	(15.66%)
55 to 64	371	(23.84%)	173	(27.46%)	198	(21.38%)
65 and over	482	(30.98%)	174	(27.62%)	308	(33.26%)

Note: There was a statistically significant difference between players and non-players regarding the distribution by income status of the respondents.
*More respondents reported that they participated in any of the Texas lottery games during the past year for the 2011 survey than did for 2010.

SOURCE: "Table 1. Demographics," in *Demographic Study of Texas Lottery Players 2011*, University of Houston, Hobby Center for Public Policy, December 2011, http://www.txlottery.org/export/sites/lottery/Documents/Texas-Lottery-Report-2011.pdf (accessed August 25, 2012). Courtesy of the Texas Lottery Commission.

successful advertising; publicity about jackpot winners; ignorance of probability theory; televised drawings; overestimating the positive outcomes and underestimating the negative ones; the credibility of government backing; and players' belief in their own luck. However, perhaps the most important finding by Griffiths and Wood concerns the role of entrapment. According to the researchers, many people select the same numbers week after week. As time goes by and their numbers are not selected, they do not become discouraged. Instead, they think their chances of winning are getting better. Often, players experience near misses, in which two or more of their numbers come up in the jackpot drawing. This only convinces them that they are getting closer to the big win. They become increasingly entrapped in playing their numbers and fear skipping even one drawing. According to Wood and Griffiths, this mind-set has its roots in a common myth that the probability of winning increases the longer a losing streak lasts.

In "Wins, Winning, and Winners: The Commercial Advertising of Lottery Gambling" (*Journal of Gambling Studies*, vol. 25, no. 3, September 2009), John L. McMullan and Delthia Miller of Saint Mary's University find that lottery advertisements play on the perceived benefits of playing the lottery to entice people to play. Advertisements emphasize what the researchers call an "ethos of winning" by embedding words and symbols into advertisements that convey "imagery of plentitude and certitude" without referencing the extremely long odds of winning. McMullan and Miller conclude that lottery advertisements exploit some factors that are associated with problem gambling.

Emily Haisley, Romel Mostafa, and George Loewenstein of Carnegie Mellon University find in "Subjective Relative Income and Lottery Ticket Purchases" (*Journal of Behavioral Decision Making*, vol. 21, no. 3, July 2008) that people who perceive themselves as poor are more likely to buy lottery tickets and are more likely to buy

TABLE 7.3

Percentage of Texas residents who played a lottery game in the past year, by demographic characteristics and median dollars spent per month, 2009–11

Year	Percentage played	Median dollars spent
2011	40.5	$13.00
2010	33.8	10.00
2009	41.7	10.00
Demographic factors 2011		
Education		
Less than high school diploma	34.7	25.00
High school degree	40.5	15.00
Some college	45.1	18.00
College degree	38.5	10.00
Graduate degree	38.3	4.50
Income		
Under $12,000	25.3	11.00
$12,000 to $19,999	33.3	22.00
$20,000 to $29,999	48.7	18.00
$30,000 to $39,999	36.2	20.00
$40,000 to $49,999	45.7	20.00
$50,000 to $59,999	44.3	8.00
$60,000 to $74,999	52.7	10.50
$75,000 to $100,000	48.9	15.00
More than $100,000	40.6	11.00
Race		
White	39.1	10.00
Black	43.6	25.50
Asian	30.6	20.00
Native American Indian	50.0	17.00
Other	45.5	20.00
Hispanic origin		
Yes	44.1	20.00
No	39.8	11.00
Gender		
Female	37.5	15.00
Male	44.1	12.00
Age		
18 to 24	19.4	11.50
25 to 34	37.4	15.00
35 to 44	42.9	14.50
45 to 54	47.3	14.50
55 to 64	46.6	15.00
65 or older	36.1	12.00
Employment status		
Employed full/part time	42.2	14.00
Unemployed	40.9	14.50
Retired	38.0	13.00

Note: In some categories, the number of respondents contributing to cell percentages is small. This has the effect of making generalizations from these figures more tenuous. Due to greater uncertainty, small sample size also requires larger discrepancies among categories to attain acceptable levels of statistical significance.

SOURCE: "Table 2. Any Game: Past-Year Lottery Play and Median Dollars Spent per Month by Demographics," in *Demographic Study of Texas Lottery Players 2011*, University of Houston, Hobby Center for Public Policy, December 2011, http://www.txlottery.org/export/sites/lottery/Documents/Texas-Lottery-Report-2011.pdf (accessed August 25, 2012). Courtesy of the Texas Lottery Commission.

more lottery tickets than people who do not perceive themselves as poor. The researchers find that buying lottery tickets sets up a vicious cycle for poor people: it exploits individuals' desires to escape poverty, but it also contributes to their inability to improve their financial situation.

THE EFFECTS OF LOTTERIES
Economic Effects

Lottery proponents usually use economic arguments to justify their position. They point out that lotteries provide state governments with a relatively easy way to increase their revenues without imposing more taxes. The games are financially beneficial to the many small businesses that sell lottery tickets and to the larger companies that participate in merchandising campaigns or that provide advertising or computer services. In addition, lottery advocates suggest that the games provide cheap entertainment to people who want to play, while raising money for the betterment of all.

Lottery opponents also have economic arguments. They contend that lotteries contribute only a small percentage of total state revenues and, therefore, have a limited effect on state programs. Lotteries cost money to operate and lure people into parting with their money under false hopes. In addition, opponents contend that those targeted by lotteries come particularly from lower-income brackets and may not be able to afford to gamble.

THE DIVISION OF LOTTERY MONEY. The sales amount is the total amount taken in by the lottery. This sales amount is then split between prizes, administrative costs, retailer commissions, and state profits. In general, 50% to 60% of U.S. lottery sales are paid out as prizes to winners. Administrative costs for advertising, employee salaries, and other operating expenses usually account for 1% to 10% of sales. On average, retailers collect 5% to 8% of sales in the form of commissions and approximately 2% as bonuses for selling winning tickets. The remaining 30% to 40% is turned over to the state.

According to the NASPL, U.S. state lotteries reported $68.8 billion in sales in FY 2012. (See Table 7.1.) By comparison, in 2011 sales topped $63.1 billion. In FY 2012 New York ($8.4 billion) had the highest lottery sales, followed by Massachusetts ($4.7 billion), Florida ($4.5 billion), and California ($4.4 billion). These four states accounted for 31.9% of national lottery sales. Twenty-one states had lottery sales of more than $1 billion in FY 2012.

The states took in $19.4 billion in profits from the lottery in FY 2012, a 5% increase over total profits of $18.4 billion generated in 2011. (See Table 7.1.) As the NASPL reports, by June 2009 a total of $291.9 billion had been given to various beneficiaries since the beginning of lotteries in each state. (See Table 7.4.) New York topped the list with $36.7 billion in profits allocated to education. California followed with $21.8 billion to education, while Florida allocated $20.3 billion to the state's Education Enhancement Trust Fund. In 2012 New York again led all states, granting $2.9 billion in lottery profits to state education programs. (See Table 7.5.)

TABLE 7.4

Cumulative lottery contributions to beneficiaries, by state or province, from start to June 30, 2009

[In millions]

Arizona (1982)

Local transportation assistance fund	$625.85
County assistance fund	$175.20
Heritage fund	$358.53
Economic development fund	$60.47
Mass transit	$92.67
Healthy Arizona	$103.54
General fund (by category)	
Education	$531.54
Health and welfare	$218.00
Protection and safety	$98.80
General government	$51.57
Inspection and regulation	$8.52
Natural resources	$7.98
Department of Gaming (Responsible gaming support)	$1.50
Court appointed special advocate fund (unclaimed prizes)	$36.76
Clean air fund (unclaimed prizes)	$0.50
State general fund (unclaimed prizes)	$1.50
Homeless shelters	$1.00
Total	**$2,373.93**

Arkansas (2009)

Educational trust fund	**$22.20**

California (1985)

Education	**$21,796.23**

Colorado (1983)

Capital construction fund	$440.00
Division of parks and outdoor recreation	$208.00
Conservation trust fund	$835.00
Great outdoors Colorado trust fund	$676.00
General fund	$1.20
School fund	$50.00
Total	**$2,210.20**

Connecticut (1972)

General fund (to benefit education, roads, health and hospitals, public safety, etc.)	**$6,692.68**

D.C. (1982)

General fund	**$1,600.00**

Delaware (1975)

General fund	$3,078.50
Health & social services-problem gambler programs	$18.40
Total	**$3,096.90**

Florida (1987)

Education enhancement trust fund	**$20,265.40**

Georgia (1993)

Lottery for education account	**$12,300.00**

Idaho (1989)

Public schools (K–12)	$218.65
Public buildings	$218.65
Total	**$437.30**

Illinois (1974)

Illinois common school fund (K–12)	$15,470.65
Illinois veterans assistance fund	$7.24
Ticket for the Cure fund	$6.85
Quality of Life Endowment fund	$1.43
Multiple sclerosis research fund	$2.38
Total	**$15,488.55**

Indiana (1989)

Build Indiana fund	$2,700.00
Teachers' retirement fund	$637.60
Police & fire pension relief fund	$449.70
Other state funds	$1.80
Total	**$3,789.10**

Iowa (1985)

Iowa plan (economic development)	$170.32
CLEAN fund (environment and agriculture)	$35.89
Gambling treatment fund	$15.73
Special appropriations	$13.77
General fund	$1,007.50
Veterans trust fund	$5.44
Total	**$1,248.65**

Kansas (1987)

Economic development initiatives fund	$731.85
Correctional institutions building fund	$86.26
County reappraisal project (Fiscal year 1988–1990)	$17.20
Juvenile detention facilities fund	$30.19
State general fund (Fiscal year 1995–2004)	$157.70
Problem gambling grant fund	$0.64
Veterans programs	$5.40
Total	**$1,029.24**

Kentucky (1989)

Education	$214.00
Vietnam veterans	$32.00
General fund	$1,449.50
Post-secondary & college scholarships	$1,270.30
Affordable housing trust fund	$20.80
Literacy programs & early childhood reading	$30.00
Total	**$3,016.60**

Louisiana (1991)

Various state agencies	$147.30
State general fund	$69.20
Minimum foundation program—funding elementary & secondary education in public schools	$1,906.80
Problem gambling	$7.00
Total	**$2,130.30**

Maine (1974)

General fund	$985.85
Outdoor heritage fund	$16.16
Total	**$1,002.01**

Maryland (1973)

General fund	$10,724.00
Subdivisions (for one year only Fiscal year 1984–1985)	$31.25
Stadium authority	$507.00
Total	**$11,262.25**

Massachusetts (1972)

Cities and towns	$12,786.84
Arts council	$199.51
General fund	$3,070.04
Compulsive gamblers	$10.95
Total	**$16,067.34**

Michigan (1972)

Education (K–12)	$15,177.97
General fund	$600.63
Total	**$15,778.60**

RETAILER PAYMENTS. According to the U.S. Census Bureau in "Income and Apportionment of State-Administered Lottery Funds: 2010" (December 14, 2011, http://www.census.gov/govs/state/10lottery.html), $32.8 billion was given out as prizes in state lotteries in 2010. That was 62% of the total lottery revenue in that year. Administrative costs, including retailer compensation, made up approximately $2.6 billion (4.9%) of the total revenue, whereas state profit was $17.8 billion (33.5%).

TABLE 7.4

Cumulative lottery contributions to beneficiaries, by state or province, from start to June 30, 2009 [CONTINUED]

[In millions]

Minnesota (1989)

General fund	$1,031.24
Environmental and natural resources trust fund	$490.03
Game & fish fund	$93.59
Natural resources fund	$93.59
Other state programs	$39.84
Compulsive gambling	$28.20
Total	**$1,776.49**

Missouri (1986)

Public education (1994–present)	$3,800.00
General revenue fund (1986–1993)	$542.54
Total	**$4,342.54**

Montana (1987)

State of Montana general fund	$121.21
Property tax relief	$15.32
School equalization aid account	$34.87
Board of crime control	$1.75
Study of socioeconomic impact on gambling	$0.10
Total	**$173.25**

Nebraska (1993)

Compulsive gamblers assistance fund	$7.90
Education innovation fund	$123.95
Environmental trust fund	$143.42
Solid waste landfill closure assistance fund	$18.46
General fund	$5.00
State fair support & improvement fund	$12.69
Nebraska scholarship fund	$37.93
Total	**$349.35**

New Hampshire (1964)

Education	**$1,303.24**

New Jersey (1970)

Education and institutions	**$18,000.00**

New Mexico (1996)

Public school capital outlay	$66.55
Lottery tuition fund	$336.01
Total	**$402.56**

New York (1967)

Education	**$36,700.00**

North Carolina

Education	**$413.93**

North Dakota (2004)

Compulsive gambling fund	$1.20
State general fund	$30.93
Drug task force	$0.85
Total	**$32.98**

Ohio (1974)

Education	**$17,093.90**

Oklahoma (2005)

Education	**$279.16**

Oregon (1985)

Economic development	$1,850.00
Public education	$4,130.00
Natural resource programs	$660.00
Total	**$6,640.00**

TABLE 7.4

Cumulative lottery contributions to beneficiaries, by state or province, from start to June 30, 2009 [CONTINUED]

[In millions]

Pennsylvania (1972)

Older Pennsylvanians	**$17,742.19**

Rhode Island (1974)

General fund	**$3,642.00**

South Carolina (2002)

Education lottery fund	**$1,990.39**

South Dakota (1989)

General fund	$395.79
Capital construction fund	$35.61
Property tax reduction fund	$1,375.43
Grant to human services	$2.57
Total	**$1,809.40**

Tennessee (2004)

Lottery for education account	$1,706.40
After school program	$68.00
Total	**$1,774.40**

Texas (1992)

Health and human services commission's graduate medical program	$40.00
General revenue fund	$5,168.50
Foundation school fund	$11,674.37
Multicategorical teaching hospital	$140.00
Total	**$17,022.87**

Vermont (1978)

General fund	$212.46
Education fund	$218.41
Total	**$430.87**

Virginia (1988)

General fund (Fiscal year 1989–1998)	$2,788.42
Direct aid to public education K–12 (Fiscal year 1999–present)	$4,335.37
Total	**$7,123.79**

Washington (1982)

General fund	$1,858.80
Education funds	$782.20
Seattle Mariners Stadium (Safeco Field)	$52.40
King County Stadium and Exhibition Center (Qwest Field)	$80.90
Economic devel. strategic reserve	$12.10
Problem gambling	$0.94
Total	**$2,787.34**

West Virginia (1986)

Education	$1,500.00
Senior citizens	$627.00
Tourism	$665.00
General fund	
Other	
Total	**$5,600.00**

Wisconsin (1988)

Public benefit such as property tax relief	**$2,900.00**
Total–US ($US millions)	**$291,938.1**

Atlantic lottery (1976)

Lotteries Commission of New Brunswick	$1,982.36
Provinces of Newfoundland and Labrador	$1,780.49
Nova Scotia Gaming Corporation	$2,627.98
Prince Edward Island Lotteries Commission	$295.57
Total	**$6,686.40**

The primary means of retailer compensation is a commission on each ticket sold. In other words, a lottery retailer keeps a certain percentage of the money that is taken in from lottery sales. Most states also have incentive-based programs for retailers that meet particular sales criteria. For example, the Wisconsin Lottery explains in "Wisconsin Lottery Questions for Prospective Retailers" (2013, http://retailer.wilottery.com/new/faq.aspx) that it pays

TABLE 7.4

Cumulative lottery contributions to beneficiaries, by state or province, from start to June 30, 2009 [CONTINUED]

[In millions]

British Columbia (1974)	
Government of British Columbia	**$9,554.30**
Loto-Québec (1970)	
Consolidated fund	$24,747.00
Government of Canada	$382.03
Special commissions to non-profit organizations	$97.30
Independent community action support fund	$217.50
Agricultural ministry	$58.60
Culture & communication ministry	$3.00
Municipal affairs	$2.60
Social services ministry	$403.00
Total	**$25,911.03**
Ontario (1975)	
Province of Ontario	**$30,300.00**
Western Canada (1974)	
Member provinces and associate territories	**$5,318.00**
Total-Canada ($CDN millions)	**$77,769.73**
Puerto Rico (1991)	
Contingency fund to subsidize rent for elders economically disadvantaged	$40.00
Municipality fund	$437.20
Public health reform	$70.60
General fund	$1,028.20
Total	**$1,576.00**
Mexico (1991)	
Education & health programs	**$9.40**

	2006	2008
West Virginia (1986)	$773.72	$1,013.02
Education	$328.30	$413.19
Senior citizens	$318.33	$365.98
Tourism	$0.00	$0.00
Bonds covering profit areas	$457.74	$613.54
General fund	$802.01	$1,432.07
Other	$2,680.10	$3,837.80

Note: At the time of publication, some data may be unaudited.

SOURCE: "Cumulative Lottery Contributions to Beneficiaries, from Start up Date to 6/30/09," North American Association of State and Provincial Lotteries, April 2011, http://www.naspl.org/UploadedFiles/files/new_cumulative_lottery_contributions_to_beneficiaries.pdf (accessed August 26, 2012)

retailers a 6.3% commission on scratch-off tickets and a 5.5% commission on lottery tickets; retailers that are part of the Retail Performance Program receive a bonus for increasing ticket sales by particular amounts. Lottery officials believe the incentive program, which encourages retailers to ask customers if they would like to buy lottery tickets, is more effective than an increase in commission.

UNCLAIMED LOTTERY WINNINGS. Unclaimed lottery winnings add up to hundreds of millions of dollars each year, and each state handles them differently. Some states, such as New York, require that unclaimed winnings be returned to the prize pool. Other states allocate such funds to lottery administrative costs or to specific state programs. For example, in Texas unclaimed prizes

go to funds that benefit hospital research and payment of indigent health care. As the California State Lottery reports in "Unclaimed Prizes" (2013, http://www.calottery.com/win/unclaimed-prizes), as of FY 2012 almost $750 million in unclaimed money had been allocated to school funding.

TAXES AND OTHER WITHHOLDING FROM LOTTERY WINNINGS. Lottery winnings are usually taxable as personal income. All prizes greater than $600 are reported by the lotteries to the Internal Revenue Service. In general, the lottery agencies subtract taxes before awarding large prizes. For example, in 2012 the New York Lottery withheld federal, state, and local income taxes on prizes greater than $5,000. The lottery withheld 25% for federal taxes and 6.9% for state taxes. An additional 3.7% was withheld if the winner was a New York City resident. Non-U.S. residents faced even higher tax withholding rates. In addition, the New York Lottery is required by law to subtract past-due child support payments and collect repayment of public assistance from prizes of $600 or more.

Education

Lottery proponents often advocate lotteries for their economic benefits to education. Some lotteries dedicate all or a portion of their profits to primary, secondary, or higher education. For example, Washington's Lottery explains in "Beneficiaries" (2013, http://www.walottery.com/Beneficiaries/WhoBenefits/Default.aspx) that a portion of the proceeds from ticket sales go to the Washington Opportunity Pathways Account to provide college scholarships. Opponents, however, often argue that these profits do not provide additional dollars for education but simply replace general fund dollars that would have been spent on education anyway.

Donald E. Miller of Saint Mary's College argues in "Schools Lose out in Lotteries" (*USA Today*, April 14, 2004) that educational spending per student gradually decreases once a state starts a lottery. He examines data for 12 states that had enacted lotteries for education between 1965 and 1990. According to Miller, before lotteries were established the average education spending in those states increased each year by approximately $12 per student. In the first year following the initiation of the lotteries, the states increased their education spending on average by nearly $50 per student. However, the increase fell sharply in subsequent years and eventually lagged behind states without lottery-generated education funds. Miller suggests that legislators use lottery funds "to replace rather than add to existing sources of education funding."

In contrast, Stodghill and Nixon note that in 2006 only 1% to 5% of public education money came from lotteries. Most of the money raised by lotteries is spent on marketing, prizes, and retail commissions. In addition, as

TABLE 7.5

Lottery contributions to beneficiaries, by state or province, fiscal year 2012

[In millions]

Arizona

Heritage Fund	$10.00
Commerce Authority Arizona Competes Fund	$3.50
Mass Transit	$11.20
Healthy Arizona	$19.27
General Fund	$106.15
Court Appointed Special Advocate Fund (Unclaimed prizes)	$2.99
Homeless Shelters	$1.00
Department of Gaming	$0.30
University Bond Fund	$10.29

Arkansas

Educational Trust Fund	$97.50

California

Education	$1,320.73

Colorado

Division of Parks and Wildlife	$12.30
Conservation Trust Fund	$49.30
Great Outdoors Colorado Trust Fund	$57.10
School Fund	$4.50

Connecticut

General Fund (to benefit education, roads, health and hospitals, public safety, etc.)	$310.00

Delaware

General Fund	$269.00
Health & Social Services-Problem Gambler Programs	$2.33

District of Columbia

General Fund	$66.00

Florida

Education Enhancement Trust Fund	$1,321.60

Georgia

HOPE Scholarships	$612.70
Pre-Kindergarten Program	$300.60

Idaho

Public Schools (K–12)	$20.75
Public Buildings	$20.75

Illinois

Illinois Common School Fund (K–12)	$639.88
Illinois Veterans Assistance Fund	$0.80
Ticket For The Cure Fund	$0.70
Quality of Life Endowment Fund	$1.00
Multiple Sclerosis Research Fund	$0.90
Capital Projects Fund	$65.20

Indiana

Build Indiana Fund	$147.59
Teachers Pension Fund	$30.00
Police & Firefighters Pension Fund	$30.00

Iowa

General Fund	$76.01
Veterans Trust Fund	$2.72

Kansas

Not Provided	

Kentucky

General Fund	$45.10
Post-Secondary & College Scholarships	$168.30
Literacy Programs & Early Childhood Reading	$3.00

Louisiana

State Treasury	$156.90

Maine

General Fund	$53.70
Outdoor Heritage Fund	$0.53

TABLE 7.5

Lottery contributions to beneficiaries, by state or province, fiscal year 2012 [CONTINUED]

[In millions]

Maryland

General Fund—Lottery Proceeds	$536.26
Stadium Authority—Lottery Proceeds	$20.00
Education Trust Fund—VLT Proceeds	$94.62
Purse Dedication Account—VLT Proceeds	$13.66
Local Impact Grants—VLT Proceeds	$10.73
Race Tracks Facility Renewal Fund—VLT Proceeds	$4.88
Small, Minority Woman Owned Businesses—VLT Proceeds	$2.92

Massachusetts

Cities and Towns	$833.90
Arts Council	$6.10
General Fund	$78.60
Compulsive Gamblers	$1.20

Michigan

Education (K–12)	$770.00
General Fund	$7.50

Minnesota

General Fund	$66.08
Environmental and Natural Resources Trust Fund	$31.01
Game & Fish Fund	$12.24
Natural Resources Fund	$12.24
Other State Programs	
Compulsive Gambling	$2.08

Missouri

Public Education in Missouri	$280.04

Montana

State of Montana General Fund	$13.10

Nebraska

Compulsive Gamblers Assistance Fund	$0.86
Education Innovation Fund	$7.03
Environmental Trust Fund	$15.83
State Fair Support & Improvement Fund	$3.56
Nebraska Opportunity Grant Fund	$8.80

New Hampshire

Education	$66.77

New Jersey

Education and Institutions	$950.00

New Mexico

Public School Capital Outlay	$66.50
Lottery Tuition Fund	$462.30

New York

Education	$2,887.99

North Carolina

Education	$456.76

North Dakota

Compulsive Gambling Fund	$0.20
State General Fund	$7.00
Drug Task Force	$0.42

Ohio

Education	$771.03

Oklahoma

Education	$69.99

Oregon

Economic Development	$137.00
Public Education	$325.00
Parks and Natural Resource Programs	$82.00

more lotteries are created, they are competing for players, leading lotteries to increase the size of their prizes, which shrinks the percentage of money that goes to education.

THE HELPING OUTSTANDING PUPILS EDUCATIONALLY SCHOLARSHIP PROGRAM. The Georgia Lottery Corporation explains in "Proceeds to Education" (2013, http://www.galottery.com/education) that it funds three educational programs: the Helping Outstanding Pupils Educationally (HOPE) Scholarship Program for college-bound

TABLE 7.5

Lottery contributions to beneficiaries, by state or province, fiscal year 2012 [CONTINUED]

[In millions]

Pennsylvania	
Older Pennsylvanians	$1,060.89
Rhode Island	
General Fund	$377.70
South Carolina	
Education Lottery Fund	$297.70
South Dakota	
General Fund	$6.83
Capital Construction Fund	$6.00
Property Tax Reduction Fund	$87.44
Grant to Human Services	$0.14
Tennessee	
Lottery for Education Account	$310.30
After School Program	$13.00
Texas	
General Revenue Fund	$46.02
Foundation School Fund	$1,096.49
Multicategorical Teaching Hospital	$5.75
Texas Veterans Commission (Veterans Assistance Fund)	$5.31
Vermont	
Education Fund	$22.33
Virginia	
Direct aid to Public Education K–12	$487.10
Washington	
Washington Opportunity Pathways Account	$121.80
Seattle Mariners Stadium (Safeco Field-King County)	$2.70
King County Stadium and Exhibition Center (Qwest Field)	$10.00
Economic Development Strategic Reserve	$3.00
Problem Gambling	$0.30
Veterans Innovations Program	$0.20
West Virginia	
All profits generated transferred to the state less operating and administrative costs.	
Wisconsin	
Public Benefit—Total Available for Property Tax Relief	$175.94
Atlantic	
Lotteries Commission of New Brunswick	$120.01
Provinces of Newfoundland and Labrador	$107.80
Nova Scotia Gaming Corporation	$126.96
Prince Edward Island Lotteries Commission	$14.87
British Columbia	
Government of British Columbia	$289.40
Loto-Quebec	
Government of Canada	$105.00
Special Commissions to Non-Profit Organizations	$17.10
Independent Community Action Support Fund	$15.40
Agricultural Ministry	$6.30
Culture & Communication Ministry	$8.50
Fight Against Excessive Gambling	$30.30
Ministry of Health and Services	$30.00
Ministry of Finance	$0.30
Sponsorships	$14.00
Assistance for International Humanitarian Action	$2.60
Ontario	
Province of Ontario (FY2012)	$1,879.96
Western Canada	
Member Provinces and Associate Territories	$31.20

Note: At the time of publication, some data may be unaudited.

SOURCE: "FY 2012 Contributions to Lottery Beneficiaries by Program," North American Association of State and Provincial Lotteries, January 2013

students, the HOPE PROMISE Teacher Scholarship Program for aspiring teachers, and the HOPE Teacher Scholarship Program for teachers seeking graduate degrees in critical areas of need. The Georgia Lottery Corporation notes that HOPE scholarships and grants are available to Georgia residents who enroll in certain programs at public and private institutions in the state. Students must have at least a 3.0 grade point average to qualify for HOPE money and must maintain their eligibility in subsequent years. Most recipients are recent high school graduates who pursue college degrees.

In "Georgia's HOPE Program" (2009, http://www.gacollege411.org/Financial_Aid_Planning/HOPE_Program/_default.aspx), the Georgia Student Finance Commission explains that the HOPE scholarship pays for tuition, fees, and a $300 book allowance per academic year at public schools. Room and board expenses are not covered. In 2009 the HOPE scholarship provided $4,000 per academic year to full-time students and $2,000 per academic year to part-time students at private schools; public school tuition was paid in full. Georgia students who earned a general equivalency diploma could receive a one-time $500 award that could be used toward tuition or books at a public or private school in Georgia. According to the Georgia Lottery Corporation, as of 2013 the state had given more than $7 billion to 1.4 million recipients through its HOPE scholarship program.

The HOPE scholarship program is one of the country's largest state-financed merit-based aid programs and is credited with significantly increasing the attendance of in-state residents at Georgia colleges. Similar programs include the Kentucky Educational Excellence Scholarship (https://www.kheaa.com/website/kheaa/kees?main=2) and the Florida Bright Futures Scholarship (http://www.floridastudentfinancialaid.org/ssfad/bf/).

Social Effects

According to the NASPL in "Lottery History" (2013, http://www.naspl.org/index.cfm?fuseaction=content&menuid=11&pageid=1016), lotteries operate on every continent except Antarctica. In the United States lotteries enjoy unprecedented popularity. They are legal in 43 states and the District of Columbia and are generally considered a benign form of entertainment with two enormous selling points: they seem to offer a shortcut to the so-called American Dream of wealth and prosperity, and they are a voluntary activity that raises money for the public good in lieu of increased taxes. Opposition to lotteries is generally based on religious or moral reasons. Some people consider all forms of gambling to be wrong, and state-sponsored lotteries may be particularly abhorrent to them.

The National Gambling Impact Study Commission (NGISC) complains in *Final Report* (June 1999, http://govinfo.library.unt.edu/ngisc/reports/fullrpt.html) about the appropriateness of state governments pushing luck, instant gratification, and entertainment as alternatives to hard work, prudent investment, and savings. It suggests that such a message might be particularly troubling if it is directed toward lower-income people.

POVERTY, RACE, AND ETHNICITY. One of the most common criticisms leveled against state lotteries is that they unfairly burden the poor—that they are funded mostly by low-income people who buy tickets, but benefit mostly higher-income people. In economics terminology, a tax that places a higher burden on lower-income groups than higher-income groups (in terms of percentage of their income) is called regressive. Even though the lottery is not really a tax, many people consider it a form of voluntary taxation because the proceeds fund government programs. The economist Philip J. Cook, one of the coauthors of the NGISC's *Final Report*, states that "the tax that is built into lottery is the most regressive tax we know."

The NGISC expresses serious concern about the heavy reliance of lotteries on less-educated, lower-income people. It also mentions that an unusually large number of lottery outlets are concentrated in poor neighborhoods.

Joseph McCrary and Thomas J. Pavlak of the Carl Vinson Institute of Government at the University of Georgia review in *Who Plays the Georgia Lottery?: Results of a Statewide Survey* (2002, http://www.cviog.uga.edu/free-downloads/51.pdf) a number of nationwide and state studies on the relationship between income and lottery participation. The researchers find that "the regressivity finding remains largely consistent throughout the literature." McCrary and Pavlak cite a common belief among lower-income people that playing the lottery is their only chance to escape poverty.

In "Illinois Lottery: The Poor Play More" (*Chicago Reporter*, October 2002), Leah Samuel analyzes the lottery sales in Illinois between FY 1997 and FY 2002 by comparing lottery sales figures around the state with income and demographic data from the 2000 census. The 10 zip codes with the highest lottery sales from FYs 1997 to 2002 were all in Chicago. The residents of all 10 zip codes had average incomes of less than $20,000 per year, compared with the city average of $24,000 per year. Eight of the zip code areas had unemployment rates that were higher than the city average of 10%. Five of the zip codes had a racial breakdown of at least 70% African-Americans. Samuel finds that average lottery sales per capita in the city's mostly African-American zip codes were 29% to 33% higher than in mostly white or Hispanic zip code areas. The zip code with the highest lottery sales in the state, 60619, coincided with predominantly African-American and Latino low-income communities on the city's south side. Residents of that zip code spent nearly $23 million on lottery tickets during FY 2002. Samuel also finds that residents in poorer communities spent a larger portion of their income on lottery tickets than did people in more affluent neighborhoods. Lottery spending during FY 2002 was $224 per person in zip codes that were at least 70% African-American and $173 per person in zip codes that were at least 70% white.

Robert Gebeloff and Judy DeHaven report similar findings in "Who Really Pays for the Lottery" (*Star-Ledger* [Newark, New Jersey], December 6, 2005). Gebeloff and DeHaven gathered data on lottery sales in New Jersey by zip code and compared those data to income and population data for each zip code from 2000 to 2004. The results clearly show that those who lived in poorer areas bought far more lottery tickets than those living in wealthy ones. People who resided in zip codes where the average income was less than $52,151 spent an average of $250 per year on the lottery, whereas those who lived in zip codes with an average income of $117,503 to $141,132 spent an average of $115 per year on lottery tickets. Residents of extremely wealthy neighborhoods—where the average income was more than $141,132—spent an average of $89 per year on lottery tickets. In addition, less wealthy neighborhoods had more lottery retailers per capita. The ratio of lottery retailers per 5,000 people was 4 to 1 in low-income areas, compared with roughly 1.5 to 1 in wealthy neighborhoods.

In "Poor Areas Fuel Lottery" (*Tucson Citizen*, April 6, 2006), Brad Branan notes that the same pattern holds true in Arizona. In lower-income zip codes, Tucson residents spent an average of $177 per year for lottery tickets in FY 2005, which was $35 more per year than residents of upper-income zip codes. Furthermore, there were three times as many retailers selling lottery tickets in lower-income neighborhoods than in higher-income neighborhoods. Steven Levin reports similar findings in "Poverty Leads to Playing Lottery, Study Says" (July 25, 2008, http://www.post-gazette.com/stories/news/education/poverty-leads-to-playing-lottery-study-says-403531/). Citing a study conducted by researchers at Carnegie Mellon University, Levin notes that individuals who perceived themselves to be poor were twice as likely to purchase lottery scratch tickets than those who believed themselves to be relatively affluent. According to Levin, poor people sometimes view the lottery as providing a more "balanced playing field," in contrast to the basic economic inequities they perceive in society in general. In some cases, people living in poverty make their financial situations considerably worse by pinning their hopes on the lottery. As Geoff Williams finds in "Poor People Spend 9% of Income on Lottery Tickets; Here's Why" (May 31, 2010, http://www.dailyfinance.com/2010/05/31/poor-people-spend-9-of-income-on-lottery-tickets-heres-why/?icid=sphere_copyright), people with annual household incomes of under $13,000 spent an average of $645, or nearly 10% of their earnings, on lottery tickets each year. In "Hope and Hard Luck" (December 17, 2010, http://www.ncpolicywatch.com/2010/12/17/hope-and-hard-luck/), Sarah Ovaska reports that lottery ticket sales in Lenoir County, North Carolina—one of the poorest areas of the state—averaged more than $432 per adult resident for FY 2009–10, more than double the state average of just over $200 per adult.

Haisley, Mostafa, Loewenstein, and others back up their studies by finding that people who perceive themselves as poor are more likely to buy lottery tickets than other people. Poor people see the lottery as a way to improve their financial situation. The researchers determine that poor people spending money on the lottery is a factor in their inability to improve their relative finances.

Even when a poor individual does win the lottery, it does not necessarily change their perception of their economic condition. In "Lincoln Park Lottery Winner on Welfare Gets 9 Months of Probation" (July 24, 2012, http://www.freep.com/article/20120724/NEWS02/120724014/Lincoln-Park-lottery-winner-welfare-sentenced-today), Megha Satyanarayan reports about a Michigan woman who continued to receive public assistance, even after winning $1 million in the state lottery. According to Satyanarayan, the winner failed to report her change in income status to the Michigan Department of Human Services because she still "felt entitled to the payments because she needed the help."

RACE AND ETHNICITY OF LOTTERY BENEFICIARIES.
McCrary and Pavlak report that African-Americans and less-educated people are more likely to be active lottery players than whites and more-educated people. Proceeds from the Georgia lottery fund only education programs. If these programs provide more benefits to the poor than to the wealthy, it could be argued that this compensates for the regressive nature of the state lottery.

However, Ross Rubenstein and Benjamin Scafidi, in "Who Pays and Who Benefits: Examining the Distributional Consequences of the Georgia Lottery for Education" (*National Tax Journal*, vol. 55, no. 2, June 2002), and Christopher Cornwell and David Mustard, in *The Distributional Impacts of Lottery-Funded Aid: Evidence from Georgia's HOPE Scholarship* (August 2001, http://www.terry.uga.edu/hope/hope.lottery.pdf), criticize Georgia's lottery for providing more benefits to white households than to minority households. Cornwell and Mustard claim that counties with the highest incomes and white populations receive significantly more HOPE scholarships.

In *HOPE Scholarship: Joint Study Commission Report* (December 2003, http://www.cviog.uga.edu/free-downloads/hope-joint-study-commission-report.pdf), the Carl Vinson Institute of Government argues that a county-by-county comparison of HOPE scholarship recipients is not appropriate because other factors affect these statistics—for example, whether a particular county contains a college or university. However, the institute does conclude that minorities in Georgia are "slightly less likely" than whites to get a HOPE scholarship.

The Vinson Institute reports that lottery play was inversely related to education level. In other words, people with fewer years of education played the lottery more often than those with more years of education. It also finds that lottery spending per person was highest in counties where African-Americans made up a larger percentage of the population.

Regarding the HOPE scholarship program, the Vinson Institute indicates that white students received a disproportionately high amount of the funds, compared with African-American students. In 1999 white students made up 66% of the freshman class in Georgia's colleges and universities, but accounted for 74% of all HOPE scholars. By contrast, 26% of all freshmen were African-Americans, yet they accounted for only 21% of all HOPE scholars. The Vinson Institute notes that this disproportionate relationship was true for every year examined, back to 1994. However, the institute states that the gap narrowed substantially between 1994 and 1999.

Analysis of Georgia's lottery-funded prekindergarten program provides completely different results. The Vinson Institute finds that the rate of enrollment in the prekindergarten program was higher in lower-income areas of the state than in affluent areas. It concludes that this particular lottery program is more beneficial to poorer people, African-Americans, and those who regularly play the lottery than to other groups in the state.

In "State Lotteries: Their Effect on Equal Access to Higher Education" (*Journal of Hispanic Higher Education*, vol. 3, no. 1, January 2004), Randall G. Bowden and Henry E. Elrod confirm the Vinson Institute's findings. The researchers determine that minority and low-income students do not have proportionate access to higher education in lottery states.

COMPULSIVE GAMBLING AND COGNITIVE DISTORTION.
The vast majority of states operate lotteries, and as a result lotteries are easily accessible to large numbers of people. Surveys show that lottery play is the most popular and widely practiced form of gambling in the United States. However, does the combination of easy and widespread access and general public acceptance mean that lottery players are more likely to develop serious gambling problems?

Dean Gerstein et al. conclude in *Gambling Impact and Behavior Study: Report to the National Gambling Impact Study Commission* (April 1, 1999, http://govinfo.library.unt.edu/ngisc/reports/gibstdy.pdf) that there is a significant association between lottery availability and the prevalence of at-risk gambling within a state. At-risk gamblers are defined as those who gamble regularly and may be prone to a gambling problem. However, the researchers find that multi-visit lottery patrons had the lowest prevalence of pathological and problem gambling among the gambling types examined.

Gerstein et al. warn that the patron database used in their analysis was small, meaning that their findings may not apply universally. They note that lottery players who do have a problem may be less able to recognize it because lottery players tend to undercount their losses. Lottery players generally lose small amounts at a time, even though these small amounts may eventually total a large amount. In other words, a casino gambler who loses thousands of dollars in a day might be more likely to admit having a gambling problem than a lottery player who loses the same amount over a longer period.

In "Underlying Cognitions in the Selection of Lottery Tickets" (*Journal of Clinical Psychology*, vol. 57, no. 6, June 2001), Karen K. Hardoon et al. study undergraduate students to examine cognitive misconceptions of lottery gamblers. Sixty students were given the South Oaks Gambling Screen, which is used to determine the probability that a person has a gambling problem. (See Chapter 2.) All the students were shown 16 lotto tickets, each marked with a different sequence of six numbers. The sequences were random (e.g., 1, 13, 19, 34, 40, 47), pattern (e.g., 5, 10, 15, 20, 25, 30), long sequence (e.g., 1, 2, 3, 4, 5, 6), or nonequilibrated or unbalanced (a series not covering the whole range of possible numbers, usually limited to either high or low numbers, such as 3, 5, 9, 12, 15, 17). The students were then asked to choose the 12 tickets they would most like to play in the lottery and to rank those tickets from best to worst. Random sequences were by far the most popular: more than half of the tickets selected by the students as their first, second, third, and fourth favorite choices contained random sequences. The second-most popular choice was the pattern sequence.

Hardoon et al. point out that all the students' choices were irrational because every ticket has an equal chance of winning. However, those students who regularly played the lottery or participated in other gambling activities were more likely to display bias when choosing their favorite tickets. In other words, they had stronger opinions about what was more winnable than did infrequent players and those who did not gamble. The probable pathological gamblers were found to have more illusions about control than all other participants. Hardoon et al. conclude that there was "some level of cognitive distortion" demonstrated by all the gamblers in the study.

In fact, Nigel E. Turner of the Centre for Addiction and Mental Health in Toronto, Canada, finds in "Lottery Ticket Preferences as Indicated by the Variation in the Number of Winners" (*Journal of Gambling Studies*, vol. 26, no. 3, September 2010) strong evidence that lottery ticket buyers tend to play nonrandom numbers, despite the fact that lotteries do have random outcomes. Furthermore, Tuttle quotes Sweeney as saying, "Gambling on lotteries is not a rational act."

THE FUTURE OF U.S. LOTTERIES
New State Lotteries?

As of January 2013, only seven states did not have lotteries: Alabama, Alaska, Hawaii, Mississippi, Nevada, Utah, and Wyoming. Hawaii and Utah do not permit any types of gambling and seem unlikely to amend their constitutions. A lottery in Nevada is very unlikely because of the tremendous growth of casino gambling there. Alaskan politicians have shown minimal interest in a lottery. Even though many state lottery bills have been introduced in the Alabama and Mississippi legislatures, most of them died in committee, and the rest were soundly defeated on the floor. For several years members of the Wyoming legislature have been pushing for a bill that would allow the sale of Powerball tickets. In 2011 a lottery bill was defeated in the Wyoming House of Representatives by just four votes. When a new session opened in January 2013, Representative Dave Zwonitzer (1953–; Republican) once again introduced a bill to create a Wyoming lottery; the bill was referred to committee.

Jackpot Fatigue

A major problem facing the lottery industry is called "jackpot fatigue." Lottery consumers demand higher and higher jackpots so they can stay excited about lotto games. However, individual states cannot increase jackpot sizes without either greatly increasing sales or decreasing the portion of lottery revenue going to public funds. The first option is difficult to achieve and the second is politically dangerous. Jackpot fatigue has driven increasing membership in multistate lotteries, such as Mega Millions and Powerball.

Pressure for Increased Revenue

Besides coping with jackpot fatigue, many lotteries also face pressure to increase the amount of profit going to government programs. Several states are considering decreasing their lottery payout to raise much needed funds. Opponents argue that cutting prize payouts will reduce sales, thereby making it nearly impossible to increase state revenues.

According to Tuttle, Sweeney explains that the role that state lotteries played in state budgets shrank during the first decade of the 21st century. Growth in lottery revenues stagnated after double-digit growth in the last two decades of the 20th century. The public perception is that lotteries significantly contribute to state budgets and shrink residents' taxes; however, the reality is that lotteries account for no more than 1% or 2% of state budgets. Sweeney sees two possibilities for state lotteries' future growth: the legalization of Internet gambling, which would open the door to online games that feel more like video games than lotteries, and convincing big-box retailers such as Wal-Mart and Home Depot to carry lottery tickets.

CHAPTER 8

SPORTS GAMBLING

Wagering on sporting events is one of the oldest and most popular forms of gambling in the world. The ancient Romans gambled on chariot races, animal fights, and gladiator contests. The Romans brought sports and gambling to Britain during the first century AD, where they have flourished for hundreds of years. Cockfighting, bear- and bullbaiting, wrestling, and footraces were popular sporting events for gambling throughout Europe during the 16th and 17th centuries. Horse races and boxing matches became popular spectator and betting sports during the 18th century. During the 19th and 20th centuries sporting events became more team-oriented and organized as rugby, soccer, and cricket grew in popularity.

Many early colonists who traveled to North America brought their love of sports and gambling with them. Horse racing, in particular, became a part of American culture. However, the morals of the late 18th and early 19th centuries decreased popular support for legalized sports gambling. By 1910 almost all forms of gambling were illegal in the United States. This did not stop people from gambling on sports, however. The practice continued to flourish, and horse racing, in particular, managed to maintain some legal respectability as a betting sport.

Nevada legalized gambling again in 1931 and permitted sports wagering for two decades. Point-shaving scandals in college basketball and the exposure of the gambling industry's connections to organized crime by a federal investigation led to a crackdown during the 1950s. Legal sports gambling did not return to Nevada until 1975, when it was tightly licensed and regulated.

In the 21st century sports gambling in the United States can be broken down into three primary categories: pari-mutuel betting (in which those who have bet on the top competitors split the pool of winnings) on events such as horse and greyhound races and on the ball game jai alai, legal betting using a bookmaker, and illegal betting. As of January 2013, pari-mutuel betting was legal in 43 states and betting with a bookmaker was legal only in Nevada and, to a limited extent, in Delaware.

SOCIAL ATTITUDES TOWARD SPORTS GAMBLING

The popularity of sports gambling is attributed to several factors, including a growing acceptance of gambling in general, intense media coverage of sporting events, and emerging technologies that make wagering easier. Americans can view a wide variety of sporting events from around the world via local, cable, and satellite television stations (with networks dedicated solely to sports) and the Internet (through computers and mobile phones). Also, sports bars and restaurants feature multiple television sets that are tuned in to various sporting events.

Betting on sports is one of the less popular forms of gambling in the United States. Jeffrey M. Jones of the Gallup Organization reports in *One in Six Americans Gamble on Sports* (February 1, 2008, http://www.gallup.com/poll/104086/One-Six-Americans-Gamble-Sports.aspx) that as of 2007 the percentages of survey respondents who had gambled on sports were near the low end. Only 14% had bet on a sporting event in an office pool, 7% had bet on a professional sporting event, and 4% had bet on college sports. Approximately 5% had bet on a horse race, and 3% had bet on a boxing match. These figures were near 20-year lows.

According to Paul Taylor, Cary Funk, and Peyton Craighill of the Pew Research Center, in *Gambling: As the Take Rises, So Does Public Concern* (May 23, 2006, http://pewresearch.org/assets/social/pdf/Gambling.pdf), the demographic makeup of those who bet on sports between March 2005 and March 2006 was slightly different from the demographic makeup of the average gambler. Whereas 71% of those with some college education gambled, only 23% of them had bet on sports during the previous year. Similarly, 65% of college graduates gambled, but only 25% bet on sports; and 66% of those who had high school diplomas or less had gambled, but only 22% had bet on sports. African-Americans (24%) and whites (23%) were more likely than Hispanics (16%) to have bet on sports. The American Gaming Association (AGA) reports in *2012 State of the States: The AGA Survey of Casino Entertainment* (2012, http://www.americangaming.org/files/aga/uploads/docs/sos/aga_sos_2012_web.pdf) that in 2011 Americans bet $2.9 billion on sporting events, up from $2.8 billion in 2010. According to the AGA, football was the most popular sport on which to wager in the legal Nevada sports books. Nearly half (47%) of all wagers were placed on football games in 2011; by comparison, 26% of money wagered on sports was bet on basketball games, and 19% on baseball games.

Taylor, Funk, and Craighill note that 50% of people approved of legalized offtrack betting on horse races in 2006. In contrast, only 42% approved of legalized betting on professional sports. A higher percentage of sports fans approved of legalized betting on professional sports: 55% of adults who claimed to follow sports news very closely in 2006 approved of legalized betting on professional sports, compared with only 38% of those who did not follow sports news very closely or at all.

PARI-MUTUEL GAMBLING

Pari-mutuel is a French term meaning "mutual stake." In pari-mutuel betting all wagers on a particular event or race are combined into a pool that is split between the winning bettors, minus a percentage for the management. Consequently, the larger the pool, the bigger the payoff. In pari-mutuel gambling patrons bet against each other, not against the house. The principles of the pari-mutuel system were developed in France by Pierre Oller during the late 19th century.

The pari-mutuel system has been used for horse races in the United States since about 1875, but it did not really catch on until the 1920s and 1930s, when the totalizator, an automatic odds calculator, came into use. The totalizator took money, printed betting tickets, and continuously calculated odds based on betting volume.

Previously, horse betting had been conducted mostly by bookmakers who were notoriously corrupt. In 1933 California, Michigan, New Hampshire, and Ohio legalized pari-mutuel gambling on horse racing as a means of regulating the industry and gaining some revenue. Dozens of states followed suit over the next decade. Pari-mutuel gambling was also adopted for greyhound racing and jai alai matches. As of January 2013, 43 U.S. states allowed pari-mutuel gambling. A handful of states permit pari-mutuel gambling by law but do not have facilities or systems in place to conduct it.

In pari-mutuel gambling the entire amount wagered is called the betting pool, the gross wager, or the handle. The system ensures that event managers receive a share of the betting pool, regardless of who wins a particular race or match. The management's share is called the takeout. The takeout percentage is set by state law and is usually about 20%.

Breakage refers to the odd cents that are not paid out to winning bettors because payoffs are rounded. For example, the payout on a $2 bet is typically rounded down in $0.10 or $0.20 increments. The cents left over are the breakage. Even though breakage amounts to only pennies per bet, it adds up quickly with high betting volume. For example, the California Horse Racing Board (CHRB) notes in *41st Annual Report of the California Horse Racing Board: A Summary of Fiscal Year 2010–2011 Revenue and Calendar Year 2011 Racing in California* (2012, http://www.chrb.ca.gov/annual_reports/2011_annual_report.pdf) that California horse racetracks accumulated approximately $6.4 million in breakage in fiscal year (FY) 2011. Each state has its own rules about breakage, but usually the funds are split between the state, the track operators, and the winning horse owners. Breakage is subtracted from the betting pool before payouts are made.

Pari-mutuel wagering can be performed in person at the event or at offtrack betting (OTB) facilities. The New York legislature approved the state's first OTB operation in 1970. Some states also allow betting by telephone or by Internet when an account is set up before bet placement. Many races are broadcast as they occur by televised transmission to in-state and out-of-state locations (including OTB sites). This process, known as simulcasting, allows intertrack wagering to take place. In other words, bettors at one racetrack can place bets on races taking place at another racetrack.

A race book is an establishment (usually a room at a casino or racetrack) in which intertrack wagering takes place on pari-mutuel events such as horse races and greyhound races. A race book typically features many television monitors that show races as they occur. Race books are included in many Nevada and Atlantic City, New Jersey, casinos as well as in some tribal casinos.

HORSE RACING

Horse racing has been a popular sport since the time of the ancient Greeks and Romans. It was popularized in western Europe during the Middle Ages, when knights returned from the Crusades with fast Arabian stallions. These horses were bred with sturdy English mares to produce a new line of horses now known as Thoroughbreds. Thoroughbreds are tall, lean horses with long, slender legs. They are renowned for their speed and grace while running.

Thoroughbred racing became popular among the British royalty and aristocrats, earning it the nickname the "sport of kings." The sport was transplanted to North America during colonial times. In *Thoroughly Thoroughbred* (2006, http://www.jockeyclub.com/pdfs/thoroughly _thoroughbred.pdf), the Jockey Club, the governing body of Thoroughbred horse racing in North America, indicates that races were run on Long Island, New York, as early as 1665. However, the advent of organized Thoroughbred racing in the United States is attributed to Governor Samuel Ogle (1702–1752) of Maryland, who staged a race between pedigreed horses in "the English style" in Annapolis, Maryland, in 1745. The Annapolis Jockey Club, which sponsored the race, later became the Maryland Jockey Club. Among its members were George Washington (1732–1799) and Thomas Jefferson (1743–1826).

Thoroughbred breeding was prominent in Maryland and Virginia until the Civil War (1861–1865), when many operations were moved to Kentucky. Thoroughbred racing had already grown popular throughout the agricultural South. In 1863 the Saratoga racecourse opened in northern New York. It is considered the oldest Thoroughbred flat track in the country. (A flat track is one with no hurdles or other obstacles for a racehorse to jump over.) The Jockey Club, which maintains the official breed registry for Thoroughbred horses in North America, was established in 1894 in New York City.

Horse racing remained popular in the United States until World War II (1939–1945), when it was severely curtailed. The decades since the war have seen a sharp decline in the popularity of horse racing. Three reasons are commonly mentioned:

- Competition increased from other entertainment venues and leisure activities, such as theme parks, shopping malls, and television.

- The horse racing industry avoided television coverage of races during the 1960s for fear it would keep people away from the tracks. (This is now seen as a failure to take advantage of a major marketing tool.)

- The legalization of state lotteries and casinos created competition for gambling dollars.

However, even though attendance declined, the amount of money gambled on horse races increased overall. According to the Jockey Club in *2012 Online Fact Book* (2012, http://www.jockeyclub.com/factbook.asp), the pari-mutuel handle from Thoroughbred horse racing was approximately $10.8 billion in 2011. This figure represented a 27% decrease since 2006, when the handle was $14.8 billion. Approximately $9.5 billion (88%) of the total amount gambled on horse races in 2011 was bet at OTB facilities. Analysts believe attendance at live racing will continue to decline as more OTB opportunities become available, although states such as California are upgrading racetracks in an attempt to bring fans back to live races.

Thoroughbred Racetracks and Races

The Daily Racing Form states in "Racing Links: Race Tracks" (2011, http://www.drf.com/racing_links/ links_tracks.html) that 94 Thoroughbred racetracks of varying sizes operated throughout the United States in 2011. Some are open seasonally, whereas those in warm climates are open year-round. Some are owned by the government, and some are owned by public or private companies. Thoroughbred horse racing in the United States is controlled by a relatively small group of participants. Two publicly traded companies, Churchill Downs and MI Developments (the parent company of Magna Entertainment, which filed for bankruptcy in 2009), along with the New York Racing Association, control much of the business. The New York Racing Association is a not-for-profit group that controls the Belmont, Saratoga, and Aqueduct racetracks. Analysts predict that the industry will continue to undergo consolidation, with corporations taking over most of the business.

The three most prestigious Thoroughbred races in the United States are the Kentucky Derby at the Churchill Downs racetrack in Kentucky, the Preakness Stakes at the Pimlico racetrack in Maryland, and the Belmont Stakes at the Belmont Park racetrack in New York. The races are held during a five-week period between May and June of each year. A horse that wins all three races in one year is said to have won the Triple Crown. As of January 2013, only 11 horses had captured the Triple Crown—the most recent was by a horse named Affirmed in 1978.

According to the Jockey Club in *2012 Online Fact Book*, there were 45,418 Thoroughbred horse races in 2011. Pennsylvania hosted the most events, with 4,464 races, followed by California (4,184), West Virginia (4,123), New York (3,692), Louisiana (3,531), and Florida (3,387). The total gross purses amounted to nearly $1.1 billion in 2011. The gross purse is the amount awarded to the owners of the winning horses. California racetracks had the highest gross purse of $140.5 million, followed by Pennsylvania ($123.5 million), New York ($122.9 million), Florida ($90.3 million), Kentucky ($89.7 million), and Louisiana ($86.1 million). The number of Thoroughbred races held each year has steadily declined since 2000.

Non-Thoroughbred Horse Racing

Even though Thoroughbred horse racing is the most popular, other types of horse racing also attract pari-mutuel wagering. In harness racing, specially trained horses trot or pace rather than gallop. Usually, the horse pulls a sulky (two-wheeled cart), which carries a jockey who controls the reins. Sometimes the jockey is seated on the horse rather than in the sulky. Harness racing is performed by standardbred horses, which are shorter, more muscled, and longer in body than Thoroughbreds. The National Association of Trotting Horse Breeders in America established the official registry for standardbred horses in 1879. At the time, Thoroughbred horses were the favorite of high society, and standardbred horses were popular among the common folk. In "Track Information" (2013, http://www.ustrotting.com/trackside/trackfacts/trackfacts.cfm), the U.S. Trotting Association indicates that in 2013 there were 41 licensed harness racetracks that offered pari-mutuel betting. Harness racing is also an attraction at state and county fairs, although wagering is not always allowed.

A third type of horse known for racing is the quarter horse, so named because of its high speed over distances of less than a quarter of a mile. North American colonists originally bred quarter horses to be both hardworking and athletic. The American Quarter Horse Association (AQHA) reports in its *2011 Annual Report* (2012, http://www.pageturnpro.com/American-Quarter-Horse-Association/37682-American-Quarter-Horse-Annual-Report-2011/index.html#16) that there were 8,450 American Quarter Horse races in 2011, with a total handle of $301.4 million and total purses of $129.3 million.

Arabian horses are considered the only purebred horses in the race circuit. The Arabian Jockey Club indicates in "Mark Your Calendar: 2012 Arabian Race Meets" (2012, http://www.arabianracing.org/upload/Mark_Your_Calendar_2012_Race_Meets.pdf) that in 2012 they raced at 14 tracks in the United States. In "2012 Arabian Stakes Calendar" (2012, http://www.arabianracing.org/upload/2012_Stakes_Calendar.pdf), the Arabian Jockey Club notes that 43 stake races were held in 2012.

Betting on Horse Races

The betting pool for a particular horse race depends on how much is wagered by bettors on that race. Each wager affects the odds. The more money bet on a horse, the lower that horse's odds and the potential payoff become. The payout for winning tickets is determined by the amount of money bet on the winner in relation to the amount bet on all the other horses in that particular race.

First, the takeout is subtracted from the betting pool. This money goes toward track expenses, taxes, and the purse. Most states also require that a portion of the takeout be put into a breeder incentive fund to encourage horse breeding and health in the state. Figure 8.1 shows the breakdown of each takeout dollar in California in FY 2011. (Note: In this graphic, "other states takeout" refers to wagering fees that are paid to betting facilities in other states that take bets on California races.) After the takeout

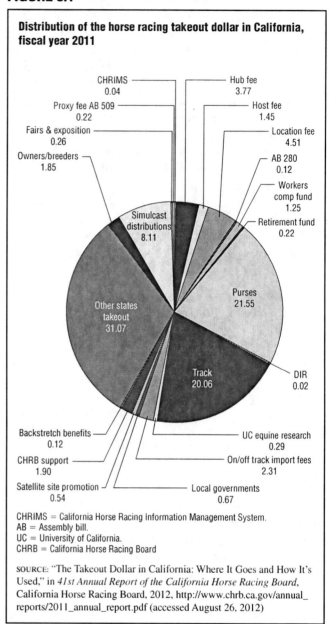

FIGURE 8.1

Distribution of the horse racing takeout dollar in California, fiscal year 2011

CHRIMS = California Horse Racing Information Management System.
AB = Assembly bill.
UC = University of California.
CHRB = California Horse Racing Board

SOURCE: "The Takeout Dollar in California: Where It Goes and How It's Used," in *41st Annual Report of the California Horse Racing Board*, California Horse Racing Board, 2012, http://www.chrb.ca.gov/annual_reports/2011_annual_report.pdf (accessed August 26, 2012)

and the breakage are subtracted from the betting pool, the remaining money is divided by the number of bettors to determine the payoff, or return, on each wager.

The odds on a particular horse winning first, second, or third place are estimated on the morning of a race and then are constantly recalculated by computer during the betting period before the race. The odds are posted on a tote board and on television screens throughout the betting area. The tote board also tallies the total amount paid into each pool. Bettors can wager that a particular horse will win (come in first), place (come in first or second), or show (come in first, second, or third). The payoff for a win is higher than payoffs for place or show, because the latter two pools have to be split more ways. For example, the show pool must be split between all bettors who selected win, place, or show.

Betting on horse races is considered more a game of skill than a game of chance. Professional racing bettors spend many hours observing individual horses and consider previous race experience when they make their picks. This gives them some advantage over bettors who pick a horse based on whim—for example, because they like its name. Even though bettors do not play directly against each other, an individual bettor's skill does affect other bettors because the odds are based on the bets of all gamblers.

Horse Racing in California

In 2011 California topped all states in purses paid to winning horses. The state has allowed pari-mutuel gambling on horse races since 1933, when voters passed a constitutional amendment. California has six privately owned racetracks and nine racing fairs. Racing fairs are county and state fairs—often held at racetracks—where wagering on horse races is one of many fair events. The fairs usually last only a week or two and are conducted several times a year. Gamblers can also bet on horse races at 20 simulcast facilities in the state.

The CHRB indicates in *41st Annual Report of the California Horse Racing Board* that in FY 2010–11 industry revenue reached $11.4 million on total handle of $2.9 billion. Figure 8.2 shows the handle broken down by ontrack, offtrack, and out-of-state wagers. According to the CHRB, only $410 million (14%) of all wagers occurred at the track in FY 2010–11. More than a quarter of the wagers ($816 million, or 28%) were placed at offtrack locations throughout the state. Winning bettors received $2.3 billion (79%) of the total betting pool of $2.9 billion.

The Economic Effects of Horse Racing

The industry provides direct income to horse owners, trainers, and jockeys through purses. In *2012 Online Fact Book*, the Jockey Club notes that in 2011 California tracks paid out the highest gross purse for the year ($140.5 million), followed by Pennsylvania ($123.5 million) and New York ($122.9 million). The largest portion of a Thoroughbred race purse (typically 60%) goes to the owner of the first-place horse. The owner is responsible for paying the horse's trainer and jockey. The owners of the horses finishing second and third typically receive about 20% and 12%, respectively, of a race purse.

The horse racing industry also supports a large business in horse breeding. In 1962 Maryland was the first state to establish a program to encourage breeders within the state through direct money payments. The practice spread quickly to other states involved in horse racing.

In *Economic Impact of Horse Racing in Maryland* (January 20, 1999), Wesley N. Musser et al. of the University of Maryland determine that the sport's main

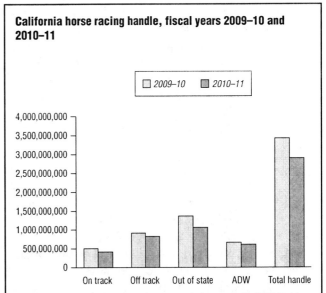

FIGURE 8.2

California horse racing handle, fiscal years 2009–10 and 2010–11

Notes: The on-track handle represents wagers at the host track. For FY 2010–11, on-track wagers accounted for 14.13 percent of the total handle. Off-track handle represents wagering at California simulcast locations and accounted for 28.11 percent of the total. Out-of-state handle represents commingled wagers from other US and international sites. Out-of-state wagers accounted for 36.64 percent of the total. Advance Deposit Wagering (ADW) represents the handle generated through the four licensed California ADW companies. The ADW handle accounted for 21.11 percent of the total.

SOURCE: "Sources of Handle, Fiscal Years 2009–10 and 2010–11," in *41st Annual Report of the California Horse Racing Board*, California Horse Racing Board, 2012, http://www.chrb.ca.gov/annual_reports/2011_annual_report.pdf (accessed August 26, 2012)

impact is not the cash flow between the wagering public, the racetracks, OTB sites, horse owners, jockeys, breeders, trainers, and government regulatory agencies. Rather, the researchers suggest that the true economic effects of the sport occur outside the industry from expenditures on goods and services. Racetrack and OTB operators spend money on land, labor, and other goods and services from various businesses. In addition, horse owners, breeders, and trainers spend money on land, labor, veterinary care, and horse feed and supplies. All of this spending pumps money into the general economy.

Unlike the casino industry, the horse racing industry has only a minor impact on tourism. Most racetracks are not typical tourist destinations that attract overnight visitors who spend money on lodging, food, and other entertainment. The exceptions are the races that are held as part of the Triple Crown. These racing events attract visitors from all over the world and bring a significant number of tourist dollars to local businesses.

Horse Fatalities and Injuries

Horse racing does have a price in terms of horse fatalities and injuries. The plight of Eight Belles at the 2008 Kentucky Derby focused national attention on these issues. Eight Belles finished second in the race, but collapsed shortly after with broken ankles on both front legs and was euthanized on the track. According to T. D. Thornton in "Injured Racehorses You Didn't See" (*New York Times*, May 7, 2008), Eight Belles was just one of many racehorses that are euthanized each year because of injuries on the track. For example, in *41st Annual Report of the California Horse Racing Board*, the CHRB notes that in FY 2010–11 California had 265 racehorse fatalities: 100 of the deaths occurred during races, 86 occurred during training, and 79 occurred during other activities.

Besides racing fatalities, two other horse health issues of major concern are mare reproductive loss syndrome (MRLS) and exercise-induced pulmonary hemorrhage (EIPH). In "Eastern Tent Caterpillars Now Wandering, Populations up Sharply from 2007" (May 9, 2008, http://www.ca.uky.edu/gluck/mrls/2008/050908ETCupdate.htm), the University of Kentucky's College of Agriculture reports that MRLS is an illness that killed 30% of Kentucky foals (horses less than one year old) between 2001 and 2002. Since then, scientists have determined that MRLS is caused by eastern tent caterpillars, which can find their way into horse food. Manu M. Sebastian et al. estimate in "Review Paper: Mare Reproductive Loss Syndrome" (*Veterinary Pathology*, vol. 45, no. 5, September 2008) that between 2001 and 2002 MRLS had an economic impact on the horse racing industry of approximately $500 million.

EIPH is a common condition in racehorses: they bleed from the lungs during strenuous exercise, probably because increased blood pressure ruptures tiny blood vessels in their lungs. Up to 80% of racehorses are affected. Horses that experience EIPH can be temporarily or permanently barred from racing, depending on state regulations and the severity of the problem.

GREYHOUND RACING

Greyhounds are mentioned in many ancient documents. English noblemen used greyhounds to hunt rabbits, a sport known as coursing. Greyhound racing was given the nickname the "sport of queens" because Queen Elizabeth I (1533–1603) of England established the first formal rules for greyhound coursing during the 1500s. Greyhounds were brought to the United States during the late 1800s to help control the jackrabbit population on farms in the Midwest. Eventually, farmers began holding local races, using live rabbits to lure the dogs to race. During the early 1900s Owen Patrick Smith (1867–1927) invented a mechanical lure for this purpose. The first circular greyhound track opened in Emeryville, California, in 1919.

Three major organizations manage greyhound racing in the United States: the National Greyhound Association (NGA), which represents greyhound owners and is the official registry for racing greyhounds; the American Greyhound Track Operators Association (AGTOA); and the American Greyhound Council (AGC), a joint effort of the NGA and the AGTOA, which manages the industry's animal welfare programs, including farm inspections and adoptions.

Wagering on greyhound races is similar to wagering on horse races. However, greyhound racing is not nearly as popular as horse racing, and its popularity has declined dramatically in the past few decades. During the 1990s seven states banned greyhound racing: Idaho, Maine, Nevada, North Carolina, Vermont, Virginia, and Washington. Pennsylvania became the eighth state to ban greyhound racing in 2004, Massachusetts banned greyhound racing in 2008, and Rhode Island and New Hampshire banned greyhound racing in 2010.

Florida's Greyhound-Racing Industry

According to the Florida Department of Business and Professional Regulation's Division of Pari-mutuel Wagering, in *80th Annual Report, Fiscal Year 2010–2011* (2012, http://www.myfloridalicense.com/dbpr/pmw/documents/AnnualReport2010-2011.pdf), greyhound races were the most attended pari-mutuel event in Florida in FY 2010–11, attracting 406,089 visitors. However, this figure represented a 16% decrease from 2009–10 attendance numbers of 480,877. There were 3,681 greyhound races in FY 2010–11, down 4.5% from 3,857 the previous fiscal year. The greyhound racing handle in FY 2010–11 was approximately $264.7 million, a 9% decrease from $291.8 million the previous fiscal year. Purses totaled $25.6 million in FY 2010–11, an amount comparable to what was paid in FY 2008–09 ($25.9 million) and FY 2009–10 ($25 million).

The Division of Pari-mutuel Wagering indicates that Florida's greyhound racetracks paid $3.4 million to the state in FY 2010–11, accounting for 29% of the state's total $11.6 million in revenue from pari-mutuel gambling. Greyhound racing is declining as a percentage of all state revenue derived from racing.

Concerns about Greyhound Welfare

The Greyhound Protection League explains in *"Isolated Incidents" and Documented Deaths of Some of the Half Million Racing Greyhounds Who Have Died in the Last Two Decades* (November 2004, http://www.greyhounds.org/gpl/contents/PDFs/abuse_cases_11-04.pdf) that during the 1990s there were dozens of well-documented cases of cruelty and abuse in the greyhound industry involving thousands of dogs that were shot, starved, abandoned, or sold to research laboratories. Because of the work of animal rights groups such as the Humane Society of the United States (HSUS), the cruelty of the greyhound industry was revealed to the American public. Many greyhound racing organizations changed the way they treated greyhounds and initiated adoption programs for dogs that were too old to race. Nevertheless, animal rights groups maintain that greyhounds continue to be killed if they are unsuitable or too old for racing.

According to the Division of Pari-mutuel Wagering in *80th Annual Report, Fiscal Year 2010–2011*, Florida's greyhound tracks are legally required to actively sponsor greyhound adoption programs, and many have onsite adoption booths. The tracks are required to pay 10% of the credit they receive for uncashed winning tickets to organizations that promote or encourage greyhound adoptions. These mandatory contributions amounted to $195,407 in FY 2010–11.

JAI ALAI

Jai alai is a court game in which players bounce a ball against a wall and catch it using a *cesta* (a long curved basket) that is strapped to the wrist. The term *jai alai* comes from the Spanish Basque phrase for "merry festival." The first permanent jai alai arena, called a *fronton*, was built in Florida in 1926.

The game's scoring system has been adjusted over the years to make it more attractive to gamblers. Typical games include eight players, with two players competing for a point at one time. The game continues until one player obtains seven points. Win, place, and show positions are winning bets, just as in horse racing.

The Division of Pari-mutuel Wagering notes in *80th Annual Report, Fiscal Year 2010–2011* that only six frontons in Florida offered pari-mutuel gambling on jai alai in FY 2010–11. As of January 2013, Florida was the only state in the nation to conduct jai alai performances. Admittance to jai alai events was free in 2010–11. The state received $462,126 in taxes and fees from the jai alai industry in FY 2010–11.

Jai alai peaked in popularity during the early 1980s, when more than $600 million was wagered on the sport. However, during the first decade of the 21st century the sport's popularity declined precipitously. By FY 2010–11 the total handle had declined to $32.8 million.

THE FUTURE OF PARI-MUTUEL GAMBLING
Decreasing Popularity and Income

Pari-mutuel gambling is decreasing in popularity as it faces increasing competition from other gambling options, particularly casinos. The horse racing industry experienced a 40% decline in attendance during the 1990s. As a result, racetracks found it increasingly difficult to attract a large enough betting pool to afford to run races. According to the Jockey Club in *2012 Online Fact Book*, the number of Thoroughbred races run each year in the United States fell from 74,071 in 1989 to 45,418 in 2011, a decrease of nearly 39%.

Attempts to Attract New Gamblers

Gambling industry analysts suggest that horse races have a relatively small hard-core group of attendees, most of whom are older people. The industry is trying to attract a larger and younger fan base (25 to 45 years old) with disposable income. Some racetracks have tried to become entertainment venues by offering food courts, malls, and music concerts. Even though these attractions may increase attendance, the newcomers do not necessarily gamble. Meanwhile, devoted race fans complain that such promotions are too distracting and draw attention away from the racing.

Increasingly, pari-mutuel facilities are offering other gambling choices to patrons. The AGA indicates in *2012 State of the States* that 12 states had slot machines and/or video lottery terminals at their racetracks in 2011: Delaware, Florida, Indiana, Iowa, Louisiana, Maine, New Mexico, New York, Oklahoma, Pennsylvania, Rhode Island, and West Virginia. The racinos (racetracks at which slot machines are available) in these states have become a huge success. The AGA reports that revenues at the nation's 10 most lucrative racinos topped $4.4 billion in 2011. Philadelphia topped the list, with $842.1 million in revenues. Indeed, four of the top 10 racinos were in Pennsylvania, and accounted for $1.7 billion in revenues, or nearly 39% of overall earnings at the top 10 racinos.

Most of Florida's racetracks and jai alai frontons have card rooms in which gamblers wager on card games, mainly poker. In *80th Annual Report, Fiscal Year 2010–2011*, the Division of Pari-mutuel Wagering notes that the gross revenue in the state's card rooms was $125.1 million in FY 2010–11, an increase of more than 19% from FY 2009–10. The number of card room tables decreased from 746 in FY 2009–10 to 718 in FY 2010–11. The card rooms contributed $13.2 million in taxes and fees to state and local governments in FY 2010–11.

LEGAL SPORTS GAMBLING

Besides the sports involved in pari-mutuel gambling, legalized sports gambling is extremely limited in the United States. Only two states, Nevada and Delaware, allow high-stakes gambling on sports.

In 1992 Congress passed the Professional and Amateur Sports Protection Act, which banned sports betting nationwide except in four states (Delaware, Montana, Nevada, and Oregon) that had offered it at some point between 1976 and 1990. Delaware was exempted from the law because it ran a National Football League (NFL) lottery in 1976 that allowed only parlay bets (bets in which the bettor had to pick the winners of at least three different NFL games in a single wager). In 2009 Delaware began taking bets on NFL games and hoped to expand to other sports as a way to solve a state budget crisis that was caused by the recession that began in late 2007 and ended in mid-2009.

However, a federal appeals court ruled in August 2009 that Delaware's sports betting plan violated federal law and must be limited to betting that was allowed in 1976 (i.e., parlay bets on only the NFL). As a result of this ruling, Delaware's three slot parlors could only take parlay bets on NFL games. Nevertheless, even limited parlay betting turned out to be profitable. Chris Sieroty reports in "Delaware Wins by Betting on Sports" (January 5, 2013, http://www.lvrj.com/business/delaware-wins-by-betting-on-sports-185738631.html) that through January 2013 the state had netted more than $22 million on NFL games (including the preseason), a 42.4% increase over revenues of $15.4 million for the same period in 2011–12.

In March 2009 organizations representing New Jersey's gaming and horse racing industries filed suit in federal court with the intention of overturning the Professional and Amateur Sports Protection Act. The suit charged that the law discriminated against the people of New Jersey because sports betting is allowed in four other states. As the Associated Press reports in "New Jersey Sued over Sports Betting" (August 7, 2012, http://espn.go.com/espn/story/_/id/8243013/ncaa-4-pro-leagues-sue-new-jersey-sports-betting), in August 2012 the nation's four major professional sports leagues–the National Football League (NFL), Major League Baseball (MLB), the National Basketball Association (NBA), and the National Hockey League (NHL)—joined the National Collegiate Athletic Association (NCAA) in a lawsuit filed against New Jersey, asserting that the state's plan to legalize sports betting was in violation of federal law. According to Hoa Nguyen in "Federal Judge in New Jersey Sports Betting Case to Hear Arguments in February Whether Federal Ban Is Constitutional" (January 3, 2013, http://www.pressofatlanticcity.com/news/breaking/federal-judge-in-new-jersey-sports-betting-case-to-hear/article_1e4ff14a-55d1-11e2-af47-001a4bcf887a.html), lawyers representing the state of New Jersey maintained that the Professional and Amateur Sports Protection Act should be overturned on constitutional grounds. The case was scheduled to take place before a U.S. District Court judge beginning in February 2013.

Sports and Race Books in Nevada

Sports books are establishments that accept and pay off bets on sporting events. Bettors must be over the age of 21 years and be physically present in the state.

According to the Nevada Gaming Control Board (November 5, 2012, http://gaming.nv.gov/modules/show document.aspx?documentid=7366), there were 185 licensed sports pools and 160 licensed race books in Nevada as of September 30, 2012. More than 200 of these were in Las Vegas, and most were operated by casinos. The typical casino book is a large room with many television monitors showing races and games from around the world. Most casinos have combined race/sports books, although the betting formats are usually different. Race book betting is mostly of the pari-mutuel type, whereas sports book betting is by bookmaking.

Bookmaking

Bookmaking is the common term for the act of determining odds and receiving and paying off bets. The person performing the service is called the bookmaker or bookie. Bookmaking has its own lingo, which can be confusing to those who are not familiar with it. For example, a dollar bet is actually a $100 bet, a nickel bet is a $500 bet, and a dime bet is a $1,000 bet. To place a bet with a bookmaker, the bettor lays down (pays) a particular amount of money to win a particular payoff.

Bookmakers make money by charging a commission called "vigorish" (often shortened to just "vig"). Vigorish is an important yet misunderstood concept by most bettors. Most gambling literature describes vigorish as a 4.55% commission that a bookie earns from losers' bets. In "A Crash Course in Vigorish…and It's Not 4.55%" (December 7, 2012, http://www.professionalgambler.com/vigorish.html), J. R. Martin, a sports handicapper (a person who analyzes betting odds and gives advice to bettors), provides a different interpretation of vigorish. Statistically, only bettors who win exactly half of their bets pay exactly 4.55% in vigorish. Other bettors pay different percentages. Martin explains that a bettor must win 53% of all equally sized bets to break even. This bettor, however, would wind up paying a vigorish of at least 4.82%.

Some sports bets are simple wagers based on yes or no logic. Examples include under and over bets, in which a bettor wagers that a particular game's final score will be under or over a specific number of points.

Most sports bets are based on a line that is set by the bookmaker. For example, the line for an NFL game between the Miami Dolphins and the Tennessee Titans might say that the Dolphins are picked by seven points. A bettor picking the Dolphins to win the game wins money only if the Dolphins win the game by more than seven points.

The line does not reflect a sports expert's assessment of the number of points by which a team will win. Rather, it is a concept designed to even up betting and to ensure that the bookmaker gets bets on both sides. This reduces the bookie's financial risk. Bookmakers will change lines if one side receives more betting action than the other. The skill of sports gambling comes in recognizing the accuracy of the line. Experienced bettors choose games in which they believe the posted lines do not accurately reflect the expected outcomes. This gives them an edge. The odds for most licensed sports books in Nevada are set by Las Vegas Sports Consultants, Inc. (http://www.lvsc.com/).

Developments in Legal Sports Gambling in Nevada

Nevada legalized gambling during the Great Depression (1929–1939) as a means of raising revenue. During that time, Charles K. McNeil (1903–1981), a Chicago securities analyst, developed the handicapping system, in which bookmakers establish the betting line. The new system provided an incentive for gamblers to bet on the underdog in a contest and made gambling more appealing. During the 1940s the Nevada legislature legalized offtrack betting on horse racing, and sports and race books were popular in the state's casinos.

Then in 1950 and 1951 a series of U.S. Senate hearings led by Senator Estes Kefauver (1903–1963; D-TN) investigated the role of organized crime in the gambling industry. The televised hearings focused the nation's attention on gangsters, corrupt politicians, and legal and illegal gambling. One of the results was the passage of a 10% federal excise tax on "any wager with respect to a sports event or a contest." Because of the tax, the casino sports books, which were making only a small profit, were forced to shut down.

In 1974 the federal excise tax was reduced to 2%, and the sports books slowly made a comeback. Frank "Lefty" Rosenthal (1929–2008), a renowned handicapper, was credited with popularizing the sports book in Las Vegas during the 1970s. The 1980s were boom years for the sports and race books: in 1983 the federal excise tax was reduced to 0.3%. Jimmy "the Greek" Snyder (1919–1996) brought some legitimacy to sports gambling through his appearances on televised sports shows. The amount of money wagered in the Nevada sports books increased dramatically until the mid-1990s, when it began to level off.

Money and Games

Wagering in Nevada is only allowed on professional and college sports; it is not allowed on high school sporting events or Olympic events. Nevada law also restricts the sports books to wagering on events that are athletic contests—betting is not allowed on related events, such as who will win the most valuable player awards.

According to the AGA in *2012 State of the States*, Nevada's sports books had a betting handle of $2.9 billion in 2011. The profit made on sports betting is actually quite low. In 2011 the sports books had a revenue of only $140.7 million, or just under 5% of the total amount wagered.

The AGA indicates that football wagers accounted for $1.3 billion of Nevada's sports book wagering in 2011. The Super Bowl alone generated $93.9 million in wagers in 2012.

Low-Stakes Sports Gambling

MONTANA. Montana allows five types of sports gambling: sports pools, Calcutta pools, sports tab games, fantasy sports leagues, and fishing derbies.

Calcutta pools operate much like pari-mutuel betting, in that all the money wagered on a sporting event is pooled together. In a Calcutta pool, an auction is held before a sporting event, and bettors bid for the opportunity to bet on a particular player. For example, before a golf tournament the pool participants bid against each other for the right to bet on a particular golfer. The money collected during the auction becomes the wagering pool. It is divided among the "owners" of the best finishing players and the pool sponsor. Calcutta pools are most often associated with rodeos and golf tournaments.

A sports tab game is one in which players purchase a numbered tab from a game card containing 100 tabs with different number combinations. Bettors win money or prizes if their numbers match those that are associated with a sporting event—for example, digits in the winning team's final score. The cost of a sports tab is limited by law to less than $5. Operators of sports tab games (except charities) are allowed to take no more than 10% of the total amount wagered to cover their expenses (charities are allowed to take 50%). Sports tab sellers must obtain a license from the state and pay licensing fees and gaming taxes.

OTHER STATES. Other states that offer limited sports gambling are Washington, which permits $1 bets on race cars, and New Mexico, where small bets on bicycle races are legal. Office pools on sporting events are legal in a few states as long as the operator does not take a commission. Despite these examples of sports betting in other parts of the United States, the big money in legal sports gambling is in Nevada.

Fantasy Sports

During the first decade of the 21st century a new type of legal sports betting emerged: fantasy sports. In fantasy sports players choose real professional players for fictional teams; the teams compete against one another based on real-world performance. The Unlawful Internet Gambling Enforcement Act of 2006, which made bank transactions to online gaming websites illegal, specifically exempted fantasy sports games. By 2013 over a hundred companies—including ESPN—facilitated fantasy sports contests over the Internet. In 2007 the U.S. Court of Appeals for the 8th Circuit ruled that such companies do not need to pay license fees to professional sports leagues because the First Amendment guarantees their right to use players' names and statistics. As a result of this ruling, and the U.S. Supreme Court's refusal to hear the case in June 2008, fantasy sports continued to expand. According to the Fantasy Sports Trade Association (FSTA) website (2013,

ILLEGAL SPORTS GAMBLING

The AGA estimates in the fact sheet "Sports Wager-ing" (2013, http://www.americangaming.org/industry-resources/research/fact-sheets/sports-wagering) that in 2011 Nevada sports books accounted for less than 1% of all sports gambling in the country and that the vast majority of sports bets were illegal. This makes it difficult to determine exactly how much money is involved.

Illegal sports gambling encompasses a wide variety of activities. Most illegal bets on sporting events are placed with bookies, although illegal Internet gambling is increasing in popularity, according to the article "The Big Business of Illegal Gambling" (CNBC.com, December 10, 2009). In addition, some illegal "sporting" events are popularly associated with gambling, such as cockfighting and dogfighting.

The Link to the Nevada Sports Books

Most illegal books use the odds posted by the Nevada sports books because these are well publicized. Nevada sports books also provide illegal bookies with a means for spreading the risk on bets: illegal bookies who get a lot of action on one side of a bet often bet the other side with the Nevada sports books to even out the betting.

Transmitting gambling information across state lines for the purpose of placing or taking bets is illegal. News items about point spreads (the predicted scoring difference between two opponents) can be reported for informational and entertainment purposes only, but betting lines are still published by many U.S. newspapers. The Newspaper Association of America, which represented nearly 2,000 daily circulation newspapers in the country in 2013, defends the practice as free speech that is protected under the First Amendment of the U.S. Constitution. The association claims that readers want to see the lines for informational purposes (to learn which teams are favored to win) and not necessarily for betting purposes. Even though the NCAA argues that a ban on all college sports wagering would pressure newspapers to stop publishing point spreads, the AGA and others counter that betting lines would still be accessible through independent sports analysts, offshore Internet gambling sites, and other outlets.

The Link to Organized Crime

Illegal sports gambling has long been associated with organized crime in the United States. During the 1920s and early 1930s mobsters set up organized bookmaking systems across the country, including two illegal wire services, Continental Wire Service and Trans America

Wire, which operated under the direction of the gangster Al Capone (1899–1947). The legal wire service, Western Union, was prohibited by law from transmitting race results until the races were officially declared over. Sometimes this declaration was delayed for several minutes following the completion of the races, so mobsters reported the winners on the illegal wire services to prevent bettors from taking advantage of these delays by posting winning bets before the official results were wired.

During the 1950s the federal government cracked down on organized crime and eventually drove mobsters out of the Nevada casino industry. As the casinos were taken over by corporations, organized crime strengthened its hold on illegal bookmaking. Even though law enforcement officials acknowledge that many "independent" bookies operate throughout the country, the big money in illegal sports gambling is still controlled by organized crime.

ANIMAL FIGHTING

Gambling on animal fights has a long history in the United States. Most staged animal fights involve cocks (roosters) or dogs that are specially bred and trained. Even though such fighting is usually associated with rural areas, urban police reports about cockfighting and dogfighting have increased since the early 1990s, mostly because the contests have become popular among street gangs. Animal fights are of particular concern to law enforcement authorities because large amounts of cash and weapons are usually present.

Official national statistics are not available on animal fighting. However, Pet-Abuse.com, a website that is operated by a nonprofit organization in New York, collects and documents information about animal abuse cases. As of January 2013, the website's database included 1,582 documented cases of animal fighting that took place in the United States between 1975 and 2012.

Cockfighting

Cocks fight and peck one another naturally to establish a hierarchy within their social order. These altercations rarely lead to serious injury. By contrast, fighting cocks are specially bred and trained by humans to be extremely aggressive. They are given stimulants, steroids, and other drugs to heighten their fighting nature. Before a fight, the cocks have sharp spikes, called gaffs, attached to their legs, and then they are thrown into a pit. They slash and peck at one another, often until death. Spectators wager on the outcome of these fights.

In "Cockfighting Fact Sheet" (2013, http://www.humanesociety.org/issues/cockfighting/facts/cockfighting_fact_sheet.html), the HSUS indicates that cockfighting was illegal in all 50 states in 2013. According to the

HSUS, as of 2011 cockfighting was a felony in 39 states and the District of Columbia and a misdemeanor offense in 11 others, although states differed in their treatment of cockfight spectators and those caught possessing birds for cockfighting. The federal Animal Welfare Act prohibits the interstate transport of birds for cockfighting.

As of January 2013, Pet-Abuse.com listed 481 documented cases of cockfighting in the United States between 1977 and 2012. For example, in June 2005 in Sevierville, Tennessee, the Federal Bureau of Investigation broke up a cockfighting ring, known as the Del Rio, one of the oldest and largest in the country. About 300 birds and more than 700 spectators were discovered in the raid. Individual bets were said to be as high as $30,000. According to officials, it was common to have 250 fights per night at the location, resulting in dozens of dead chickens; 143 people were charged in the incident.

In September 2010 police raided a cockfighting ring in Philadelphia, Pennsylvania. Twenty-three roosters were seized at a private home, where fights were staged in the basement with up to 100 spectators at a time. Bullet-proof glass was installed over the windows of the home. George Bengal of the Pennsylvania Society for the Prevention of Cruelty to Animals called the operation "the top of the food chain, very extensive" and said, "I haven't seen this in the 15 years or more that I've been doing this kind of work." In February 2012, police responding to a disturbance in Good Hope, California, discovered more than 125 live fighting roosters, along with 21 dead roosters, at a private residence. The home owner, 53-year-old Jesus Salazar, was subsequently arrested on charges of illegal cockfighting, possession of cockfighting instruments, and animal cruelty.

Dogfighting

Spectators huddle around pits or small, boarded arenas to watch dogfights. They place bets on the outcome of the contests, which can go on for hours, sometimes to the death. Dogs are specially bred and trained for such fights—the American pit bull terrier is the most common breed because of its powerful jaws. Authorities report that the dogs are often draped in heavy chains to build muscle mass and systematically deprived of food and water. Stolen and stray pet dogs and cats are commonly used as bait to train the fighters. The smaller animals are stabbed or sliced open and thrown to the fighting dogs to enhance their blood lust. Dogs are often drugged to increase their aggressiveness.

Dogfighting is a felony in all 50 states. Dogfighting rings are often intermingled with other criminal activities. For example, Pet-Abuse.com notes that in May 2005 Louisiana authorities broke up one of the larger dogfighting rings in the state. Police said more than 140 dogs were seized from two kennels in the rural towns of Church Point and Franklinton. The owners of the kennels had been under investigation for money laundering (the act of engaging in transactions that are designed to hide or obscure the origin of illegally obtained money) and drug dealing when authorities uncovered the dogfighting ring. Four people were arrested.

Dogfighting is not limited to southern states and rural areas. The HSUS indicates in "Ranking of State Dogfighting Laws" (January 2013, http://www.humanesociety.org/assets/pdfs/animal_fighting/dogfighting_statelaws.pdf) that New York has one of the weakest animal fighting laws in the Northeast, which attracts animal fighters to the state. According to T. J. Pignataro in "Betting on Cruelty" (*Buffalo News*, February 8, 2004), drug and weapons raids by police accidentally uncovered well-organized dogfighting operations around Buffalo, New York. Authorities reported that thousands of dollars in cash and other valuables, such as car titles, guns, and drugs, were commonly wagered at the dogfights. Authorities also described gruesome scenes in which owners chopped off the heads of dogs that disgraced them by losing or backing down during a fight. City authorities have found trash bags full of mangled pit bulls in vacant fields or along city streets. Pet-Abuse.com indicates that in October 2009, 21 dogs were removed from four homes on Laurel Street in the city—a street from which 300 pit bulls had been removed because of suspected dogfighting since 2000.

One of the highest profile cases of dogfighting is that of Michael Vick (1980–), a former professional quarterback for the Atlanta Falcons. In July 2007 Vick was indicted on charges linked to dogfighting, including federal conspiracy charges involving crossing state lines to participate in illegal activity and buying and sponsoring pit bulls in fighting ventures. Vick and his associates were charged with having bought property in Virginia on which to stage dogfights; the dogs were fought over a six-year period. Dogs who performed poorly were killed violently by the dogfighting ring. Vick himself admitted to killing several dogs. He pleaded guilty and was sentenced to 23 months in prison. Following his release from prison, Vick joined the Philadelphia Eagles at the beginning of the 2009–10 NFL season.

THE EFFECTS OF ILLEGAL SPORTS GAMBLING ON SOCIETY

Money and Crime

Because the vast majority of sports gambling that occurs in the United States is illegal, it is difficult to determine its economic effects. However, the only people definitely benefiting from illegal sports gambling are the bookmakers. Large bookmaking operations that are overseen by organized crime groups take in billions of dollars each year. The betting stakes are high and the consequences for nonpayment can be violent. Small independent bookies typically operate as entrepreneurs, taking bets only from local people they know well. Illegal bookmaking cases reported in the media range from multimillion-dollar enterprises to small operations run by one person.

Sports Tampering

In *National Incident-Based Reporting System—Volume 1: Data Collection Guidelines* (August 2000, http://www.fbi.gov/about-us/cjis/ucr/nibrs/nibrs_dcguide.pdf), the Federal Bureau of Investigation defines sports tampering as "to unlawfully alter, meddle in, or otherwise interfere with a sporting contest or event for the purpose of gaining a gambling advantage." The most common form is point-shaving, which occurs when a player deliberately limits the number of points scored by his or her team in exchange for payment of some sort. For example, if a basketball player purposely misses a free throw in exchange for a fee, that player is participating in a point-shaving scheme.

Gambling has led to some famous sports scandals, mostly in college basketball games. However, any link between an athlete and gambling gives rise to suspicions about the integrity of the games in which that athlete participates.

The professional baseball player Pete Rose (1941–) is an example. On September 11, 1985, at Riverfront Stadium in Cincinnati, Ohio, Rose broke Ty Cobb's (1886–1961) all-time hit record. Before the end of the decade, however, Rose was under investigation by the MLB commissioner and by federal prosecutors for betting on sporting events and associating with known bookies. He agreed to leave baseball, and the case was dropped. At the time, Rose denied ever betting on baseball games. However, in January 2004 he admitted that he had bet on baseball games while he managed the Cincinnati Reds during the late 1980s.

THE INTEGRITY OF COLLEGE SPORTS. The popularity of sports gambling among college students leads to suspicions that athletes, coaches, and officials associated with collegiate sports could be wagering on the very games in which they are participating. In May 2004 the extent of gambling among college athletes was examined in "Pushing the Limits: Gambling among NCAA Athletes" (*Wager*, vol. 9, no. 21, May 26, 2004). The article summarizes the findings of two major studies: *2003 NCAA National Study on Collegiate Sports Wagering and Associated Health Risks* (December 2004) by the NCAA and "Correlates of College Student Gambling in the United States" (*Journal of American College Health*, vol. 52, no. 2, September–October 2003) by Richard A. LaBrie et al. of the Harvard School of Public Health. The results indicate that as of 2004 approximately one-quarter of male student athletes had gambled on college sporting events.

The NCAA reports in *Results from the 2008 NCAA Study on Collegiate Wagering* (November 13, 2009, http://www.ncaa.org/wps/wcm/connect/public/ncaa/pdfs/2012/2008+collegiate+wagering+study) that between 2004 and 2008 there were some declines in gambling among student athletes. Regardless, 29.5% of male student athletes had gambled on sports in 2008, up from 23.5% in 2004. The proportion of female student athletes who had gambled on sports remained about the same in 2008, at 6.6%. Rates of probable pathological gambling had increased among male student athletes, from 2.1% in 2004 to 2.9% in 2008.

The NCAA opposes both legal and illegal sports gambling in the United States. Bylaw 10.3 of the NCAA prohibits staff members and student athletes from engaging in gambling activities that are related to college and professional sporting events. It also forbids them from providing any information about collegiate sports events to people involved in organized gambling activities.

The NCAA opposes sports gambling for the following reasons:

- It attracts organized crime.

- The profits fund other illegal activities, such as drug sales and loan-sharking (lending money at an excessive rate of interest).

- Student athletes who become involved can become indebted to bookies, leading to point-shaving schemes.

CHAPTER 9
INTERNET GAMBLING

Internet gambling is a relatively new phenomenon. The first gambling websites were launched during the mid-1990s and soared in popularity, particularly in the United States. Millions of Americans have gambled online, even though the practice is illegal. The American Gaming Association (AGA) estimates in "Online Gambling" (2013, http://www.americangaming.org/government-affairs/key-issues/online-gambling) that by 2012 Americans accounted for between $4 billion and $6 billion in global Internet gambling revenue. As Alan McGlade reports in "What eSports Can Tell Us about the Future of Online Gambling" (October 1, 2012, http://www.forbes.com/sites/alanmcglade/2012/10/01/what-esports-can-tell-us-about-the-future-of-online-gambling/), online gaming revenues topped $30 billion worldwide in 2011.

Exact figures on Internet gambling revenue are not known because the sites have not been permitted to operate within the United States and because most of the countries that do allow them to operate do not collect or report revenue statistics. According to David O. Stewart in *An Analysis of Internet Gambling and Its Policy Implications* (May 31, 2006, http://www.americangaming.org/files/aga/uploads/docs/whitepapers/wpaper_internet_0531.pdf), by 2005 two-thirds of Internet gambling operations were located in small Caribbean and Central American countries that provide little or no government oversight of the industry.

Many Internet gambling sites either do not pay taxes to their home countries or pay lower taxes than land-based gambling establishments. For example, Stewart notes that in March 2005 the island nation of Antigua and Barbuda in the Caribbean served as the headquarters for 536 gambling sites, the most of any country. The sites were only required to pay 3% of their gambling revenues (winnings after payout to customers) to the government with a ceiling of $50,000 per month. John L. McMullan and Aunshul Rege explain in "Online Crime and Internet Gambling"

(*Journal of Gambling Issues*, vol. 24, July 2010) that other popular locations for online gambling sites include Australia, Gibraltar, the United Kingdom, and the Kahnawake Mohawk Native American reserve in Canada.

Unlike most land-based casinos, the vast majority of Internet gambling sites are operated by small, virtually unknown companies. A land-based casino costs several hundred million dollars to build and operate and requires hundreds of employees, whereas an online casino is set up and operated by a handful of people for an initial investment of a few million dollars. The relatively low setup and operating costs make the businesses extremely profitable and allow them to offer higher payoffs to winners than land-based casinos.

The future of Internet gambling in the United States remains uncertain. Under the Unlawful Internet Gambling Enforcement Act (UIGEA) of 2006 banks and credit card companies are prohibited from transferring Americans' money to Internet gambling sites. Many casual gamblers turned away from online gambling sites when the law was enacted, although serious Internet gamblers continued to find ways of transferring funds to online casinos and card rooms. By late 2006, many of the larger, publicly traded Internet gambling companies, such as PartyPoker, had stopped accepting American customers altogether to avoid any conflicts with the U.S. government.

The landscape for online gambling in the United States changed dramatically in December 2011, however, when the U.S. Department of Justice issued an opinion stating that the Federal Wire Act of 1961 "does not cover communications related to non-sports wagering" (September 20, 2011, http://www.justice.gov/olc/2011/state-lotteries-opinion.pdf). As Nathan Vardi relates in "Department of Justice Flip-Flops on Internet Gambling" (December 23, 2011, http://www.forbes.com/sites/nathanvardi/2011/12/23/department-of-justice-flip-flops-on-internet-gambling/), the opinion arose in response to requests from the New

York and Illinois state lotteries, which were seeking clarification on the legality of selling lottery tickets over the Internet. According to Vardi, the opinion represented a clear reversal of the Justice Department's previous interpretation of the law, which had maintained that the Wire Act applied to all forms of Internet gambling. Indeed, as Vardi notes, the Justice Department ruling opened the door for other forms of online gambling, including poker and casino games, to become legal.

THE DEVELOPMENT OF INTERNET GAMBLING

There is no consensus on when the first Internet casino began operating and who started it. However, it is generally agreed that the first online casinos began operating sometime in 1995 or 1996. Among the first was Intercasino, based in Antigua and Barbuda. In 1996 Antigua and Barbuda legalized and licensed online gambling sites. The companies that operate these websites are trade-zone corporations—that is, foreign-owned corporations operating in specific areas of the country as if they were on foreign soil. In Antigua and Barbuda, trade-zone corporations cannot produce products for domestic consumption, so the citizens of Antigua and Barbuda are not allowed to participate in online gambling with any trade-zone companies that are located there.

Various agencies and private entities have attempted to estimate the extent of the online gambling industry, including the National Gambling Impact Study Commission (NGISC), the U.S. Department of Justice, and industry researchers such as Bear Stearns & Co. Even though their estimates differ, these analysts agree that the growth of online gambling has been phenomenal. In 1997 there were 50 to 60 Internet casinos in operation (most based in the Caribbean) that earned approximately $300 million to $350 million. By 2000 an estimated 600 to 700 sites were operating and revenues approached $2 billion. The AGA estimates in "Online Gambling" that in 2012 there were approximately 1,700 online gambling sites. Some sources cite a much higher figure for online gaming sites. In *Teen Gambling: Understanding a Growing Epidemic* (2012), Jeffrey L. Derevensky cites a survey indicating that, as of June 2010, 665 companies were operating 2,679 Internet gambling sites worldwide. According to Derevensky, this total included 865 online casinos, 616 online poker games, 516 sports wagering pages, 426 Internet bingo halls, and 187 pages devoted to lotteries and other forms of gambling.

ONLINE GAMES

Online casinos offer many of the same games that are available in land-based casinos, such as poker, blackjack, roulette, and slot machines. Bet denominations range from pennies to thousands of dollars. Poker websites have card rooms where players compete against each other rather than against the house. This is an example of person-to-person betting. To make a profit on these sites, the casino operators take a small percentage of the winning hand.

Online casino games operate in much the same way as the electronic games found in actual casinos. Both depend on random number generators: slot machines have a computer chip built in, and online games have random number generators written into their programming. Slot machine payoff percentages at actual casinos are dictated by the state in which they are located, whereas online payoffs are not. However, online providers who never have winners would not have return customers, so their programs are designed to pay out a particular percentage. Online games are particularly appealing to people who enjoy card games because the betting limits are much lower than they are in actual casinos. For example, an online gambler can play blackjack for $1 per hand, whereas many land-based casinos set a $10- or $25-per-hand minimum.

Some sites require players to download software onto their personal computer. The software still runs through a program at the website, so the user must be online to play. Other games are played right at the website. Many sites use high-tech software that allows players to gamble in virtual reality: they can "look" around the table or around the casino room. Players can even "chat" with each other via online messaging during a game. Both of these effects make online gambling more interactive for the user.

Many sites offer free play to introduce visitors to the types of games offered and to give them a chance to practice. Visitors who decide to play for money must register, open an account, and deposit money into that account. This requires input of personal information, including name and address. The user usually sets up a user name and password for future access. Money is transferred to the gambling site via credit or debit card, through an account with an online bank or payment service, or via electronic check or wire transfer.

Most online sites offer bonuses of 5% to 20% of the amount of the initial deposit. These bonuses usually require that the gambler wager an amount two to three times the size of the bonus. Other sites offer prizes, such as trips, for repeat business. Winnings are typically deposited into the user's online account or paid via a certified check that is mailed to the winner.

Stewart indicates that sports book betting constituted 35% of all Internet gambling in 2005. Casino games made up about 25%, and online poker accounted for 18% of all online gambling. As Joseph Menn reports in "Rushing for Online Poker Spoils, Some US Firms Tie up with Partners with a Past" (May 14, 2012, http://openchannel.nbcnews.com/_news/2012/05/14/11699454-rushing-for-online-poker-spoils-some-us-firms-tie-up-with-partners-with-a-past?lite), by 2012 the global online poker industry topped $5 billion in annual revenues. Of this figure, $400 million, or approximately 8%, was generated by players in the United States.

ONLINE GAMBLERS

Peter D. Hart Research Associates and Luntz Maslansky Strategic Research conducted an extensive poll of online gaming habits in the United States in 2006, which was presented by the AGA in *2006 State of the States: The AGA Survey of Casino Entertainment* (May 2006, http://www.americangaming.org/files/aga/uploads/docs/sos/aga-sos-2006.pdf). The poll finds that nearly 4% of Americans gambled online in 2006. Online gamblers (68%) were much more likely than casino gamblers (53%) to be male. The AGA also reports that 43% of online gamblers were aged 21 to 29 years, compared with only 9% of casino gamblers. Interestingly, people aged 60 years and older made up the largest proportion of casino gamblers (37%) and the smallest proportion of online gamblers (2%). Among online gamblers surveyed in 2006, 35% had four-year college degrees, and another 17% had postgraduate degrees. Among casino gamblers, a lower proportion had four-year college degrees (28%) and postgraduate degrees (15%). Online gamblers also tended to have incomes that were higher than the median U.S. household income (half of all households earned more and half earned less). In 2006, 24% had an income of between $75,000 and $99,999, and 17% had an income of more than $100,000.

The poll indicates that 38% of those who gambled online in 2006 started betting online a year before, and 32% said they started one to two years before. The largest number of online gamblers (80%) reported playing poker against other people during the previous year. Nearly as many online gamblers (78%) played casino games for money, and far fewer people (56%) made online bets on sports. Of those people who played online poker, nearly two-thirds (65%) said Texas Hold 'Em was their favorite game, followed by seven-card stud (13%), five-card draw (13%), and Omaha (8%). For online casino gamblers, people reported playing blackjack (78%) most often, followed by video poker (65%), slot machines (60%), roulette (37%), and craps (29%).

Robert T. Wood, Robert J. Williams, and Paul K. Lawton examine in "Why Do Internet Gamblers Prefer Online versus Land-Based Venues? Some Preliminary Findings and Implications" (*Journal of Gambling Issues*, vol. 20, June 2007) why gamblers patronize Internet gambling sites. The researchers find that gamblers' top reasons for betting on the Internet rather than at a casino involved convenience (12.9%), ease (12.2%), and comfort (11.7%). One out of 10 (10%) gamblers surveyed said they gambled online because of their distance from a casino or because they wanted privacy (9.8%). Other reasons given included dislike of casino clientele (5.1%), crowds (4.7%), noise (4.1%), or cigarette smoke (3.9%).

In *Online Gambling Five Years after UIGEA* (May 18, 2011, http://www.americangaming.org/files/aga/uploads/docs/final_online_gambling_white_paper_5-18-11.pdf), David O. Stewart notes that, in spite of legal prohibitions, approximately 10 million Americans had gambled online in the previous decade. According to Stewart, between 2003 and 2010 Americans wagered roughly $30 billion on Internet gambling. This money was bet on a variety of games and contests, including sports betting, online poker, and electronic casino games such as blackjack, roulette, and slots. The AGA indicates in *2012 State of the States: The AGA Survey of Casino Entertainment* (2012, http://www.americangaming.org/files/aga/uploads/docs/sos/aga_sos_2012_web.pdf) that 4% of American adults placed some form of Internet wager in 2011.

THE LEGAL ISSUES

Regulating any activity on the Internet has turned out to be extremely challenging for authorities. Every country wants jurisdiction (the authority to enforce its own laws) over content that its citizens can access on the Internet. This has proved to be difficult, however, because the Internet has no boundaries. A business based on a host computer might be legal in the country in which it is physically located but illegal in other countries where it can be accessed on the Internet.

Most countries restrict gambling activity much less than the United States does, but in the United States the individual states and not the federal government regulate gambling. Even though there are federal antigambling laws, they defer to the 10th Amendment of the U.S. Constitution, which guarantees the rights of the states to govern their own affairs. Every state allows or disallows different forms of gambling. For example, Hawaii and Utah prohibit all types of gambling. Commercial casino gambling is legal in 13 states. Pari-mutuel wagering on horse and greyhound races is legal in 43 states. Gambling on sporting events through a bookmaker is legal only in Nevada and, to a limited extent, in Delaware. Internet gambling, however, is not subject to state boundaries. A user in any state can access online gambling sites that are operated from countries around the world where gambling is legal.

Determining jurisdiction is a major problem for authorities. Does online gambling occur at the location where the website is hosted or at the location where the gambler is located? The Department of Justice states that gambling occurs in both places. The problem becomes even more complicated when one or the other is not on U.S. soil. Even though an international treaty with extradition rights could settle such matters, it is unlikely that one would be written and signed.

Various forms of gambling are legal in many parts of Europe, Central and South America, the Caribbean, Australia, and New Zealand. Most of these areas have established regulatory measures that are similar to the laws regulating land-based casinos in the United States. For example, in June 2001 the Australian senate passed the Interactive Gambling Act, which prohibits online casinos in the country from taking bets from Australians. The law has provisions allowing interactive sports gambling and wagering services. Foreign residents can gamble at the Australian-based online casinos unless their governments sign up to be excluded from the program. In 2005 the parliament of the United Kingdom passed the Gaming Act, which set up regulations and licensing procedures for online casinos. Even though online casinos in the United Kingdom would pay higher taxes than those in the Caribbean, the UK had several advantages over Caribbean locations, including an advanced communications infrastructure, a stable political environment, and an educated workforce.

The Interstate Wire Act

In 1961 President John F. Kennedy (1917–1963) signed the Interstate Wire Act—widely known as the Wire Act—which makes it a crime to use telephone lines (wire communication) in interstate or foreign commerce for the placement of sports bets or even to transmit information assisting in the placement of bets on sporting events. The act applies only to the gambling business, not to gamblers themselves.

The article "Gambling on the Internet: Crossing the Interstate Wire" (*Wager*, vol. 6, no. 6, February 7, 2001) examines the legal issues involved in Internet gambling, particularly criticisms of the Wire Act. It finds that many legal experts say the law does not directly apply or is too ambiguous to apply to offshore Internet gambling sites. The states have interpreted the Wire Act to mean that online wagering is illegal if it occurs in any state in which gambling is illegal.

In 1999 the issue was addressed by the New York Supreme Court in *People v. World Interactive Gaming Corporation* (185 Misc.2d 852, 714 N.Y.S.2d 844). The state of New York brought suit against the World Interactive Gaming Corporation (WIGC) and the Golden Chips Casino for offering online gambling to New York residents. The Golden Chips Casino operated a legal land-based casino in Antigua and Barbuda. The company was wholly owned by the WIGC, a Delaware-based corporation with corporate offices in New York. The suit alleged that the casino had installed interactive software

on its computer servers in Antigua and Barbuda that allowed Internet users from around the world to gamble. Users in states where gambling was illegal had only to give a false address to access the website. The state of New York did not consider this a "good faith effort" to keep New Yorkers from gambling, as required by law.

The WIGC argued that the federal and state laws in question did not apply to an offshore casino that operated in full compliance with the law in the country in which it was located. The court ruled in favor of the state, saying that the act of entering the bet and transmitting the betting information originated in New York and constituted illegal gambling activity. The legality of gambling in Antigua and Barbuda was not an issue.

Furthermore, the court said the gambling activity violated three federal laws: the Wire Act; the Foreign Travel or Transportation in Aid of Racketeering Enterprising Act (U.S. Code §1952), known as "the Travel Act"; and the Interstate Transportation of Wagering Paraphernalia Act (U.S. Code §1953), known as "the Paraphernalia Act." According to the court, "the Travel Act…prohibits the use of 'any facility in interstate or foreign commerce' with intent to promote any unlawful activity." The Paraphernalia Act is specific to gambling activity, prohibiting the interstate or foreign transmission of any item for use "in (a) bookmaking; or (b) wagering pools with respect to a sporting event; or (c) in a numbers, policy, bolita, or similar game." The court ruled that the WIGC violated this law because it used the U.S. mail to send literature to potential investors and to send computers to the operations in Antigua and Barbuda.

One issue was still not settled: Which types of gambling sites were covered by the Wire Act? The Wire Act only states that people cannot make sports bets over communication lines. In 2002 the Appeals Court for the Fifth Circuit ruled in *In regarding MasterCard International, Inc.* (313 F.3d 257) that the Wire Act applies specifically to online sports gambling (also known as sports books) and not to online casinos or poker sites.

During the late 1990s the Department of Justice went after the operators of offshore sports books that had taken bets from U.S. citizens via the Internet and telephone. Despite some high-profile arrests, many online sports books operating outside the United States continued to openly market their websites to Americans and allow Americans to place bets.

In 2006 the Department of Justice cracked down once again on the owners of Internet sports book sites when it arrested David Carruthers (1957–), who was the chief executive officer of the Costa Rican–based BetOnSports. Federal agents arrested Carruthers when he changed planes in Dallas, Texas. He was charged with violating the Wire Act and committing mail fraud. After the arrest, BetOnSports shut down the division of its operations that took bets from U.S. gamblers and fired Carruthers. In January 2010 Carruthers pleaded guilty to racketeering and was sentenced to 33 months in prison. Several other BetOnSports executives were also arrested, notably its founder, Gary Kaplan (1959–), who was sentenced to 51 months in prison.

Jacob Sullum reports in "Some Bets Are Off: The Strangely Selective and Self-Defeating Crackdown on Internet Gambling" (*Reason*, June 2008) that in 2003 Antigua and Barbuda claimed that the stance the United States took on online gambling was in violation of several free trade agreements laid down by the World Trade Organization (WTO), a multinational trading organization with limited power that sets up and enforces trading agreements between its members. When they appealed to the WTO in an effort to end U.S. restrictions, Antigua and Barbuda maintained that thousands of jobs in their nation depended on online gambling and that the United States was harming their economy by attempting to restrict access by U.S. citizens. The WTO ruled against the United States in 2004, claiming that several U.S. laws regarding online gambling violated WTO free trade agreements. After two years of talks, the United States refused to change its position on online gambling. Antigua and Barbuda approached the WTO again, and in July 2006 the WTO convened a panel to further investigate U.S. laws regarding online gambling. In February 2007 the panel found that the United States was in violation of international trade agreements. In December of that year an arbitrator found that Antigua and Barbuda had lost $21 million as a result of the U.S. laws and that they could impose trade sanctions against the United States. As Geno Laurenzi Jr. reports in "Antigua-Barbuda Declare Gaming Trade War on U.S." (December 29, 2012, http://www.thestkittsnevisobserver.com/2012/12/28/gaming-trade-war.html), in December 2012 Antigua Finance Minister Howard Lovell filed a lawsuit with the WTO, charging that the United States had violated international law by continuing to deny online gaming operations the right to do business with American citizens. While Antigua was seeking $3.4 billion as part of the lawsuit, the WTO imposed a limit of $21 million a year in potential damages. A formal hearing on the dispute was scheduled for January 2013.

The UIGEA

Because of the shortcomings of the Wire Act and its failure to address modern gambling technologies, the NGISC recommended in *Final Report* (June 1999, http://govinfo.library.unt.edu/ngisc/reports/fullrpt.html) that Congress enact federal legislation that prohibits wire transfers from U.S. banks to online gambling sites and their banks. The UIGEA, which was signed into law in October 2006, outlaws the use of credit cards to pay for online gambling. More specifically, the law prohibits credit card companies from conducting transactions with online gambling establishments and authorizes the U.S. secretary of the treasury to prohibit any future, unforeseen payment methods that might be used for online gambling.

Michael Blankenship notes in "The Unlawful Internet Gambling Enforcement Act: A Bad Gambling Act? You Betcha!" (*Rutgers Law Review*, vol. 60, no. 2, 2008) that even after the UIGEA became law, many questions remained about how it would be enforced. It was clear that banks and credit card companies were prohibited from transferring money directly to online casinos and poker sites, such as PartyPoker. However, whether banks and credit card companies could transfer money for gambling to online payment processors, such as Neteller and PayPal, was considerably murkier. Many online gamblers set up accounts with payment processors, which function as online banks, and then transfer money in and out of online casinos. The new law prohibited U.S. banks and credit card companies from sending money to payment processors that deal exclusively with casinos. However, the law was less clear about payment processors that cater to a wide array of businesses and to payment processors or casinos that are located in other countries or are privately held: foreign businesses are not regulated by U.S. law and privately held companies are not required by law to divulge publicly how they make money. According to Blankenship, many people believe that those who are determined to gamble online will find a way, probably by going to foreign, private payment processors and casinos. In fact, banks and credit card companies were not required to comply with the law until June 1, 2010, because there were so many potential problems with enforcement.

However, since the UIGEA did not specifically ban gambling over the Internet, U.S. lawmakers continued to wrestle with the legality of online gaming. In 2007 two bills were introduced in Congress that sought to regulate, rather than outlaw, online gambling. In April 2007 the Internet Gambling Regulation and Enforcement Act (H.R. 2046) was introduced in the U.S. House of Representatives. The bill would license and regulate Internet gambling sites. It was referred to the House Subcommittee on Commerce, Trade, and Consumer Protection, where it died. In June 2007 the Internet Gambling Regulation and Tax Enforcement Act (H.R. 2268) was introduced to establish licensing requirements and fees for Internet gambling sites and was referred to the House Ways and Means Committee. The bill was subsequently reintroduced three times: in March 2008, in May 2009, and in June 2011; in all three instances it was buried in committee, and never received a vote on the House floor. In May 2009 another bill, the Internet Gambling

Regulation, Consumer Protection, and Enforcement Act (H.R. 2267) was introduced in the House. The bill would legalize online poker and other nonsports betting. It was referred to the House Ways and Means Committee in July 2010. Sewell Chan reports in "Congress Rethinks Its Ban on Internet Gambling" (*New York Times*, July 28, 2010) that supporters of this bill estimate that tax revenues could be as much as $42 billion over 10 years. The bill was reintroduced as H.R. 1174 in March 2011, but it never received a vote.

During this time, the U.S. Senate also considered bills that would legalize some forms of online gambling. The Senate considered the Internet Skill Game Licensing and Control Act (S. 3616) in September 2008 and the Internet Poker and Game of Skill Regulation, Consumer Protection, and Enforcement Act (S. 1597) in August 2009. S. 3616 was referred to the Committee on Banking, Housing, and Urban Affairs and S. 1597 was referred to the Committee on Finance. Both bills ultimately died in committee.

Meanwhile, the federal government continued its aggressive attempts to shut down online gambling operations. One of the biggest crackdowns in the history of the Internet gaming industry took place on April 15, 2011, when the U.S. Department of Justice issued indictments against the world's three leading online poker sites: PokerStars, Full Tilt Poker, and Absolute Poker. As Caroline Winter reports in "Bitcoin: Making Online Gambling Legal in the U.S.?" (January 3, 2013, http://www.business week.com/articles/2013-01-03/bitcoin-making-online-gam bling-legal-in-the-u-dot-s-dot), 11 individuals affiliated with the companies were charged with money laundering, bank fraud, and illegal gambling. Within the online gaming industry, the day the indictments were released became known as "Black Friday." In the aftermath of the bust, thousands of online poker players based in the United States had more than $100 million in assets frozen by the federal government. According to Winter, these players, who were not formally charged with crimes, had not been reimbursed for lost funds as of January 2013.

In June 2011 Representative Joe Barton (R-Texas; 1949–) introduced the Internet Gambling Prohibition, Poker Consumer Protection, and Strengthening UIGEA Act (H.R. 2366), a bill calling for the legalization of online poker. Under the bill, the federal government would establish a new division within the Department of Commerce charged with regulating the industry. Although the bill was subsequently referred to committee, other attempts to legalize online poker soon followed. As the news agency UPI reports in "Ruling Ups Stakes for Online Poker in U.S." (August 24, 2012, http://www.upi.com/Top_News/US/2012/08/24/Ruling-ups-stakes-for-online-poker-in-US/UPI-52281345811626/), proponents of online poker received a boost in August 2012, when a U.S. District

Court Judge ruled that poker could not technically be considered gambling because it is not "predominated by chance," but rather requires skill on the part of the player. In October 2012, Senators Harry Reid (D-NV; 1939–) and Jon Kyl (R-AZ; 1942–) co-authored the Internet Gambling Prohibition, Poker Consumer Protection, and Strengthening UIGEA Act, with the aim of creating a regulatory framework allowing for U.S. citizens to play online poker. As of January 2013, the bill had yet to be introduced to the Senate.

State Laws

Both Hawaii and Utah outlaw any acts of gambling within state borders, which by default includes Internet gambling. As of 2011, eight states had laws in place that expressly banned online gambling: Illinois, Indiana, Louisiana, Montana, Nevada, Oregon, South Dakota, and Washington. Furthermore, the attorneys general in Florida, Kansas, Minnesota, Oklahoma, and Texas maintained that Internet gambling in their states is illegal under existing state laws. In the aftermath of the U.S. Justice Department's December 2011 opinion stating that the prohibition on Internet wagering applied only to sports betting, a number of states began to explore ways to legalize online gaming. Michael Cooper reports in "As States Weigh Online Gambling, Profit May Be Small" (January 17, 2012, http://www.nytimes.com/2012/01/18/us/more-states-look-to-legalize-online-gambling.html?_r=0) that by January 2012 lawmakers in Iowa, California, Nevada, and Washington, D.C., had already begun to pursue new legislation opening the way for Internet gambling. As Doug Denison reports in "Delaware to Allow Online Gambling" (June 28, 2012, http://usatoday30.usa today.com/news/nation/story/2012-06-28/delaware-online-gambling/55897914/1), in June 2012 Delaware became the first state to legalize gambling over the Internet; the statute included online casino games such as blackjack and roulette, as well as online poker. In "N.J. Bill Allowing Atlantic City Online Gambling Gets Final Approval" (December 20, 2012, http://www.nj.com/politics/index.ssf/2012/12/nj_bill_allowing_atlan tic_city.html), Christopher Baxter reports that the New Jersey State Legislature passed a bill in December 2012, allowing licensed casino operators in Atlantic City to begin accepting wagers online.

Credit Cards

Between 1997 and 1998 a California woman named Cynthia Haines charged more than $70,000 in online gambling losses to her credit cards. Providian National Bank, which issued the cards, sued her for nonpayment. In June 1998 Haines countersued the bank, claiming that it had engaged in unfair business practices by making profits from illegal gambling activities. At that time all casino gambling was illegal in California. Haines's lawyers argued that her debt was void because it arose from an illegal contract. Providian ultimately settled out of court, forgave her debt, and paid $225,000 of her attorneys' fees. Consequently, the company decided not to accept online gambling transactions in the future.

This settlement caught the attention of other major credit card issuers. Nonpayment of outstanding credit card charges results in serious losses, called charge-offs in the industry. Faced with the potential for massive charge-offs and legal uncertainties, many credit card issuers—including Bank of America, Capital One Bank, Chase Manhattan, Citibank, Direct Merchants, Fleet, and MBNA—stopped accepting financial transactions from online gambling sites. Issuers that continued to accept online gambling transactions decided to delay payment of part or all the money to the online sites for several months in case the user decided to dispute the charges.

The U.S. General Accounting Office (now the U.S. Government Accountability Office) explains in *Internet Gambling: An Overview of the Issues* (December 2002, http://www.gao.gov/new.items/d0389.pdf) that all the major credit card companies (Discover, American Express, Visa, and MasterCard) had enacted measures to restrict the use of their cards for Internet gambling by 2002. Discover and American Express accomplished this primarily by preventing Internet gambling sites from becoming merchants in the first place. All potential merchants are screened, and existing merchants are spot-checked to make sure they are not engaged in online gambling. Visa and MasterCard are issued by a large network of financial institutions that have credit card associations. These associations set policies for member institutions and provide the computer systems that are used to process financial transactions. The associations have a coding system that merchants must use to distinguish the different types of transactions. It was refined in 1998 so that online gambling sites have to enter a special two-part code that tells the issuer the nature of their business and gives the issuer a chance to deny authorization. However, the coding system does not distinguish between legal and illegal transactions. For example, Americans visiting countries in which online gambling is legal may find their credit cards rejected there when they try to gamble over the Internet. According to the credit card associations, the coding system can also be tricked by unscrupulous merchants who intentionally enter the wrong code for their business.

Because credit card transactions were blocked at online gambling sites, merchants and gamblers turned to alternative payment systems, called online payment providers. These services allow customers to transfer money from their credit cards into accounts that can then be debited to pay for a variety of online goods and services, including gambling. Money going to and from these intermediary accounts is not easily traced. Online payment providers include PayPal, Neteller, and ECash. Some credit card associations are refusing to do business with online payment providers unless they receive assurances that money will not be transferred to Internet gambling sites.

Between 2002 and 2003 PayPal paid millions of dollars to settle allegations that it violated the Uniting and Strengthening America by Providing Appropriate Tools Required to Intercept and Obstruct Terrorism Act of 2001 (also called the Patriot Act) during 2001 and early 2002 by processing online gambling transactions from U.S. citizens. The Patriot Act forbids the electronic transmission of funds known to be associated with criminal acts. PayPal stopped handling online gambling transactions in November 2002. Neteller processed these funds until January 2007, when its Canadian founders were arrested in the United States on charges of conspiracy and money laundering (the act of engaging in transactions that are designed to hide or obscure the origin of illegally obtained money).

Federal Crackdown on Advertising

Under the Wire Act, advertisements for online gambling are illegal in the United States. According to the Department of Justice, media outlets that run advertisements for online gambling are aiding and abetting the gambling websites. However, during the first years of the 21st century online gambling companies advertised extensively online, in magazines and newspapers, and on television. In 2003 the Department of Justice mounted an offensive against the U.S. media to stop the proliferation of such advertisements. One salvo was a letter to the National Association of Broadcasters in which the department outlined its position on advertising for online gambling websites. Then in 2004 the Department of Justice intervened when Discovery Communications agreed to run $3.9 million in ads for Paradise Poker, mostly during *World Poker Tour* episodes on the Travel Channel. Discovery Communications aired $600,000 worth of the ads and refused to air the rest. Before Paradise Poker could recover the remainder of the balance paid to Discovery Communications for the ads (about $3.3 million), the Department of Justice seized the money. The obvious message was that online gambling sites that advertised in the United States could have their ads canceled and their assets seized.

In April 2004 major Internet search engines, including Yahoo and Google, announced that they would no longer display ads for online gambling sites that targeted U.S. citizens. The companies reportedly acted to head off plans by the Department of Justice to pursue legal action against them. However, many other websites did not heed the department's warning. For example, in 2005 the parent company of the *Sporting News* was forced to surrender $4.2 million in advertising revenue after running ads for several online gambling sites. Furthermore, the company agreed to spend $3 million to create and run antigambling advertisements online. The Department of Justice also intervened in 2005 when *Esquire* ran ads for the Costa Rican poker site Bodog.com. *Esquire* agreed not to run any more online casino ads.

One way Internet gambling sites have subverted these prohibitions is to create dot-net sites that mirror the dot-com sites, except that users play with fake money. For example, PartyPoker.com created PartyPoker.net, which bills itself as the "world's largest poker school." Media outlets have accepted advertising for these dot-net sites.

THE EFFECTS OF ONLINE GAMBLING

Because the Internet gambling medium is relatively new, a limited number of studies have been conducted to determine its effects on people and their gambling habits. Economic factors are also difficult to assess because most online gambling sites operate in foreign countries with little government oversight.

Economics

Unlike traditional casinos, online gambling sites are not licensed or taxed by state governments. Therefore, they provide no revenue for educational and social programs. The primary financial beneficiaries are the online gambling companies themselves, the foreign countries in which they are located, and the companies that process their financial transactions.

Other businesses that benefit directly or indirectly from online gambling include Internet service providers, phone and cable companies, nongambling websites that feature advertisements for online gambling sites, and software companies. Major software providers to online gambling sites include GTECH G2, Microgaming, Virgin Gaming, and WagerLogic Limited.

Mobile phone companies expect cellular gambling to become commonplace in the future, particularly for phones with video streaming. Ladbrokes and William Hill are traditional British bookmakers that accept wagers via cellular phones using wireless application protocol. The company Eurobet launched wireless betting in 2000. Other companies, such as Slotland.com, allow people to play slots and win jackpots on their mobile phones. In the press release "Mobile Gambling Wagers to Surpass $48bn by 2015, Spurred by Chinese Lottery Deployments, Juniper Research Finds" (September 2, 2010, http://www.juniperresearch.com/viewpressrelease.php?pr=204), Juniper Research, an analyst firm for the wireless industry, predicts that revenues from cellular gambling will grow to $48 billion by 2015. Experts believe this growth will be fueled by expansions of mobile gambling services in Asia and by a liberalization of gambling laws in the United States.

Ryan D. Hammer discusses the economic effects of online gambling in "Does Internet Gambling Strengthen the U.S. Economy? Don't Bet on It" (*Federal Communications Law Journal*, vol. 54, no. 1, December 2001). Hammer argues that people who do not gamble on the Internet still suffer financially from online gambling. He notes that the credit card companies pass the high costs of litigation and unpaid bills on to their customers in the form of higher interest rates and fees. Taxpayer money also funds federal and state lawsuits against online gambling sites. State governments receive no licensing fees or tax revenue from online gambling sites but must fund treatment programs for pathological gamblers, a growing number of whom are online gamblers. The federal government collects income taxes from the big winners of lotteries and traditional casino games, but taxes are not collected from online gambling winners.

Crime

MONEY LAUNDERING. Law enforcement agencies are concerned about the possible use of online gambling sites for money laundering. In his testimony before the U.S. Senate Committee on Banking, Housing, and Urban Affairs, John G. Malcolm (March 18, 2003, http://banking.senate.gov/03_03hrg/031803/malcolm.htm), the former U.S. deputy assistant attorney general, explained that once the money has been stashed with an online casino, criminals can use the games themselves to transfer money to their associates. Some criminals set up private tables at online casino sites and then intentionally lose their money to business associates at the table. In other instances, the casino is part of the crime organization, so all the criminal has to do is lose money to the casino.

According to law enforcement officials, the factors that make online gambling susceptible to money laundering include the speed and anonymity with which financial transactions take place and the offshore locations of the gambling companies. McMullan and Rege document several ways that money laundering can take place through online gambling. For example, criminal networks can swamp online poker rooms with inferior "bots" and then play against these bots, allowing dirty money to be divided and exchanged through the online game. Bots can also be programmed to wager and fold to flood online games with illegal money. In such instances, criminals can take the last seat at the table, beat the bots, and cash out the winnings, thereby "cleaning" the money through the online poker room accounts.

CYBERNOMADS AND "DOT-CONS." The proliferation of online poker sites has led to increasingly sophisticated methods of "cheating" at the game. McMullan and Rege call these cheating individuals "cybernomads"—people who illegally make money from online poker sites, but not as part of criminal networks. The researchers explain that these players use artificial intelligence software that gives them a huge edge in online poker games. This software is used to monitor opponents to determine their betting patterns and styles and to calculate the odds. Other "cheaters" are hackers themselves who harvest personal information from online gambling sites and sell it on the black market.

McMullan and Rege note that criminals sometimes work in "dot-con" teams to cheat online poker sites. A notable case happened in 2007 during an online poker tournament at FullTiltPoker.com. During the middle of the tournament Chris "BluffMagCV" Vaughn sold his seat to Sorel "Imper1um" Mizzi, a more experienced player. As a result, the other tournament players were unable to recognize Mizzi's playing style and defeat him. However, Mizzi/Vaughn were denied the $1 million prize when FullTiltPoker.com discovered the deception. Dot-con teams also work together to modify game events or commands or to steal usernames, passwords, and account information.

Compulsive Gambling

Experts suggest that online gambling is more addictive than other types of gambling because of its fast pace and instant gratification. Online gambling is quite different from traditional casino gambling because it is a solitary and anonymous activity. By contrast, casino gambling is a social activity that is usually conducted in the company of family or friends. The Council on Compulsive Gaming of New Jersey estimates that a large percentage of online gamblers gamble alone. Online gamblers who contact the organization for help are usually younger than traditional gamblers and have built up large amounts of debt in a shorter time than traditional gamblers.

George T. Ladd and Nancy M. Petry of the University of Connecticut conducted a study of Internet gamblers and published their results in "Disordered Gambling among University-Based Medical and Dental Patients: A Focus on Internet Gambling" (*Psychology of Addictive Behaviors*, vol. 16, no. 1, March 2002). Between August 1999 and September 2000 the researchers surveyed 389 patients seeking free or reduced-cost services at the university's health and dental clinics. All the patients who participated in the study had gambled at some point during their life. About 90% had gambled during the previous year, and 42% had gambled during the previous week. About 8% had gambled online at some point during their lifetime, and 3.7% gambled online weekly. The younger respondents were more likely to have Internet gambling experience than were the older respondents: the median age of the online gamblers was 31.7 years, compared with 43.5 years for traditional gamblers. Ethnicity also made a difference. Non-whites made up only 15.8% of the total group surveyed but 35.8% of the Internet gamblers.

All participants were given the South Oaks Gambling Screen (SOGS), a standard series of questions that are used to determine the probability that a person has a gambling problem. (See Chapter 2.) Results showed that the mean SOGS score of online gamblers was 7.8, compared with 1.8 for those who had no online gambling experience. Researchers categorized all respondents into levels depending on their SOGS scores. Level 1 gamblers had SOGS scores of 0 to 2 and were considered not to have a gambling problem. Level 2 gamblers had SOGS scores of 3 to 4 and were considered probable problem gamblers. Level 3 gamblers had SOGS scores of 5 or greater and were considered probable pathological gamblers. Ladd and Petry note that Internet gamblers were much more likely to have gambling problems than non-Internet gamblers. Slightly more than 74% of Internet gamblers were rated at Levels 2 or 3, compared with 21.6% of the traditional gamblers.

Ladd and Petry then retrieved the medical records for those who participated in the study. The researchers find that Internet gamblers had poorer mental and physical health than did non-Internet gamblers. In detailing their study, Ladd and Petry write that "the availability of Internet gambling may draw individuals who seek out isolated and anonymous contexts for their gambling behaviors." Even though problem gamblers are able to resist traveling to another state to play in casinos, Ladd and Petry determine that online gambling is more difficult to avoid because Internet sites are always open and accessible.

Nancy M. Petry reports the results of a follow-up study in "Internet Gambling: An Emerging Concern in Family Practice Medicine" (*Family Practice*, vol. 23, no. 4, August 2006). In this study, 1,414 adults in waiting areas of health clinics were given the SOGS test. Some 6.9% of adults reported ever gambling on the Internet, and 2.8% said they gambled online frequently. Of those who gambled frequently, nearly two-thirds (65.9%) were categorized as problem gamblers, as compared with 29.8% of those who reported ever gambling on the Internet and 7.6% of those who were classified as non-Internet gamblers.

Thomas Holtgraves of Ball State University finds in "Gambling, Gambling Activities, and Problem Gambling" (*Psychology of Addictive Behaviors*, vol. 23, no. 2, June 2009) that Internet gambling and betting on sports and horse races have higher "conversion rates" than other gambling activities; in other words, people who gamble on the Internet or bet on sports are more likely than other gamblers to continue doing so frequently. Holtgraves identifies the Internet's availability as a causal factor in this high conversion rate, writing, "Nothing is more available than the Internet; a player doesn't even need to leave home."

Underage Gambling

In January 2001 the American Psychiatric Association was already warning the public about Internet gambling. In a public health advisory, it noted that because online sites were not regulated, measures were not being taken to prevent underage gamblers from participating. It considered children, who already play nongambling games on the Internet, to be at significant risk of being lured to gambling sites. It also noted that few safeguards were in place to ensure the fairness of the Internet games or to establish exactly who had responsibility for operating them.

In "FTC Warns Consumers about Online Gambling and Children" (June 26, 2002, http://www.ftc.gov/opa/2002/06/onlinegambling.shtm), the Federal Trade Commission (FTC) also warns parents about children and online gambling. The FTC states "that minors can... access these sites easily, and that minors are often exposed to ads for online gambling on non-gambling websites." Furthermore, the agency notes that it examined over 100 Internet gambling websites and found that 20% did not have any warnings directed toward children and that many lacked measures to block minors from gambling.

Each year the Annenberg Public Policy Center at the University of Pennsylvania releases the National Annenberg Survey of Youth. The center states in "Internet Gambling Grows among Male Youth Ages 14 to 22" (October 14, 2010, http://www.annenbergpublicpolicycenter.org/ Downloads/Releases/ACI/Card%20Playing%202010%20 Release%20final.pdf) that 6.2% of male high school students between the ages of 14 and 17 gambled online at least once per month in 2010; in 2008 this figure was only 2.7%. At the same time, 1.5% of female high school students aged 14 to 17 reported gambling over the Internet at least once per month in 2010, up from 0.5% in 2008. Among older students, these numbers were significantly higher, with 16% of college-aged males and 4.4% of college-aged females gambling online at least once per month in 2010. In October 2011 Daniel Romer, director of the Adolescent Communication Institute at the Annenberg Public Policy Center, testified before the House Subcommittee on Commerce, Manufacturing, and Trade on the subject of online gambling. At the hearing ("Internet Gambling: Is There a Safe Bet?," October 14, 2011, http://www.annenbergpublicpolicycenter.org/Downloads/ Adolescent_Risk/NASY/Dan%20Romer%20Testimony .pdf), Romer argued that online gambling presented a particularly challenging situation because it involved illegal entities operating outside of the United States, making it more difficult for the U.S. government to implement legal safeguards protecting young people from engaging in this potentially self-destructive behavior. Nevertheless, he encouraged the adoption of "a new regime of online licensing and control" that would help to "minimize the harm that this activity can inflict on the young and their families."

IMPORTANT NAMES
AND ADDRESSES

American Gaming Association
1299 Pennsylvania Ave. NW, Ste. 1175
Washington, DC 20004
(202) 552-2675
FAX: (202) 552-2676
E-mail: info@americangaming.org
URL: http://www.americangaming.org/

Annenberg Public Policy Center
202 S. 36th St.
Philadelphia, PA 19104-3806
(215) 898-9400
FAX: (215) 573-7116
E-mail: info@annenbergpublicpolicycenter
.org
URL: http://www.annenbergpublicpolicy
center.org/

Arizona Department of Racing
1110 W. Washington, Ste. 260
Phoenix, AZ 85007
(602) 364-1700
FAX: (602) 364-1703
E-mail: support@azracing.gov
URL: http://www.azracing.gov/

Arizona Lottery
4740 E. University Dr.
Phoenix, AZ 85034
(480) 921-4400
URL: http://www.arizonalottery.com/

Arkansas Racing Commission
1509 W. Seventh St.
Little Rock, AR 72201
(501) 682-1467
FAX: (501) 682-5273
E-mail: racing@dfa.arkansas.gov
URL: http://www.dfa.arkansas.gov/offices/
racingCommission/Pages/default.aspx

Arkansas Scholarship Lottery
PO Box 3238
Little Rock, AR 72203-3239
(501) 683-2000

E-mail: aslinfo@arkansas.gov
URL: http://myarkansaslottery.com/

California Horse Racing Board
1010 Hurley Way, Ste. 300
Sacramento, CA 95825
(916) 263-6000
URL: http://www.chrb.ca.gov/

California Lottery
4106 East Commerce Way
Sacramento, CA 95834
(916) 830-0292
URL: http://www.calottery.com/

Colorado Division of Gaming
17301 W. Colfax Ave., Ste. 135
Golden, CO 80401
(303) 205-1355
FAX: (303) 205-1342
E-mail: gamingweb@spike.dor.state.co.us
URL: http://www.revenue.state.co.us/
Gaming/home.asp

Colorado Lottery
225 N. Main St.
Pueblo, CO 81003
(719) 546-2400
FAX: (719) 546-5208
URL: http://www.coloradolottery.com/

**Connecticut Department of Consumer
Protection, Gaming Division**
165 Capitol Ave.
Hartford, CT 06106-1630
(860) 713-6100
FAX: (860) 713-7239
E-mail: dcp.gaming@ct.gov
URL: http://www.ct.gov/dosr/site/
default.asp

Connecticut Lottery Corporation
777 Brook St.
Rocky Hill, CT 06067
(860) 713-2000
FAX: (860) 713-2805

E-mail: ctlottery@ctlottery.org
URL: http://www.ctlottery.org/

The Connection, Inc.
100 Roscommon Dr.
Middletown, CT 06457
1-888-TCI-1972
FAX: (860) 343-5517
E-mail: info@theconnectioninc.org
URL: http://theconnectioninc.org/

**DC Lottery and Charitable Games
Control Board**
2101 Martin Luther King Jr. Ave. SE
Washington, DC 20020
(202) 645-8000
FAX: (202) 645-7914
URL: http://lottery.dc.gov/

Delaware Lottery
1575 McKee Rd., Ste. 102
Dover, DE 19904
(302) 739-5291
FAX: (302) 739-6706
URL: http://lottery.state.de.us/

**Florida Department of Business and
Professional Regulation
Division of Pari-mutuel Wagering**
1940 N. Monroe St.
Tallahassee, FL 32399-1035
(850) 487-1395
FAX: (850) 488-0550
E-mail: communications@dbpr.state.fl.us
URL: http://www.myflorida.com/dbpr/pmw/
index.shtml

Florida Lottery
250 Marriott Dr.
Tallahassee, FL 32301
(850) 487-7787
FAX: (850) 488-8049
URL: http://www.flalottery.com/

Gamblers Anonymous
PO Box 17173
Los Angeles, CA 90017
(626) 960-3500
FAX: (626) 960-3501
E-mail: isomain@gamblersanonymous.org
URL: http://www.gamblersanonymous.org/

Georgia Lottery Corporation
250 Williams St., Ste. 3000
Atlanta, GA 30303
(404) 215-5000
E-mail: glottery@galottery.org
URL: http://www.galottery.com/

Greyhound Protection League
PO Box 669
Penn Valley, CA 95946
1-800-446-8637
URL: http://www.greyhounds.org/

Hoosier Lottery
1302 N. Meridian St.
Indianapolis, IN 46202
1-800-955-6886
URL: http://www.hoosierlottery.com/

Humane Society of the United States
2100 L St. NW
Washington, DC 20037
(202) 452-1100
URL: http://www.humanesociety.org/

Idaho Lottery
1199 Shoreline Ln., Ste. 100
Boise, ID 83702
(208) 334-2600
E-mail: info@idaholottery.com
URL: http://www.idaholottery.com/

Idaho State Police Racing Commission
700 S. Stratford Dr.
Meridian, ID 83642
(208) 884-7080
FAX: (208) 884-7090
URL: http://www.isp.idaho.gov/race/index.html

Illinois Gaming Board
160 N. LaSalle, Ste. 300
Chicago, IL 60601
(312) 814-4700
FAX: (312) 814-4602
URL: http://www.igb.illinois.gov/

Illinois Lottery
101 W. Jefferson St.
Springfield, IL 62702
(217) 524-6435
E-mail: LotteryInfo@NorthstarLottery.net
URL: http://www.illinoislottery.com/

Illinois Racing Board
100 W. Randolph, Ste. 7-701
Chicago, IL 60601
(312) 814-2600
FAX: (312) 814-5062

E-mail: IRB.Info@illinois.gov
URL: http://www.state.il.us/agency/irb/

Indiana Gaming Commission
East Tower, Ste. 1600
101 W. Washington St.
Indianapolis, IN 46204
(317) 233-0046
FAX: (317) 233-0047
URL: http://www.in.gov/igc/

Indiana Horse Racing Commission
Hoosier Park
4500 Dan Patch Cir.
Anderson, IN 46160
(765) 609-4855
URL: http://www.in.gov/hrc/

Institute for the Study of Gambling and Commercial Gaming
1664 N. Virginia St.
Reno, NV 89557-0025
(775) 784-6850
FAX: (775) 784-1057
URL: http://www.unr.edu/gaming/

Iowa Lottery
2323 Grand Ave.
Des Moines, IA 50312-5307
(515) 725-7900
URL: http://www.ialottery.com/

Iowa Racing and Gaming Commission
Capitol Medical Office Bldg.
1300 Des Moines St., Ste. 100
Des Moines, IA 50309-5508
(515) 281-7352
FAX: (515) 242-6560
E-mail: irgc@iowa.gov
URL: http://www.state.ia.us/irgc/

Jockey Club
40 E. 52nd St.
New York, NY 10022
(212) 371-5970
FAX: (212) 371-6123
URL: http://www.jockeyclub.com/

Kansas Lottery
128 N. Kansas Ave.
Topeka, KS 66603
(785) 296-5700
E-mail: lotteryinfo@kslottery.net
URL: http://www.kslottery.com/

Kansas Racing and Gaming Commission
Dwight D. Eisenhower State Office Bldg., Aud. A
700 SW Harrison, Ste. 500
Topeka, KS 66603-3754
(785) 296-5800
FAX: (785) 296-0900
E-mail: krgc@krgc.ks.gov
URL: http://krgc.ks.gov/

Kentucky Horse Racing Commission
4063 Iron Works Pkwy., Bldg. B
Lexington, KY 40511

(859) 246-2040
FAX: (859) 246-2039
E-mail: Marc.Guilfoil@ky.gov
URL: http://www.khrc.ky.gov/

Kentucky Lottery
1011 W. Main St.
Louisville, KY 40202
(502) 560-1500
URL: http://www.kylottery.com/

Louisiana Gaming Control Board
7901 Independence Blvd., Bldg. A
Baton Rouge, LA 70806
(225) 925-1846
1-888-295-8450
FAX: (225) 925-1917
E-mail: LGCB@dps.la.gov
URL: http://www.dps.state.la.us/lgcb/

Louisiana Lottery Corporation
555 Laurel St.
Baton Rouge, LA 70801-1813
(225) 297-2000
URL: http://www.louisianalottery.com/

Maine Harness Racing Commission
Deering Bldg.—AMHI Complex
28 State House Station
Augusta, ME 04333-0028
(207) 287-3221
URL: http://www.maine.gov/agriculture/hrc/

Maine State Lottery Commission
Bureau of Alcoholic Beverages and Lottery Operations
8 State House Station
Augusta, ME 04333-0008
(207) 287-3721
1-800-452-8777
FAX: (207) 287-6769
URL: http://www.mainelottery.com/

Maryland Racing Commission
300 E. Towsontowne Blvd.
Towson, MD 21286
(410) 296-9682
FAX: (410) 296-9687
E-mail: racing@dllr.state.md.us
URL: http://www.dllr.state.md.us/racing/

Maryland State Lottery Agency
Montgomery Business Park
1800 Washington Blvd., Ste. 330
Baltimore, MD 21230
(410) 230-8800
URL: http://www.mdlottery.com/

Massachusetts State Lottery Commission
60 Columbian St.
Braintree, MA 02184
(781) 849-5555
URL: http://www.masslottery.com/

Massachusetts State Racing Commission
1000 Washington St., Ste. 710
Boston, MA 02118

(617) 727-2581
FAX: (617) 727-6095
E-mail: racing.commission@state.ma.us
URL: http://www.state.ma.us/src/

Michigan Gaming Control Board
3062 W. Grand Blvd., Ste. L-700
Detroit, MI 48202-6062
(313) 456-4100
FAX: (313) 456-4200
E-mail: MGCBweb@michigan.gov
URL: http://www.michigan.gov/mgcb

Michigan Lottery
101 E. Hillsdale
PO Box 30023
Lansing, MI 48909
(517) 335-5600
FAX: (517) 335-5644
E-mail: onlinehelp@michiganlottery.com
URL: http://www.michigan.gov/lottery

Minnesota Gambling Control Board
1711 W. County Rd. B, Ste. 300 S
Roseville, MN 55113
(651) 639-4000
URL: http://www.gcb.state.mn.us/

Minnesota Racing Commission
15201 Zurich St. NE, Ste. 212
Columbus, MN 55025
(651) 925-3951
FAX: (651) 925-3953
URL: https://ww.mrc.state.mn.us/index.htm

Minnesota State Lottery
2645 Long Lake Rd.
Roseville, MN 55113-2533
(651) 635-8100
FAX: (651) 635-8188
E-mail: lottery@mnlottery.com
URL: http://www.mnlottery.com/

Mississippi Gaming Commission
620 North St., Ste. 200
Jackson, MS 39202
(601) 576-3800
1-800-504-7529
FAX: (601) 576-3929
E-mail: info@mgc.state.ms.us
URL: http://www.mgc.state.ms.us/

Missouri Gaming Commission
3417 Knipp Dr.
Jefferson City, MO 65109
(573) 526-4080
FAX: (573) 526-1999
E-mail: PublicRelation@mgc.dps.mo.gov
URL: http://www.mgc.dps.mo.gov/

Missouri Lottery
1823 Southridge Dr.
PO Box 1603
Jefferson City, MO 65109-1603
(573) 751-4050
FAX: (573) 751-5188
URL: http://www.molottery.com/

Montana Department of Livestock Board of Horse Racing
PO Box 520
Stevensville, MT 59870
(406) 777-5409
E-mail: tomptucker@gmail.com
URL: http://liv.mt.gov/hr/default.mcpx

Montana Gambling Control Division
2550 Prospect Ave.
PO Box 201424
Helena, MT 59620-1424
(406) 444-1971
E-mail: gcd@mt.gov
URL: http://www.doj.mt.gov/gaming/

Montana Lottery
2525 N. Montana Ave.
Helena, MT 59601-0598
(406) 444-5825
E-mail: montanalottery@mail.com
URL: http://www.montanalottery.com/

Multi-state Lottery Association
4400 NW Urbandale Dr.
Urbandale, IA 50322
(515) 453-1400
URL: http://www.musl.com/

National Association of Fundraising Ticket Manufacturers
335 Atrium Office Bldg.
1295 Bandana Blvd.
St. Paul, MN 55108
(651) 644-4710
FAX: (651) 644-5904
URL: http://www.naftm.org/

National Center for Responsible Gaming
1299 Pennsylvania Ave. NW, Ste. 1175
Washington, DC 20004
(202) 552-2689
FAX: (202) 552-2676
E-mail: info@ncrg.org/
URL: http://www.ncrg.org/

National Council on Problem Gambling
730 11th St., NW, Ste. 601
Washington, DC 20001
(202) 547-9204
1-800-522-4700
FAX: (202) 547-9206
E-mail: ncpg@ncpgambling.org
URL: http://www.ncpgambling.org/

National Indian Gaming Association
224 Second St. SE
Washington, DC 20003
(202) 546-7711
FAX: (202) 546-1755
E-mail: questions@indiangaming.org
URL: http://www.indiangaming.org/

National Indian Gaming Commission
1441 L St. NW, Ste. 9100
Washington, DC 20005
(202) 632-7003
FAX: (202) 632-7066

E-mail: info@nigc.gov
URL: http://www.nigc.gov/

Nebraska Lottery
1800 O St., Ste. 101
Lincoln, NE 68509
(402) 471-6100
E-mail: lottery@nelottery.com
URL: http://www.nelottery.com/

Nebraska State Racing Commission
5903 Walker Ave.
Lincoln, NE 68507
(402) 471-4155
E-mail: diane.vandeun@nebraska.gov
URL: http://nebraskaracingcommission
.com/

Nevada Gaming Commission and State Gaming Control Board
1919 College Pkwy.
Carson City, NV 89706
(775) 684-7750
FAX: (775) 687-5817
URL: http://gaming.nv.gov/

New Hampshire Lottery Commission
14 Integra Dr.
Concord, NH 03301
(603) 271-3391
1-800-852-3324
FAX: (603) 271-1160
E-mail: webmaster@lottery.nh.gov
URL: http://www.nhlottery.org/

New Hampshire Racing and Charitable Gaming Commission
57 Regional Dr., Unit 3
Concord, NH 03301-8518
(603) 271-2158
FAX: (603) 271-3381
URL: http://www.racing.nh.gov/

New Jersey Casino Control Commission
Arcade Bldg.
Tennessee Avenue and Boardwalk
Atlantic City, NJ 08401
(609) 441-3799
URL: http://www.state.nj.us/casinos/

New Jersey Lottery
One Lawrence Park Complex
Brunswick Avenue Cir.
Lawrenceville, NJ 08648
(609) 599-5800
FAX: (609) 599-5935
E-mail: publicinfo@lottery.state.nj.us
URL: http://www.state.nj.us/lottery/

New Jersey Racing Commission
140 E. Front St.
Trenton, NJ 08625
(609) 292-0613
FAX: (609) 599-1785
URL: http://www.nj.gov/oag/racing/
index.html

New Mexico Gaming Control Board
4900 Alameda Blvd. NE
Albuquerque, NM 87113
(505) 841-9700
FAX: (505) 841-9725
E-mail: gcb.is@state.nm.us
URL: http://www.nmgcb.org/

New Mexico Lottery
4511 Osuna Rd. NE
Albuquerque, NM 87109
(505) 342-7600
URL: http://www.nmlottery.com/

New Mexico Racing Commission
4900 Alameda NE
Albuquerque, NM 87113
(505) 222-0700
FAX: (505) 222-0713
E-mail: Vince.Mares@state.nm.us
URL: http://nmrc.state.nm.us/

New York Lottery
PO Box 7500
Schenectady, NY 12301-7500
(518) 388-3300
URL: http://nylottery.ny.gov/wps/portal

New York State Racing and Wagering Board
One Broadway Ctr., Ste. 600
Schenectady, NY 12305-2553
(518) 395-5400
FAX: (518) 347-1250
E-mail: info@racing.ny.gov
URL: http://www.racing.ny.gov/

North American Association of State and Provincial Lotteries
One S. Broadway
Geneva, OH 44041
(440) 466-5630
FAX: (440) 466-5649
E-mail: info@nasplhq.org
URL: http://www.naspl.org/

North Carolina Education Lottery
2100 Yonkers Rd.
Raleigh, NC 27604
(919) 715-6886
FAX: (919) 715-8833
URL: http://www.nc-educationlottery.org/

North Dakota Lottery
1050 E. Interstate Ave., Ste. 200
Bismarck, ND 58503-5574
(701) 328-1574
1-877-635-6886
E-mail: ndlottery@nd.gov
URL: http://www.ndlottery.org/

North Dakota Office of Attorney General Gaming Division
600 E. Boulevard Ave., Dept. 125
Bismarck, ND 58505
(701) 328-2210
URL: http://www.ag.state.nd.us/Gaming/Gaming.htm

Ohio Lottery Commission
615 W. Superior Ave.
Cleveland, OH 44113
1-800-686-4208
URL: http://www.ohiolottery.com/

Ohio State Racing Commission
77 S. High St., 18th Fl.
Columbus, OH 43215-6108
(614) 466-2757
FAX: (614) 466-1900
URL: http://www.racing.ohio.gov/

Oklahoma Horse Racing Commission
Shepherd Mall
2401 NW 23rd St., Ste. 78
Oklahoma City, OK 73107
(405) 943-6472
FAX: (405) 943-6474
E-mail: ohrc@socket.net
URL: http://www.ohrc.org/INTRO.HTML

Oregon Lottery
500 Airport Rd. SE
Salem, OR 97301
(503) 540-1000
FAX: (503) 540-1001
E-mail: lottery.webcenter@state.or.us
URL: http://www.oregonlottery.org/

Oregon Racing Commission
800 NE Oregon St., Ste. 310
Portland, OR 97232
(971) 673-0207
FAX: (971) 673-0213
URL: http://racing.oregon.gov/

Penn National Gaming
825 Berkshire Blvd.
Wyomissing, PA 19610
(610) 373-2400
FAX: (610) 373-4966
E-mail: corporate@pngaming.com
URL: http://www.pngaming.com/

Pennsylvania Gaming Control Board
PO Box 69060
Harrisburg, PA 17106-9060
(717) 346-8300
FAX: (717) 346-8350
E-mail: pgcb@pa.gov
URL: http://gamingcontrolboard.pa.gov/

Pennsylvania Lottery
1200 Fulling Mill Rd., Ste. 1
Middletown, PA 17057
(717) 702-8000
1-800-692-7481
FAX: (717) 702-8024
URL: http://www.palottery.state.pa.us/

Pennsylvania State Horse Racing Commission
2301 N. Cameron St.
Harrisburg, PA 17110
(717) 787-4737
URL: http://www.agriculture.state.pa.us/

Pet-Abuse.com
PO Box 5
Southfields, NY 10975
1-888-523-7387
E-mail: info@pet-abuse.com
URL: http://www.pet-abuse.com/

Pew Research Center
1615 L St. NW, Ste. 700
Washington, DC 20036
(202) 419-4300
FAX: (202) 419-4349
E-mail: info@pewresearch.org
URL: http://www.pewresearch.org/

Rhode Island Lottery
1425 Pontiac Ave.
Cranston, RI 02920
(401) 463-6500
FAX: (401) 463-5669
URL: http://www.rilot.com/

South Carolina Education Lottery
PO Box 11949
Columbia, SC 29211-1949
(803) 737-4419
URL: http://www.sceducationlottery.com/

South Dakota Commission on Gaming
221 W. Capitol Ave., Ste. 101
Pierre, SD 57501
(605) 773-6050
FAX: (605) 773-6053
URL: http://gaming.sd.gov/

South Dakota Lottery
711 E. Wells Ave.
PO Box 7107
Pierre, SD 57501
(605) 773-5770
FAX: (605) 773-5786
E-mail: lottery@state.sd.us
URL: http://lottery.sd.gov/

Stop Predatory Gambling Foundation
100 Maryland Ave. NE, Rm. 310
Washington, DC 20002
(202) 567-6996
E-mail: mail@stoppredatorygambling.org
URL: http://stoppredatorygambling.org/

Tennessee Lottery
Plaza Tower Metro Ctr.
200 Athens Way, Ste. 200
Nashville, TN 37228
(615) 324-6500
URL: http://www.tnlottery.com/

Texas Lottery Commission
611 E. Sixth St.
Austin, TX 78701
(512) 344-5000
1-800-375-6886
FAX: (512) 344-5080
E-mail: customer.service@lottery.state.tx.us
URL: http://www.txlottery.org/

Texas Racing Commission
8505 Cross Park Dr., Ste. 110
Austin, TX 78754
(512) 833-6699
FAX: (512) 833-6907
URL: http://www.txrc.state.tx.us/

U.S. Trotting Association
750 Michigan Ave.
Columbus, OH 43215
(614) 224-2291
1-877-800-8782
FAX: (614) 228-1385
URL: http://www.ustrotting.com/

Vermont Lottery Commission
1311 U.S. Rte. 302, Ste. 100
Barre, VT 05641
(802) 479-5686
1-800-322-8800
FAX: (802) 479-4294
E-mail: satt@vtlottery.com
URL: http://www.vtlottery.com/

Virginia Lottery
900 E. Main St.
Richmond, VA 23219
(804) 692-7000
FAX: (804) 692-7102
URL: http://www.valottery.com/

**Virginia Office of Charitable and
Regulatory Programs**
Virginia Department of Agriculture and
Consumer Services
102 Governor St.
Richmond, VA 23219
(804) 371-0495

URL: http://www.vdacs.virginia.gov/
gaming/index.shtml

Virginia Racing Commission
10700 Horsemen's Rd.
New Kent, VA 23124
(804) 966-7400
FAX: (804) 966-7418
E-mail: Kimberly.Carter@VRC.Virginia
.gov
URL: http://www.vrc.virginia.gov/

Washington Horse Racing Commission
6326 Martin Way E, Ste. 209
Olympia, WA 98516
(360) 459-6462
FAX: (360) 459-6461
E-mail: whrc@whrc.state.wa.us
URL: http://www.whrc.wa.gov/

Washington's Lottery
814 Fourth Ave. E
Olympia, WA 98506
(360) 664-4720
FAX: (360) 664-2630
E-mail: director's_office@walottery.com
URL: http://www.walottery.com/

**Washington State Gambling
Commission**
4565 Seventh Ave. SE
Lacey, WA 98503
(360) 486-3440
1-800-345-2529
FAX: (360) 486-3629
E-mail: askus@wsgc.wa.gov
URL: http://www.wsgc.wa.gov/

West Virginia Lottery
900 Pennsylvania Ave.
Charleston, WV 25302
(304) 558-0500
1-800-982-2274
FAX: (304) 558-3321
E-mail: mail@wvlottery.com
URL: http://www.wvlottery.com/

West Virginia Racing Commission
900 Pennsylvania Ave., Ste. 533
Charleston, WV 25302
(304) 558-2150
FAX: (304) 558-6319
URL: http://www.racing.wv.gov/Pages/
default.aspx/

Wisconsin Division of Gaming
3319 W. Beltline Hwy., First Fl.
Madison, WI 53713
(608) 270-2555
FAX: (608) 270-2564
URL: http://www.doa.state.wi.us/gaming/
index.asp

Wisconsin Lottery
PO Box 8941
Madison, WI 53708-8941
(608) 261-4916
E-mail: info@wilottery.com
URL: http://www.wilottery.com/

Wyoming Pari-mutuel Commission
Energy II Bldg., Ste. 335
951 Werner Ct.
Casper, WY 82601
(307) 265-4015
FAX: (307) 265-4279
URL: http://parimutuel.state.wy.us/

RESOURCES

Several resources useful to this book were published by companies and organizations within the gambling industry. Most notable are *2012 State of the States: The AGA Survey of Casino Entertainment* (2012) and *Online Gambling Five Years after UIGEA* (David O. Stewart, May 2011) by the American Gaming Association, *Charity Gaming in North America: 2011 Annual Report* (2012) by the National Association of Fundraising Ticket Manufacturers, and *Profile of the American Casino Gambler: Harrah's Survey 2006* (June 2006) by Harrah's Entertainment. The Pew Research Center provided valuable insight into the industry in *Gambling: As the Take Rises, So Does Public Concern* (Paul Taylor, Cary Funk, and Peyton Craighill, May 2006).

Each state that allows gambling issues a quarterly or annual report describing revenues, employment, tax payments, and more. Reports helpful for this book included *41st Annual Report of the California Horse Racing Board: A Summary of Fiscal Year 2010–2011 Revenue and Calendar Year 2011 Racing in California* (2012) by the California Horse Racing Board; *2011 Annual Report* (2012) by the Colorado Division of Gaming; *80th Annual Report, Fiscal Year 2010–2011* (2012) by the Florida Department of Business and Professional Regulation, Division of Pari-mutuel Wagering; *2011 Annual Report* (2012) by the Illinois Gaming Board; *2012 Annual Report to Governor Mitch Daniels* (January 2013) by the Indiana Gaming Commission; *2011 Annual Report* (February 2012) by the Iowa Racing and Gaming Commission; *Annual Report to the Governor: Calendar Year 2011* (February 2012) by the Michigan Gaming Control Board; *Quarterly Reports— 2nd Quarter 2012: Property Data* (2012) by the Mississippi Gaming Commission and *Tax Revenues from Gaming* (July 2012) by the Mississippi State Tax Commission; *Missouri Gaming Commission Annual Report 2011* (2011) by the Missouri Gaming Commission; *State of Nevada Gaming Revenue Report: Year Ended December 31, 2011* (2012) by the Nevada State Gaming Control Board; *New Jersey Casino Control Commission Annual Report 2011* (2012) by the New Jersey Casino Control Commission; and *Annual Report, Fiscal Year 2011* (2011) by the South Dakota Commission on Gaming.

The Bureau of Labor Statistics published *Occupational Outlook Handbook, 2012–13 Edition* (2012), which provided information on career opportunities in the gaming industry. Information on gambling policy and legislation is available from the National Conference of State Legislatures. The Legislative Analyst's Office, which provides fiscal and policy advice to the California legislature, has published information papers on gambling on tribal lands. The Federal Bureau of Investigation published *Crime in the United States, 2011* (2012), which provided information on the numbers of gambling arrests, while *WISQARS Injury Mortality Reports, 1999–2010* (September 2011) published by the Centers for Disease Control and Prevention provided information on suicide rates per state.

The National Indian Gaming Commission published "2011 Indian Gaming Revenues Increased 3%" (July 2012). The National Indian Gaming Association published *The Economic Impact of Indian Gaming* (March 2010). *Gambling in Connecticut: Analyzing the Economic and Social Impacts* (June 2009) and "Gaming Revenue and Statistics" (December 2012) by the Division of Special Revenue of the state of Connecticut were helpful in analyzing the economics of Native American casinos in that state.

The Greyhound Protection League and the Humane Society of the United States provided important information on the history and status of animal racing and fighting in this country. Additional statistics on animal fighting were obtained from Pet-abuse.com. With regard to the horse racing industry, the Jockey Club and the U.S. Trotting Association issue informative materials.

The Gallup Organization provided valuable results from recent polls regarding gambling in the United

States. The Annenberg Public Policy Center at the University of Pennsylvania compiles information each year detailing the gambling habits of young people in their teens and 20s. *Demographic Survey of Texas Lottery Players 2011* (December 2011) by the Texas Lottery Commission and the Center for Public Policy at the University of Houston provided helpful information on lottery players.

Scientific and educational publications devoted to problem gambling were invaluable to this book. They include *The Wager*, which is published by Harvard Medical School and the Massachusetts Council on Compulsive Gambling, and *Journal of Gambling Issues*, which is published by the Centre for Addiction and Mental Health in Toronto, Ontario, Canada. Other scholarly journals referenced for this publication include *American Journal of Geriatric Psychiatry*, *American Journal of Psychiatry*, *American Journal on Addictions*, *Behaviour Research and Therapy*, *Federal Communications Law Journal*, *Federal Register*, *Journal of American College Health*, *Journal of Behavioral Decision Making*, *Journal of Clinical Psychology*, *Journal of Family Practice*, *Journal of Gambling Issues*, *Journal of Hispanic Higher Education*, *National Tax Journal*, *Progress in Neuro-Psychopharmacology and Biological Psychiatry*, *Psychology of Addictive Behaviors*, *Review of Economics and Statistics*, *Rutgers Law Review*, *Southern Medical Journal*, *Suicide and Life-Threatening Behavior*, and *Veterinary Pathology*.

Organizations devoted to problem gambling that provided helpful data and information include Gamblers Anonymous, the National Center for Responsible Gaming, and the National Council on Problem Gambling. Some states run their own programs to address problem gambling. One helpful report is the Iowa Department of Public Health's "Iowa Gambling Treatment Program 1-800 BETS OFF Helpline: Annual Summary for FY2010" (July 2010).

Final Report (June 1999) by the National Gambling Impact Study Commission is a critical reference for information about the effects of gambling on society. The report is based on information that was submitted by many researchers.

INDEX

Page references in italics refer to photographs. References with the letter t following them indicate the presence of a table. The letter f indicates a figure. If more than one table or figure appears on a particular page, the exact item number for the table or figure being referenced is provided.

L

"A Psychological Autopsy Study of Pathological Gamblers Who Died by Suicide" (Wong), 71

Public opinion
 on casino acceptability, 26
 on casinos, effects of, 63
 family problems related to gambling, poll respondents who have experienced, 20t
 on gambling in 1970s, 4
 on legalized gambling, 6–7
 on moral acceptability of 18 issues, 6t
 moral acceptability of 18 moral issues by political party affiliation, 7t
 on moral acceptability of gambling, 6
 poll respondents who say legalized gambling encourages people to gamble more than they can afford, 8(f1.2)
 public approval of legalized gambling, 8(f1.1)
 on sports gambling, 96
 views of gambling by demographic characteristics, 9t

Pull tabs
 in Class II gambling, 51
 definition of, 15
 description of, 79

Puritans, beliefs about gambling, 2

Purses
 of California horse racing, 99
 of greyhound races, 100
 horse racing takeout dollar in California, distribution of, 98f
 of non-Thoroughbred horse races, 98
 of Thoroughbred horse races, 97

"Pushing the Limits: Gambling among NCAA Athletes" (Wager), 106

Q

"Q&A with The Lottery Wars Author Matthew Sweeney" (Tuttle), 82

Quarter horse races, 98

R

Race book
 description of, 96
 in Nevada, 102

Race/ethnicity
 gambling participation rates by, 19
 of lottery beneficiaries, 92
 lottery participation and, 91
 of sports gamblers, 96

Racetrack casinos (racinos)
 in Iowa, 46
 number of states with, 31
 in Pennsylvania, 48, 49
 revenues of, 65
 success of, 101
 VLTs at, 80

Racetrack Table Games Act (West Virginia), 50

Racetracks
 of California, 99
 decrease in, 101
 Thoroughbred racetracks, 97
 of West Virginia, 50

Racing fairs, 99

"Racing Links: Race Tracks" (Daily Racing Form), 97

Racinos. See Racetrack casinos

Racketeer Influenced and Corrupt Organizations (RICO) Act of 1970, 14, 31

Racketeering, 4

Raffles, 79

Random number generator, 108

"Ranking of State Dogfighting Laws" (Humane Society of the United States), 105

Ravens Cash Fantasy game, 80

Recession. See Economy

Reconstruction, lotteries for, 77

Recreation Machine Program, 16

"Red Hawk Casino's Fortunes Have Disappointed So Far" (Kasler), 56

Rege, Aunshul, 107, 114–115

Region
 gambling participation rates by, 19
 tribal gaming revenue, growth in by, 56f
 tribal gaming revenues by, 55f

Regressive tax, 91

Regulation
 of Internet gambling, legal issues, 109–114
 of Nevada casinos, 31
 of tribal casinos, 52–53

Regulation 14 (Nevada), 73

Reid, Harry, 112

Religion
 disapproval of casino gambling and, 63
 gambling participation rates by, 19

Reno, Nevada, 3

Report to the Louisiana State Legislature, 2011–2012 (Louisiana Gaming Control Board), 38

Republicans, 6

Reservations
 gaming revenues, effects of, 56, 64
 history of tribal casinos on, 51
 Indian Gaming Regulatory Act and, 5
 revenues earned by tribal casinos, taxes and, 65
 social services from tribal casino profits, 54–55

"Resilience and Self-Control Impairment" (Chen & Taylor), 23

Resorts International, Atlantic City, New Jersey, 34

Responsible Gaming Education Week, 73

Results from the 2008 NCAA Study on Collegiate Wagering (NCAA), 106

Retailers
 division of lottery money, 85
 lottery retailer payments, 86–88
 lottery tickets sold by, 82

Revel casino, Atlantic City, New Jersey, 35

Revenge of the Pequots: How a Small Native American Tribe Created the World's Most Profitable Casino (Eisler), 58

Revenue Sharing Trust Fund, 61

Revenues
 of casinos, economic impact of, 65
 of casinos of Deadwood, South Dakota, 48
 of Colorado casinos, 47
 Colorado gaming revenue, 48f
 of corporate casinos, 12, 13
 of federal government from gambling, 16
 of Foxwoods and Mohegan Sun, 59
 Foxwoods and Mohegan Sun, economic impact of, 62t
 Foxwoods and Mohegan Sun, operational impact for, 61t
 gambling revenues, 11
 from greyhound racing, 100
 Illinois casino revenues, 43f
 Illinois casino revenues by casino/type, 44f
 of Illinois casinos, 43
 Illinois gaming taxes, local distribution of, 44t
 of Indiana casinos, 42
 Indiana gaming taxes, 42t, 43t
 of Internet gambling, 14, 107, 109
 Iowa casino revenue, 47f
 of Iowa casinos, 46
 of Kansas casinos, 49
 Las Vegas gaming revenue, downtown, 34(t4.3)
 Las Vegas Strip gaming revenue, 34(t4.2)
 from lotteries, pressure for increased, 93
 lottery contributions to beneficiaries, by state or province, fiscal year 2012, 89t–90t
 lottery contributions to beneficiaries, cumulative, by state or province, 86t–88t
 lottery sales, 85–88
 of Louisiana casinos, 38, 42f
 of Maryland casinos, 50
 of Michigan casinos, 45, 46f
 of Mississippi casinos, 38, 41f
 of Missouri casinos, 45
 Missouri gaming revenue, 45f
 Nevada gaming revenue, 32f, 33t
 of Nevada's commercial casinos, 31, 32, 33
 New Jersey casino industry employment statistics, 37(t4.6)

CPSIA information can be obtained
at www.ICGtesting.com
Printed in the USA
FFOW020720030613
1243FF

9 781414 481418